FATE AND FORTUNE

FATE AND FORTUNE

GEDDES & GROSSET

Published by Geddes & Grosset, an imprint of
Children's Leisure Products Limited

© 1997 Children's Leisure Products Limited,
David Dale House, New Lanark ML11 9DJ, Scotland

First published 1997
Reprinted 1998, 1999

ISBN 1 85534 891 8

Printed and bound in China

Contents

Astrology   **7**
History   7
The solar system   9
A few technicalities   12
The signs of the Zodiac   19
Groups of the Zodiac   22
The houses of the chart   25
The Sun Signs   30
The Birth Chart   42

Clairvoyance and Crystal Gazing   **45**
Clairvoyance   47
Colour and character   49
Chanting and controlling the mind   51

Fortune Telling by Numbers   **53**

The Tarot   **58**
Introduction   58
History of the tarot   58
Reading the cards   59
The Major Arcana   66
The Minor Arcana   78
Key words   109

The I Ching   **114**
Nature of the I Ching   114
The basis of the I Ching   117
The trigrams   125
Key to the hexagrams   128
The hexagrams   128

Palmistry   **251**
  Introduction   251
  The hand   251
  Interdependence of parts   252
  The skin   253
  The lines   254
  Prediction   255
  The anatomy of the hand   256
  The size and shape of the hand   257
  The elemental   259
  The spatulate or active   260
  The conical or temperamental   261
  The square or utilitarian   261
  The knotty or philosophic   262
  The pointed or idealistic   263
  The mixed   263
  The female hand   264
  The fingers and the mounts   265
  The lines of the hand   271
  Age and time calculations   272
  How to read the lines   273

Tea-leaf Fortunes   **281**

Dice and Good Luck   **285**

Astrology

History

Astrology is an ancient craft that has its origin in the mists of time. It is impossible to place accurately the beginnings, but one thing that is certain is that astrology began as a subject intimately combined with astronomy. Its history is therefore the history of astronomy until the two subjects parted company, a split that essentially began when Nicolai Copernicus (1473-1543) published his book *De revolutionibus*. In this book he postulated that, contrary to earlier thinking in which the Earth was the centre of the solar system, the Sun actually formed the focus about which all the planets orbited.

It is thought that there was some study of these subjects five to six thousand years ago when Chaldean priests made maps of the skies. The Chaldeans were the most ancient of the Babylonian peoples. It was believed that heavenly bodies exerted influence upon man and whatever could not be ascribed to man must be due to actions of the gods or the deities of the planets. Subsequent study of the solar system began as pure observation because records and other data for calculation simply did not exist. The Egyptian and Greek civilizations gave much to the theories and practice of astrology, although much remained unwritten. It is said that the Chaldeans instructed the priests of the Pharaohs in astrology, and monuments exist that show a working knowledge of the subject. This was around 400-350 BC. A little earlier, in Greece around the beginning of the sixth century BC, the philosopher Thales (*c.*643-*c.*546 BC) studied astronomy and astrology as did Pythagoras (569-470 BC) who was credited by Copernicus as the person who developed the theory that the Earth and other planets revolved around the Sun.

There were many other Greek students, notably: Plato; Hippocrates, who combined astrology with medical diagnosis; Hipparchus, the founder of observational astronomy, who in 134 BC discovered a new star; and Claudius Ptolemaeus (100-178 AD). Ptolemy wrote the *Almagest*, which is a star catalogue of just over a thousand stars, and also a consideration of the motion of the Moon and the planets. He also wrote the *Tetrabiblos*, the earliest surviving book on astrology.

In Rome and the extended empire at this time, astrology was held in very high regard, and great faith was placed in the work and advice of astrologers who were appointed to the Emperors. The Moon was considered particularly influential and can be found depicted on many of their coins. Among the many Romans active in this field were Porphyry (232-304 AD), who is said to have developed the house method, and Julius Maternus (around 300 AD), who wrote a number of books on astrology.

From about 500 AD Arabs became the prime movers in science and philosophy, but by the early Middle Ages (the thirteenth century) interest was rekindled in Europe, at which time astrology had been divided into three distinct fields: *natural* or *mundane* astrology, which is prominent in forecasting national events, weather, etc; *horary* astrology, used to answer a question through the use of a chart drawn up for the actual time of asking; and *judicial* astrology, in which the fortune of an individual is determined by using a birth chart.

The fifteenth and sixteenth centuries in Europe saw the rise of several famous names, including the Polish astronomer Copernicus. Although Copernicus concurred with the views of Pythagoras, he could not prove the theory, and many attribute the real establishment of the principle (i.e. that the planets orbit the Sun) to Johannes Kepler (1571-1630), the German astronomer. The medieval precursor of chemistry was alchemy, and one famous practitioner was Phillipus Aureolus Paracelsus (1493-1541), who also had some astrological leanings. He believed that the Sun, planets and stars influenced people, whether for good or evil. From this era also came Nostradamus (1503-1566). Michael Nostradamus has become one of the most famous of astrologists and prophets, and he also studied medicine. Almost from the outset it was thought that medical knowledge must, by necessity, include an understanding of astrology.

The work of the Dane Tycho Brahe (1546-1601) could, in some respects, be considered a watershed in the study of astrology/astronomy. Brahe became an observer of the heavens and in so doing was recognized as the most accurate since Hipparchus, centuries before. He prepared tables, designed instruments and studied the motion of the planets, particularly Mars, and it was this initial work that led Kepler to formulate his famous laws of planetary motion. Kepler was assistant to Brahe when the latter moved to Prague following the death of his patron, King Frederick. Kepler's work proved to be pivotal in advancing the understanding of astronomy. Kepler compared the work of Ptolemy, Copernicus and Tycho Brahe to produce three laws:

1. The orbit of each planet is an ellipse with the Sun at one of the foci (an ellipse has two foci.)
2. A line drawn from a planet to the Sun sweeps out equal areas in equal times.
3. The squares of the sidereal periods (time taken to orbit the Sun, measured relative to the stars) are proportional to the cubes of the mean distances from the Sun.

Kepler believed that the stars exerted an influence upon events and that astrology could predict the most mundane of happenings. During the sixteenth and seventeenth centuries there were many famous names who combined astrology with astronomy, mathematics or, commonly, medicine. These included the Italian physicist Galileo Galilei, a French professor of mathematics and doctor of medicine, Jean Morin, an Italian monk and mathematician, Placidus de Tito, and in England, William Lilly, who became famous as a practitioner of horary astrology and accurately predicted the Great Fire of London in 1666.

The poet John Dryden used astrology in predicting numerous events in his own life and the lives of his sons, including both their deaths. Following Dryden's own death in 1700, although not because of it, astrological practice declined on the continent but flourished in England. This influence extended to France at the start of the nineteenth century, where a sound scientific basis to the subject was sought.

William Allan (1800-1917), otherwise known as Alan Leo, was considered by many to be the father of modern astrology. He lectured widely throughout England and edited a magazine called *Modern Astrology*. He was also a professional astrologer and a prolific author on the subject, writing 30 books. In 1915 he founded the Astrological Lodge of London. Although the war years were disruptive to the study and practice of astrology, a large following was developed in North America. However, continental Europe suffered during the Second World War as Hitler's forces caused wholesale destruction, and Hitler himself, unhappy with adverse astrological predictions, destroyed books and records and incarcerated unfortunate practitioners.

Today astrology holds interest for many people, and growing numbers are becoming fascinated by its study. However, there is a dichotomy between astrology and astronomy.

The solar system

The early visualizations of the heavens and the stars showed the Earth at the centre of a large revolving sphere. It was thought that the stars seen in the sky were somehow fastened onto the inner surface of this sphere. The stars that appeared to revolve around the Earth but did not move in relation to each other were called the 'fixed stars'. Among the many fixed stars there are some in particular that have certain characteristics and that can be used in astrological charts. For example, Regulus (or Alpha Leonis) is the brightest star in the constellation of Leo and signifies pride, good luck and success.

From early times it was noted that while many stars remained fixed, five in particular did not, and these wandered about the sky. These were the planets of the solar system because at that time not all eight remaining planets (other than Earth) had been identified. The discovery of Uranus, Neptune and Pluto followed the invention of the telescope, and Uranus was the first planet so observed, in 1781.

For the purposes of astrology, the Sun, which is actually a star, is considered as a planet. It is approximately 150 million kilometres from Earth and has a diameter of 1.4 million kilometres. Energy is generated in the core, from nuclear fusion, where the temperature is about fifteen million degrees.

The planets

The Moon is a satellite of Earth but for convenience is also treated as a planet. It orbits the Earth roughly every 27 days, and the same face is always kept towards Earth, lit by light reflected from the Sun. The Moon seems to change size—the process known as waxing and waning—and it is called 'new' when it is situated between the Earth and the Sun and, because it is not illuminated, cannot be seen. The full Moon occurs about 14 days later, when the full face is totally illuminated.

Planets with their orbits between the Sun and the Earth's orbit are called 'inferior'. There are two planets in this category, Mercury and Venus. Mercury is the smallest planet in the solar system and takes 88 Earth days to complete one orbit, rotating slowly on its axis, and taking 58 Earth days for one revolution. Its elliptical orbit is eccentric, varying in distance from the Sun from 47 to 70 million kilometres.

Venus is the brightest planet seen from Earth and is known as the morning or evening star. It is about 108 million kilometres from the Sun and has a diameter similar to Earth's, at 12,300 kilometres. Venus spins very slowly on its axis, and a day is equivalent to 24.3 Earth days, and a year is 225 days. It is unusual in being the only planet to revolve in the opposite direction to the path of its orbit.

The remaining planets, from Mars to Pluto, are called the 'superior planets', being on the distant side of Earth from the Sun. Mars takes about 687 Earth days to complete an orbit, and a day is just a fraction longer than one Earth day. The surface is solid and mainly red in colour because of the type of rock. There are many surface features, some of which are attributed to the action of water, although none is found there now. Mars is sometimes a dominant feature of the night sky, particularly when it occasionally approaches nearer to Earth, and it has from ancient times exerted considerable fascination.

Jupiter is the largest and heaviest planet in the solar system and has a diameter of 142,800 kilometres. The planet gives out more energy than it receives from the Sun and must therefore have an internal energy source. It is due, in part, to this that the atmosphere is seen to be in steady movement. Parallel bands of colour are seen, but a particularly noticeable feature is the Great Red Spot, which is thought to be an enormous storm, larger than Earth, coloured red because of the presence of phosphorus. The magnetic field of Jupiter is thousands of times stronger than Earth's, and radio waves emanate from the planet. Jupiter has 18 satellites, or moons, of which four are called the 'Galilean satellites'—Io, Europa, Ganymede and Callisto—because they were first seen by Galileo in 1610. There are three other groups of satellites, of which the innermost contains Adastrea, Amalthea, Metis and Thebe.

The next planet out from the Sun is Saturn, the second largest in the solar system. It has a diameter of 120,800 kilometres and the orbit takes 29 Earth years at a distance of 1507 million kilometres from the Sun. Because of its rapid rotation, Saturn is flattened at the poles with a consequent bulging at its equator. A day lasts for a little over 10 hours, and the surface temperature is -170 degrees Celsius. The most obvious and interesting feature of Saturn is its rings, which consist of ice, dust and rock debris, and some of which may have derived from the break-up of a satellite. The rings are about a quarter of a million kilometres across, and there are three main ones but hundreds of smaller ones.

Saturn also has 24 satellites, or moons, of which Titan is the largest with a diameter of 5200 kilometres (larger than Mercury). Some moons were discovered by the Voyager spacecraft in 1989, including Atlas, Calypso and Prometheus.

The planets Mercury through to Saturn were all known to astrologers and astronomers for many years. The remaining planets, Uranus, Neptune and Pluto, were discovered only in modern times, after the advent of the telescope. These are therefore often called the 'modern planets' by astrologers.

Uranus is 50,080 kilometres in diameter and a day lasts 17 hours while a year is equivalent to 84 Earth years. Because of its tilted axis, some parts of the planet's surface are in light for about 40 years and then in darkness for the remainder of its year. Uranus was discovered by William Herschel in 1781 but was something of a mystery until 1986 and the approach of Voyager. It has a faint ring system and 15 moons, some of which are very small indeed (less than 50 kilometres in diameter).

Neptune was discovered in 1846, but its existence was earlier correctly postulated because of observed irregularities in the orbit of Uranus. It takes 165 Earth years to complete an orbit and is almost 4.5 billion kilometres from the Sun. It is 17 times the mass of Earth and has a diameter at its equator of 48,600 kilometres. There are three rings and eight known satellites, the largest of which, Titan, is similar in size to the Earth's Moon.

Pluto, the smallest and most distant planet from the Sun, had its existence predicted because of its effect on the orbits of Neptune and Uranus and was finally discovered in 1930, although little is known about it. A day is equivalent to almost seven days on Earth, and a year is nearly 249 Earth years. Pluto has a very wide elliptical orbit, which brings it closest to the Sun (its *perihelion*) once in each orbit. Because of its great distance from the Sun (7.4 billion kilometres at its maximum), the surface temperature is very low, about 230 degrees. In 1979, one small moon, called Charon, was discovered, but since it is about one quarter the size of Pluto itself, the two act almost as a double planet system.

A few technicalities

As has been mentioned, the orbits of the planets are elliptical rather than circular, and there is a degree of eccentricity as well. When viewed from Earth, this combination of factors produces what may appear to be peculiar effects. For example, planets may move around the sky, slow and then appear to move backwards for a time. This apparent backward motion is called *retrograde motion* and is simply caused by the Earth moving more quickly through its orbit in comparison to another planet. It *seems* as though the planet being observed is moving backwards, but in reality it is moving forwards, albeit in the line of sight at a slower rate. It is similar to a fast train moving alongside a slow train, which makes the latter appear to be moving backwards. In astronomical tables R denotes retrograde while D marks a return to direct motion.

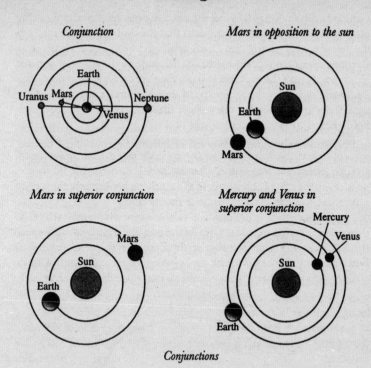

Conjunctions

Another astronomical parameter used in astrology is that of conjunctions. A *conjunction* is when two or more planets (including the Sun of course) are in a line when viewed from Earth. On occasion, Earth, Venus and the Sun will all be in a straight line. If Venus is between Earth and the Sun it is called an 'inferior conjunction'. If, however, Venus is on the other side of the Sun from Earth, it is a 'superior conjunction'. The same applies to Mercury. *Opposition* is when, for example, Earth lies between the Sun and Mars; then Mars is in opposition. Opposition is when one of the superior planets (all except Mercury, Venus and, of course, Earth) is opposite the Sun in the sky, i.e. making an angle of 180 degrees when viewed from Earth (*see* figure above).

Of vital significance to the correct interpretive study of astrology are a number of parameters that enable the relative positions of planets to be fixed. These include the three great circles, one of which is the ecliptic, and the Zodiac. (A great circle is essentially any circle projected onto the celestial sphere whose plane passes through the centre of the Earth.) The horizon and celestial equator (the Earth's equator projected outward onto the celestial sphere) form two great circles, and the ecliptic is the third. The *ecliptic* is the path that the Sun apparently forms in the heavens. Of course the Earth orbits the Sun, but it seems from Earth to mark out a path that lies at an angle to the celestial equator. This means that the two lines cross twice, at the vernal and autumn equinoxes, otherwise known as the March equinox (or first point of the sign Aries) and September equinox (or first point of the sign Libra). (*See* figure below)

The two points at which the ecliptic is farthest from the celestial equator are called the solstices, and these occur in June for the summer solstice (when the Sun enters Cancer) and December for the winter solstice (on entering Capricorn). In the southern hemisphere these equinoxes and solstices mark the reverse situation.

The ecliptic itself is divided into twelve equal divisions, each of 30 degrees, one for each Zodiac sign. As the Sun apparently moves around the Earth, it goes from one sign of the Zodiac to the next. A person's Sun sign is the sign before which the Sun seems to be at the time of birth.

The *Zodiac* is a 'band' in the heavens that extends to seven or eight

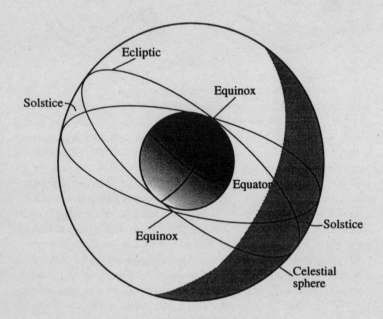

The ecliptic and the celestial sphere

degrees on either side of the ecliptic. Within this band, or path, are contained the apparent movements of the planets, except Pluto. The solar system can be considered as a relatively planar feature, and within this plane the Earth revolves around the Sun. The planes of the orbits of all the other planets are within seven degrees of Earth's, save for Pluto, which is nearer 17 degrees. The Zodiac is then split into twelve segments of 30 degrees, one for each sign of the Zodiac and each represented by a particular star constellation (*see* the figure below). These signs are essentially a means of naming the sections of the sky within which the planets move. The constellation names, Scorpio, Libra, etc, have no significance although they are bound up in the development of the subject. It should be noted that today, the 30-degree segments no longer coincide with the constellation because of a phenomenon called *precession of the equinoxes*. Precession results in the Earth's axis of rotation not remaining in the same position but forming a cone shape traced out in space. It is due to the gravitational pulls of the Sun and Moon producing a turning force, or torque. This occurs only because the Earth bulges at the equator—a perfect sphere would not be affected. The

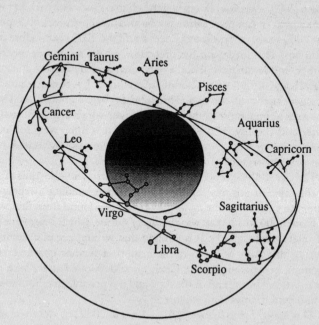

The Constellations

Earth takes almost 26,000 years (known as the Great Year) to sweep out the cone, and in astrology the point Aries 0 degrees (the First Point of Aries), where the celestial equator cuts the ecliptic, moves with time. Because of precession, the equator crossing-point moves around the ecliptic, and now the First Point of Aries (the vernal equinox of astronomy) lies in the constellation of Pisces and is soon to move into Aquarius. The 30 degrees along the ecliptic that is Aries remains the 30 degrees counted from the vernal equinox, although that equinox is farther back each year (this is, therefore, retrograde motion). Aries has been considered the first sign from hundreds of years BC, when it was believed that the Earth had a birthday.

The Great Year

The Great Year, as mentioned, is divided into twelve periods when the equinox is taken to be against each of the constellations that lie around the ecliptic. This is by no means an accurate division or placement, and the beginning of each period, or age, cannot be fixed easily as the constellations overlap and vary in size. However, each age is taken to be about 2000 years, and by tracing the characteristics of each age in history a pattern can be constructed. From available historical details, the last 2000 years are typified as Piscean and the 2000 years before that as Taurean. This links with the precession of the equinoxes mentioned earlier, and so the next period will be the *Age of Aquarius*.

Each age of the Great Year identified this far has certain characteristics associated with the sign. The *Age of Leo* began about 10000 BC and has as its animal representative the lion, with which are connected creativity and regality. The Sun is its planet. It is interesting to note the early attempts at art, by way of prehistoric cave paintings, and of course the vital importance of the Sun in those times.

The *Age of Cancer* (8000-6000 BC) is associated with the traits of home and family. At this time human beings began building dwellings, and some carvings symbolizing fertility have been found from this period.

From 6000 to 4000 BC was the *Age of Gemini*, which represents a sign of intellectual capacity. It is thought that writing began in some form during this Age, hence communication, a further characteristic of Gemini, became important. Civilization developed apace with cuneiform writing by the end of the Age, and it is possible that human beings had begun to travel and explore.

The *Age of Taurus* followed, from 4000 to 2000 BC, and there are numerous instances that relate to the Taurean features of solidity and security with beauty. These traits are seen in the Egyptian dynasties and the worship of the bull, and in the enormous and ornate temples and the pyramids.

The next age is that of *Aries* (2000 BC-0 AD). Aggressive and assertive qualities are associated with Aries, as are physical fitness and supremacy. These are balanced by courage and also harmony. All these characteristics are well exemplified by the Greeks, who dominated in battle and architecture and yet created the first democratic government. The symbol of the ram found an outlet in numerous ways, including as an emblem of the Roman army.

We are currently in the *Age of Pisces* (0-2000 AD), albeit towards the end of the period. It began with the birth of Christ, and there are numerous connections to the sign of the fish at this time. The secret symbol for the early Christians was the fish, Jesus was called *Ichthus*, the fish, and many of his disciples were fishermen. Qualities such as kindness, charity and forgiveness are typical, as is selflessness, although an element of confusion can also be discerned. We are on the brink of the new Age, that of *Aquarius* (2000-4000 AD), but in many respects the signs are already there to be seen. Aquarian influence can be seen in the strong presence of science and technology and space travel. Also Aquarian is a sense of detachment and of being impersonal.

Signs and symbols

Each sign of the Zodiac has a particular graphical representation, called a glyph, which relates to an animal or something similar. The same applies to the planets, and these symbols are used , with others, in constructing an astrological chart.

Symbol	Sign	Representation	Name
♈	Aries	the ram's horns	The Ram
♉	Taurus	the bull's head	The Bull
♊	Gemini	two children	The Twins
♋	Cancer	breasts	The Crab
♌	Leo	the heart, or the lion's tail	The Lion
♍	Virgo	the female genitalia	The Virgin
♎	Libra	a pair of scales	The Balance

Symbol	Sign	Representation	Name
♏	Scorpio	the male genitalia	The Scorpion
♐	Sagittarius	the Centaur's arrow	The Archer
♑	Capricorn	a goat's head and fish's tail	The Goat
♒	Aquarius	waves of water or air	The Water-bearer
♓	Pisces	two fish	The Fishes

The glyphs of the planets are as follows:

Planet	Symbol	Planet	Symbol
Sun	☉	Jupiter	♃
Moon	☽	Saturn	♄
Mercury	☿	Uranus	♅
Venus	♀	Neptune	♆
Mars	♂	Pluto	♇

These planetary symbols are all made up of essentially the same elements, the cross, half-circle and circle, all in different combinations. These pictorial representations are linked with the very early days of human beings, when communication was achieved using such graphical methods. As such, these elements each have a particular significance:

—the circle represents eternity, something without end, the spirit;

—a dot inside a circle represents the spirit or power beginning to come out;

—the cross represents the material world;

—and the semicircle stands for the soul.

The signs of the Zodiac

The signs appear to have got their names from the depths of history and prehistory, and do not necessarily concur with their astronomical counterparts, the constellations. In some civilizations, the signs were attributed to parts of the body. The likeliest race to have adopted this were the Greeks, who also linked the signs to various plants.

Aries	–	the head
Libra	–	the kidneys
Taurus	–	the throat
Scorpio	–	genitalia
Gemini	–	hands and arms
Sagittarius	–	hips and thighs
Cancer	–	the breasts
Capricorn	–	the knee
Leo	–	the heart
Aquarius	–	calf and ankle
Virgo	–	the intestines
Pisces	–	the feet

Below are given the main features of the signs of the Zodiac, and these will be followed later by a fuller description of the character and personal details associated with the various sun signs, i.e. when the Sun passes through each of the signs as it appears to move on the ecliptic.

Aries

The astrological new year occurs around 21 March, when the Sun enters Aries, and this new aspect is mirrored in typical Arian traits of energy, keenness and enthusiasm. The Arian can be something of a pioneer and thus somewhat self-centred with a selfish streak. Aries is the most personal of the signs.

Taurus

Taureans seek and reflect stability, security, and are generally practical with a possessive side to their character. Risks will be taken only if they are absolutely essential, and even then it will be only after a great deal of careful thought. In general Taureans are trustworthy and pleasant and yet unenterprising, which in some may lead to them become a little boring.

Gemini

This third sign of the Zodiac is that of the heavenly twins, which, not surprisingly, can surface as a certain duality, which in a negative sense may result in someone being two-faced. Geminians are intelligent, quick of mind, versatile, and are often good communicators. If the dual nature is too strongly negative then it may lead to a lack of achievement through being over-committed and trying to do too many things at once.

Cancer

Changeable, sympathetic, kind, hard on the outside but easily hurt or offended, emotional and devoted—a home and family builder. These are all Cancerian traits and paint an essentially sensitive picture but with the strengths of devotion and faithfulness. Intellectually, Cancerians are very intuitive and have a strong imagination. If these traits are over-stressed or misused, it can lead to restlessness and over-worry.

Leo

Leo is the only sign ruled by the Sun and, like the lion, so-called king of the beasts, the Leonian can be regal, dignified and magnanimous. They are faithful, trusting but strong-willed, with fixed principles and ideas, and yet if carried too far this may result in bossiness. Similarly, someone may become snobbish, conceited and domineering.

Virgo

Virgoans are typically worker types; they dislike a leading role in anything, and yet they are intellectually very capable, although with a tendency to worry. In work and at home they pay attention to detail with precision and clarity. Closeness to others may be avoided, resulting in the perception among others of Virgoans keeping to themselves, which in turn may be misinterpreted as inhospitality.

Libra

This seventh sign of the Zodiac is opposite to Aries, which makes Librans interested in relating to a partner. As such they tend to be companionable, tactful and like to be in pleasant surroundings. Librans are often unfairly dubbed as lazy. They may also have a tendency to be quite aggressive. A Libran may be of the type who sits on the fence over an issue and, seeing both sides of an argument, may be impossibly indecisive.

Scorpio

This sign is one of intense energy, with deep, passionate feelings about the object of their attention, be it a person or an issue. Scorpions can be passionate, but in excess this can result in resentment, jealousy and even hatred. However, they can equally be warm and charming, and their virtues become apparent when dealing with real life rather than more trivial matters.

Sagittarius

In the earlier days of astrology, Sagittarius was always represented by a man joined to a horse, signifying the duality of the sign—a combination of strength and intelligence. Sagittarians are often intellectuals with a thirst for a challenge and an ability of body and mind to match. Taken to extremes, these traits can mean restlessness, carelessness, extravagance and a tendency to 'horseplay'.

Capricorn

Capricornians tend to be practical, ambitious and caring, and they often possess an excellent sense of humour. In personal relationships caution is their watchword but once decided they will make good partners. Capricornians are also traditionalists and excel in routine work or in organizational capacities. On the negative side, they may become too mean and stern, and caution may turn into selfishness.

Aquarius

Aquarians are typically independent and individualistic, and also friendly. Indeed, friendships once formed tend to be faithful, although contact with others can be rather impersonal. The freedom required by an Aquarian makes them paradoxical when it comes to love. However, the enquiring mind and originality is seen to good effect in pursuit of art or working in science and technology. An excess of Aquarian traits produces someone who is rebellious, tactless and eccentric.

Pisces

The last sign of the Zodiac, Pisces, is typified by a sensitivity that may border on the inhibited unless encouraged. Pisceans can be inspired and highly intuitive, although this may be clouded by mood swings, from elation to depression. Kindness is a common trait, and there is often a strong spiritual faith. In excess, Piscean characteristics may result in muddled thinking, weakness of character and excessive worry.

Groups of the Zodiac and rulings

The twelve signs of the Zodiac are traditionally subdivided into a number of groups. The members of each group share certain characteristics that in terms of chart interpretation provide additional information rather than primary details.

The first grouping is the *triplicities*, otherwise known as the elements, and consists of the signs for fire, earth, air and water. Aries, Leo and Sagittarius are the *fire triplicity*. This sign is represented by a keenness and enthusiasm and a tendency literally to burn with excitement. Often more sensitive people will be considered slow and dealt with impatiently. While people with the fire sign may be lively and exuberant, their fault will often be that they are too lively. However, such tendencies are likely to be offset, to some extent, by features elsewhere in a chart.

The *earth triplicity* contains Taurus, Virgo and Capricorn and, as might be expected, people with this sign are 'down to earth', although the earth sign is not totally dominant. However, the beneficial aspects include practicality and caution, and although considered dull by livelier people, there is a reassuring solidity and trustworthiness about people with this sign.

Gemini, Libra and Aquarius form the *air triplicity*, and communication is one of the key attributes. An 'ideas person' would have this sign prominent in his or her chart, but a potential fault can be that schemes and ideas occupy too much time at the expense of productivity. In addition, such people can be dismissive of sensitivity or caution in others.

The final triplicity is that of *water*, and it contains Cancer, Scorpio and Pisces. Such people are naturally sensitive and intuitive, and often inspired, while also emotional and protective. Such people tend to be cautious of those with strong personalities, and their own faults may result from being too emotional.

It is often the case that people who have a shared strength in these signs will be compatible. Reference to the elements produces obvious attractions:

Fire   air fans the flames while water puts them out and earth smothers them.

Earth   water refreshes it while air and fire dry it out.

Air   fire responds to air, while earth and water restrict it.

Water   earth holds it, but air and fire diminish it.

The *quadruplicities* (otherwise known as qualities) form the second grouping. In this case the signs of the Zodiac are divided into three groups of four. The three qualities are 'cardinal', 'fixed' and 'mutable'. Aries, Libra, Cancer and Capricorn are of the *cardinal quadruplicity*. People with this sign dominant in their chart are outgoing and tend to lead. Taurus, Scorpio, Leo and Aquarius are of the *fixed quadruplicity*, which implies stability and a resistance to change. The *mutable quadruplicity* includes the remaining signs, Gemini, Sagittarius, Virgo and Pisces, and all have an adaptability. They often appear selfless.

The third grouping is into positive and negative (otherwise known as masculine and feminine). In essence these are descriptive rather than definitive terms and equate in a general sense to being self-expressive or extrovert (positive) on the one hand and receptive or introvert on the other. This does not mean that if a woman has a masculine sign she is not to be considered feminine, and vice versa.

Taking into account the three groupings, the Zodiac signs are as follows:

Aries	–	fire, cardinal, masculine
Taurus	–	earth, fixed, feminine
Gemini	–	air, mutable, masculine
Cancer	–	water, cardinal, feminine
Leo	–	fire, fixed, masculine
Virgo	–	earth, mutable, feminine
Libra	–	air, cardinal, masculine
Scorpio	–	water, fixed, feminine
Sagittarius	–	fire, mutable, masculine
Capricorn	–	earth, cardinal, feminine
Aquarius	–	air, fixed, masculine
Pisces	–	water, mutable, feminine

When interpreting charts, another useful link between signs is *polarity*. This is the relationship between a sign and the opposite sign across the Zodiac. Thus, on a circular display of the twelve signs, Aries is opposite Libra, Cancer opposite Capricorn, Taurus opposite Scorpio, etc. The signs thus opposed do not, however, have opposite tendencies; rather, the polar signs complement each other.

Before turning to the concept of ruling planets, it will be helpful to consider a few other definitions and some lines and angles that are critical in the construction of a chart. The *ascendant* is defined as the degree of a sign (or the ecliptic) that is rising above the horizon at an individual's birth and marks the junction of the first sign. This is essentially the beginning for any astrological chart construction and interpretation, and after calculation is marked on the chart, working clockwise upwards from the horizon line, which runs east-west across the chart. The ascendant is very significant and can only be constructed if a birth time is known. The significance of the ascendant is that it indicates the beginning of the personality and how an individual faces the world—his or her true self. There are many other factors that may lessen the influence of the ascendant sign, but if some characteristic comes out of a chart that reinforces one linked to the ascendant, then it will be a very significant trait.

The *descendant* is the point opposite to the ascendant, at 180 degrees to it, and is always the cusp, or junction, of the seventh house. Although it may often be left out of charts, the descendant is meant to indicate the sort of partner, friends, etc, with whom one associates and feels comfortable.

The *midheaven* is often abbreviated to MC, from the Latin *medium coeli*. At the time when one particular sign of the Zodiac is appearing over the horizon (the ascendant) there will inevitably be another sign that is at its greatest height. This sign is then said to culminate at the upper meridian of the appropriate place—in brief, the midheaven is the intersection of the meridian with the ecliptic at birth. The significance of the midheaven is that it relates to the career of an individual and the way in which it is pursued. It can also provide a general indication of aims and intentions and the type of partner that may be sought. The point opposite to the midheaven is the *imum coeli* and is connected to the subject's origins, his or her early and late life, and parental/domestic circumstances. The *imum coeli*, or IC, is sometimes referred to as the nadir, but strictly speaking this is incorrect. The nadir is actually a point in the heavens that is directly opposite the zenith, which itself is a point in the heavens directly over any place.

Influence of the planets

Every sign of the Zodiac has what is called a *ruling planet*, which is the planet that rules the ascendant sign. From the list below, it can be seen that if someone has Pisces rising, the ruling planet will be Neptune. Each planet rules one sign, save for Venus and Mercury, which each rule two. Of course, before William Herschel discovered Uranus in 1781 there were only seven planets (including the Sun and Moon) and therefore three further planets ruled two signs; Saturn ruled Aquarius in addition to Capricorn, Jupiter ruled Pisces in addition to Sagittarius, and Mars ruled Scorpio in addition to Aries.

There are also a number of planets that are termed personal. The *personal planets* are the Sun and Moon (which are always personal), the planet that rules the ascendant sign (called the chart ruler). The Sun ruler is the planet that rules the Sun sign, and the planet that rules the sign occupied by the Moon is called the Moon ruler.

These different rulings were established a long time ago. There are additional features and weight-ings given to the rulings, known as *exaltation, detriment* and *fall*. Each planet is exalted when it is in a particular sign from which it works well and with which there is a notable similarity, resulting in more significance being attributed to it in an interpretation. The exaltations are also listed below:

Planet	Ruling in	Exalted in	Detrimental in	Fall in
Sun	Leo	Aries	Aquarius	Libra
Moon	Cancer	Taurus	Capricorn	Scorpio
Mercury	Gemini and Virgo	Virgo	Sagittarius	Pisces
Venus	Taurus and Libra	Pisces	Aries	Virgo
Mars	Aries	Capricorn	Libra	Cancer
Jupiter	Sagittarius	Cancer	Gemini	Capricorn
Saturn	Capricorn	Libra	Cancer	Aries
Uranus	Aquarius	Scorpio	Leo	Taurus
Neptune	Pisces	Leo	Virgo	Aquarius
Pluto	Scorpio	Virgo	Taurus	Pisces

The ruling planets and relationships

Opposing the ruling sign of the Zodiac, each planet also has a sign of detriment. In this the planet is said to be debilitated. Finally, in this section comes the sign opposite to exaltation, which is called the fall sign. This is the sign opposite to the sign of exaltation and, is where the planet is thought to be weak. (*See* list above).

The houses of the chart

The astrological chart is divided into houses—in effect this is a way of subdividing the space around the Earth. There are numerous such systems, which have been devised over the years and which fall into three groups: the Equal House System; the Quadrant System; and a variation on these systems.

The *Equal House System* is one of the oldest and after a period of disuse

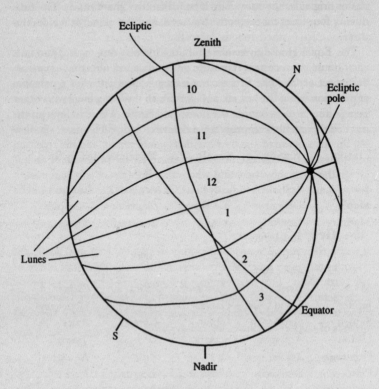

Ecliptic
Zenith
N
Ecliptic pole
10
11
12
1
Lunes
2
3
Equator
S
Nadir

The Equal House System

is now back in favour. The ecliptic is divided into twelve equal parts, and the houses are marked by great circles that meet at the poles of the ecliptic and start by going through the degree of the ecliptic ascending over the horizon, and then through every point 30 degrees farther around.

The main *Quadrant Systems* are called after the people who developed them, for example, Campanus, Regromontanus and Placidus, and appeared in the thirteenth, fourteenth and fifteenth centuries respectively. The system of Placidus was used almost exclusively until the early 1950s because it was the only system with published reference tables. It was, however, the only system that did not utilize great circles as the boundaries of the houses.

The final system, a variation, includes the system of Porphyry, which has its origins in antiquity. This is based on the Quadrant System, producing four unequal divisions that are each then equally divided into three.

The Equal House System is probably the simplest to use, and in it each house has a certain relevance or significance, affecting a particular aspect of life. The first six houses are concerned with a personal application while the last six apply more to one's dealings with other people and matters outside the home and family. There follows an expanded though not comprehensive description of each house, stipulating the association of the house with sign and planet and the resulting meanings. In this context, the planets stand for the provision of an impetus; the signs show how and where that impetus or motivation is to be used; and the houses indicate in which aspect of life the result will be seen.

The first house

This house is associated with Aries and the planet Mars, and because it includes the ascendant, or rising sign, is the most important house of the birth chart. This house refers to the person, which may include such factors as physical characteristics, nature, health, ego and so on. Planets within eight degrees of the ascendant will strongly affect all aspects of the person, including behaviour.

The second house

The second house is associated with Taurus and the planet Venus, and is concerned with the possessions and feelings of the person. As such, this house reflects attitudes to money, and since money and love are intimately entwined, this aspect will be of relevance when interpreting a chart. The second house is also concerned with priorities and the growth of things.

The third house

This is the house of Gemini and the planet Mercury, which not surprisingly means a concern for siblings and also neighbours. Other matters of a local nature, such as schooling, local travel and everyday matters of business, fall under this house. Mental attitude, also falls into the third house, meaning that many important patterns of behaviour, can be considered here. Decisions such as where to live and personal environment are typical examples. All aspects of communication also fall within this house. For anyone who is lost as to what decision to take, a positive influence from the third house will help him or her.

The fourth house

The sign of Cancer and the Moon are associated with the fourth house. The key concerns of this house are the home itself, home circumstances and the family, and caring for someone or something. The mother, or a mother figure, is a particularly strong feature of this house. The concept of the home and the protective enclosing also has analogy with the womb and the grave—thus, the beginning and end of life are also concerns.

The fifth house

This house is very different from the fourth, and the association of Leo and the Sun makes it the house of pleasure and creativity. This includes all such aspects, whether they be related to art, authors, games, gambling, and other leisure pursuits. Moving into the more personal sphere, the fifth house also accounts for lovers and love affairs, probably on a superficial level rather than a lasting, deep relationship. The other personal manifestation of creativity, that of producing children, and parents' feelings about children and procreation, fall under the rule of this house.

The sixth house

The sixth house is the last that impinges upon the person and personal acts, behaviour and relationships. Its sign is Virgo and the planet is Mercury. This is a very functional house, referring as it does to work of a routine nature, health and similar matters. The work may be in the work place, hence it also relates to employers, or at home in the daily round of chores. The concern of health also includes diet, and this house will help to assess the need and timing for a change.

The seventh house

The last six houses refer to the wider influences of one's life and to outward application. Libra and the planet Venus are associated with the seventh house, and the fundamental concern is with relationships with others. This house concerns commitment in partnership and can reflect the likely type of partner sought. It can also relate to the establishment of a business or the employment of new people, from the viewpoint of personal interaction. Because this house encompasses dealings with others, it can also include hostility and conflict.

The eighth house

This house, the opposite of the second, is associated with Scorpio and Pluto, and refers to possessions gained through others, whether as gifts or legacies. In fact, all financial matters fall within this house. It is also the house of birth and death, or alternatively beginnings and endings. Deep relationships, including those of a sexual nature, are dealt with, as are matters of the occult and the afterlife.

The ninth house

The ninth house, the house of Sagittarius and Jupiter, is from the opposite of the third, which is concerned with neighbours and matters local. The ninth focuses upon travel to foreign countries and extensive study, and also has been called the house of dreams. Longer-distance communication and matters such as the law and literature are covered by the ninth house. Indeed, all factors that potentially may increase one's experience or awareness are appropriate.

The tenth house

The tenth house is the opposite of the fourth house and looks outward to life in general, being concerned with hopes and ambitions and making one's way in life. It used to be called the house of the carer and the father, when perspectives and opportunities were more limited than today. As such this is the province of the long-term carer and also denotes responsibility in the context of the delegation, both giving and receiving. This house is pertinent when career changes are considered, and is associated with Capricorn and Saturn.

The eleventh house

The eleventh house is associated with Aquarius and Uranus. It is the house of acquaintances, social contacts and friends (but not close friends), and as such may encompass societies, clubs and similar groupings. It also provides an indication of whether a person looks favourably upon charitable causes and whether any activities in this direction are genuine or for the self—the house of social conscience in effect. It was called the house of hopes and wishes.

The twelfth house

The twelfth house, associated with Pisces and Neptune, is linked with things that are hidden, self-sacrifice, psychic matters and also matters of an institutional nature. This last aspect may refer to hospitals or prisons, and as such may include the more serious illnesses. It can also shed light on problems of a psychological nature, reflected to some extent in its previous name—the house of sorrows.

The following section on the Sun signs, provides more information on personality, characteristics, associations and aspects of personal involvement and interaction.

The Sun Signs

sign: ARIES ♈

dates: 21 March to 20 April

origin and glyph: the ram's horns, which may be traced back to Egypt

ruling planet and groupings: Mars; masculine, cardinal and fire

typical traits: Arians have several noticeable characteristics, such as courage, seemingly boundless energy, enthusiasm, initiative and enterprise, and a desire for adventure and travel. This means that when faced with a particular challenge, there is a tendency to rush in without heeding the consequences, and this can often cause problems. This impulsiveness is, of course, one of their less appealing traits, and it may also be accompanied by selfishness. This manifests itself in the need to accomplish set tasks and reach planned goals, although they tend to have the beneficial quality of being able to concentrate on the primary aim by removing anything that is unnecessary and of little importance. Competitiveness is never far from the surface for an Arian, no matter what aspect of life is involved.

family: in personal relationships, Arians can be very passionate, and Aries men look for a strong partner. Arian women are equally demanding and often prefer a career to being at home, although the two can be combined. Providing there are no adverse influences elsewhere on a person's chart, Arians are faithful but there are those who are continually moving on to new relationships and challenges.

Children of this sign tend to show the typical traits of liveliness and enthusiasm, but because there is always an underlying impatience, a child may soon lose interest and be looking for something new. Performance at school may be chequered because of this trait. However, should such a child lose his or her place or standing, his or her natural competitiveness and wish to lead usually reassert themselves, and lost ground is regained and held.

As parents Arians are, not unexpectedly, energetic and in the main will encourage their children in a variety of activities. It is all too easy, however, for the ebullience of the parent to overshadow the wishes of the child, and that can easily result in discord.

business: to satisfy the Arian character, an occupation ought to be challenging, with goals to aim for and with the opportunity to lead. Boring, routine jobs would not satisfy, but if that were the outcome then other activities would have to compensate. Large organizations with some freedom and a defined career structure, such as teaching, the police or the civil service, would be appropriate.

wider aspects: in their other pursuits, Arians import their eager approach, which in certain circumstances can be positively damaging, for example, knocks and bruises in the early years.

associations: *colour*—red; *flowers*—thistle, honeysuckle; *gemstone*—diamond; *trees*—thorn-bearing varieties; *food*—traditional rather than exotic.

sign: TAURUS ♉

dates: 21 April to 21 May

origin and glyph: the bull's head, which has links with early civilizations in Egypt.

ruling planet and groupings: Venus; feminine, fixed and earth.

typical traits: Taureans rely upon stability and security, both in an emotional and financial context, but granted this they can be extremely reliable, patient and tenacious. They tend to be persistent, methodical and see things through to the end, and this can be reflected in their steady progress through life, including their career. Their lack of flexibility can often lead to resistance to change, even when it is for the better. However, when facing the challenge, they usually cope better than most. Taureans are practical people who dislike waste, and they tend to have high standards.

family: a good partnership is important to Taureans, and this means a happy harmonious partnership. Their need to put down roots and build can render them very good at making a home, as does the practical side of their character. They usually make good husbands and wives, and parents, but they may make the mistake of getting stuck in a rut. One of the faults of Taureans is jealousy and possessiveness, which can often be applied to a partner.

Having established a good home, Taureans will probably consider children to be very important, and the parents will strive to make their children happy. Babies and toddlers can be slow to reach the obvious milestones such as walking, but in later childhood things need to be learnt only once. Discipline is important because Taureans are essentially traditional and look for rules and guidance.

business: although Taureans do not like taking risks, they are ambitious. However, they are more likely to stay with a job than to chop and change, and will quite possibly remain in uninteresting employment because the income is well nigh guaranteed. Sure handling of money and financial affairs comes easily to Taureans, and many find careers in the financial sector.

wider aspects: routine is vital, and change or uncertainty makes them uncomfortable. They enjoy leisure pursuits but must guard against becoming too lazy.

associations: *colour*—pale shades, especially blue, pink and green; *flowers*—rose, poppy and foxglove; *gemstone*—emerald; *trees*—apple, pear, ash; *food*—generally like their food.

sign: GEMINI ♊

dates: 22 May to 21 June

origin and glyph: two children, from Castor and Pollux of Classical mythology, which are bright stars.

ruling planet and groupings: Mercury; masculine, mutable and air.

typical traits: these include such characteristics as liveliness, versatility and intelligence, but these are tempered to some degree by a nervous energy and a certain inconsistency at times. They are logical, ordered and very quick of mind, seeking variety in their lives, both at home and in their work. They tend to be good communicators but at times let their desire to communicate dominate all else. They can take in information very quickly if they are concentrating enough, but run the risk of knowing a little about a lot rather than grasping one topic in great depth. This is not necessarily a bad thing, of course.

family: the Geminian curiosity and versatility render relationships a little more prone than most to disruption or diversion. However, partnerships can last, particularly if the husband/wife finds an interesting companion with whom he or she can interact intellectually. Gemini women often marry men who can deal with domestic chores, as such women have no love of housework.

As parents, they can be lively and creative but sometimes over-critical. It is not uncommon for Geminians to make poor parents because they can be too impatient, too heavily involved in their own careers and over-competitive, seeking reflected glory in their children's achievements.

Gemini children are likely to talk and walk relatively early, and it will be necessary to keep them well occupied. It is often advisable to encourage them to finish anything they have started, to ensure numerous tasks are not left in various stages of completion. Because Geminians can also be quite cunning, and although they may be very able at school, they can often put their own thoughts before hard facts.

business: Geminians are very good when dealing with money and can, therefore, be admirably suited to banking or accountancy. As might be expected, the ability to communicate and the lively personality mean they may also fit well into employment in some aspect of the media or advertising. The pitfalls inevitably are that attention to detail may be lacking and that there must be variety. Conversely, they handle pressure well and are good at handling several tasks at once.

wider aspects: change and variety remain of paramount importance, whether in leisure pursuits or retirement. Individualism will dominate over group activities, which may become routine.

associations: *colour*—yellow, although most are liked; *flowers*—lavender, lily of the valley; *gemstone*—agate; *trees*—any tree producing nuts; *food*—salads and fruit, fish.

sign: CANCER ⊕

dates: 22 June to 22 July

origin and glyph: the glyph represents the breasts; Cancer probably came from ancient Babylon.

ruling planet and groupings: Moon; feminine, cardinal and water.

typical traits: the protective nature of the Cancerian is the overriding aspect of the character, but it is tempered by a stubborn and often moody streak. Although they tend to be of the worrying type, Cancerians have a remarkably good intuition, and their instinctive reactions and decisions can usually be relied upon. There is, however, a changeability about Cancerians that manifests itself in several ways. They can rapidly adapt to pick up information, habits, etc, from others. It also means that they can be touchy and, like the crab, may be hiding a soft, easily hurt person beneath a seemingly hard shell.

family: the caring nature of Cancerians makes them excellent at building a home and good at forming long-lasting partnerships. In general Cancerians like to look back in preference to forwards and commonly stay in the same house for a long period of time. A slightly negative aspect is that their protective nature can become excessive and turn into clinging, and they may be touchy and occasionally snap for no apparent reason.

The sensitive almost retiring aspect of the character can be seen quite early in life, and this may continue to the point that they become very shy at school; they may hide behind a shell. It is commonly the case that Cancerians will eye new social contacts somewhat warily, keeping them at arm's length. However, when they get to know each other better, firm friendships can develop.

Cancerians usually like their extended family within a reasonably short distance and are keen to help anyone who may need their support.

business: Cancerians can turn their hand to most things, and their careful, intuitive approach can make them successful. They tend to work well with people and often adopt the role of mediator, where diplomacy is required. The caring professions (for example, medicine) are obviously well matched to the Cancer character, but teaching may also be suitable. Although business may prosper under a Cancerian, there is often a tendency, even a fear, to change, which may show itself as inflexibility.

wider aspects: Cancerians are extremely sensitive, and while outwardly they appear charming and friendly, they can be temperamental and subject to wide mood swings. In general they love change, and while travel appeals, home has the greatest attraction.

associations: *colour*—silver and pastel shades; *flowers*—white flowers, especially the rose, lily; *gemstone*—pearl; *trees*—none in particular; *food*—dairy foods and fish.

sign: LEO ♌

dates: 23 July to 23 August

origin and glyph: it probably originated in ancient Egypt, from the constellation; the glyph resembles the lion's tail.

ruling planet and groupings: Sun; masculine, fixed, fire.

typical traits: Leonians tend to be generous, creative and yet proud individuals who nevertheless need to keep a tight rein on themselves to avoid becoming overbearing. The creative nature needs to find an outlet in whatever guise, and it is common for Leonians to become organizers, with confidence and energy, although beneath that they may be rather nervous. The possible risk is that Leonians may end up taking over and feel they always know best, so they must learn to listen to the views of other people. They can also display a temper, if only briefly, and are prone to panic if things go badly wrong. However, they generally regain control of the situation quickly. Their impatience and tendency to go over the top are countered by the abundance of their positive qualities.

family: to their partners Leonians will be affectionate, but their strong will and urge to lead can make them rather domineering. However, they can be very sensitive, and criticism can cut deeply. As parents, Leonians understand and encourage their children and will do anything to ensure they are not unhappy. However, they are not over-compliant and often associate with traditional values when it comes to behaviour and education.

Leo children tend to have an outgoing and bright personality, but they must not be allowed to be bossy towards other children, nor must their stubborn streak be allowed to develop. However, any criticism must be levelled in such a way as not to dent the rather fragile Leo self-confidence.

business: whatever their occupation or position, Leo individuals will work hard, in part because they are happier when they have people working for them. For many, luxury or glamour will appeal, and if they can achieve this through their employment then so much the better. As such, they may turn to acting, sport or working in the jewellery trade. They will often go for highly paid jobs, which they equate with status, but, equally, they make good employers, expecting the best of their employees but generous in return.

wider aspects: the Leonian is better leading rather than following and excels where generalities rather than attention to detail are accepted.

associations: *colour*—gold and scarlet; *flowers*—marigold, sunflower; *gemstone*—ruby; *trees*—citrus, walnut, olive; *food*—honey and cereals, most meats and rice.

sign: VIRGO ♍

dates: 24 August to 22 September

origin and glyph: the Egyptian goddess of grain (Nidaba) was probably the origin, and in old pictures the Virgin is shown bearing an ear of corn and holding a child; the glyph is the female genitalia.

ruling planet and groupings: Mercury; feminine, mutable and earth.

typical traits: Virgoans are traditionally shy and modest, hard-working and practical and yet, perhaps, rather dull. They have a well-developed tendency to criticize both themselves and others, and often allow this to go too far. If a positive tenor is applied to Virgoan traits, it results in someone who works hard, is sensible and intelligent, and very good at detailed tasks.

Being essentially a worker, Virgoans are not interested in taking the lead but more in completing a task to the best of their ability. There is a likelihood that Virgoans will be worriers, and they often worry about nothing at all, which can be misconstrued or counterproductive. However, their own positive qualities are the best tools to deal with such problems.

family: Virgoans are very loyal in relationships and fond of their family, although this love may not manifest itself openly but rather in private. They may be self-effacing or even devalue themselves by

35

feeling unworthy. A more common fault would be to over-criticize, but in the main they are caring, sound partners.

Children like to be kept occupied and at school will be neat, tidy and helpful. Their natural shyness may make them seem aloof, but if they can build up their self-confidence this will help them to keep worry at bay.

A great deal of time and attention will be paid to the home to keep it nice, but care should be exercised so that standards are not kept too high.

business: as already mentioned, Virgoans are not particularly ambitious and therefore are happier when supervised at work. If attention to detail is required then they are very capable and proficient in problem-solving or working in science or medicine. Although they like to be appreciated, they are happier working as a member of a team. They have an incisive style, useful in the media and the teaching profession.

wider aspects: there is a desire for purity, perfection and happiness, which, provided that their self-esteem is strong enough, is attainable through application of their own qualities.

associations: *colour*—grey, green, brown; *flowers*—bright small flowers, e.g. buttercup; *gemstone*—sardonyx (a white/brown banded variety of onyx); *trees*—nut producing varieties; *food*—root vegetables.

sign: LIBRA ♎

dates: 23 September to 23 October

origin and glyph: The element of the scales may have several origins, possibly from their use in weighing harvests; the glyph is similar to a yoke.

ruling planet and groupings: Venus; masculine, cardinal and air.

typical traits: Librans are true to their origin—they are always trying to achieve a balance, whether between views, negotiating parties, or in their own environment. In many instances, because they prefer not to take one side or the other, they sit in the middle, and this indecision can be their greatest fault. Turned to positive effect, by combining their desire to balance with their undoubted charm, Librans make fine 'diplomats' and can often settle an argument to everyone's satisfaction. They are also easy-going and like quiet surroundings at home or work, but although they may appear vulnerable, they are in fact quite tough and ensure that they follow their own plans.

family: in relationships with a partner, Librans can be complete romantics and regard this relationship as very important, so much so that even the Libran indecisiveness can be overcome for a time. They tend to fit well into the domestic scene, being quite capable of organizing the household with their usual equable approach to all things, including money.

Librans make kind parents, although they must ensure that they are strong-willed and insist upon children doing as they are told. The Libran indecision might irritate some children, and every effort should be made to answer a child's queries. Children with this Sun sign tend to be charming and affable, and are often popular at school. Indecision and laziness should be identified and wherever possible overcome.

business: as mentioned, the tact and evenhandedness of Librans make them ideal as diplomats, in public relations, or any profession requiring these qualities. Their appreciation of art and beauty lends itself to a career in the arts or literature, and fashion, beauty and related professions are all possibilities for them. Although they like to work with other people, especially those of a like mind, they are sufficiently ambitious to reach for the top, although any isolation that this might produce would be unwelcome.

wider aspects: Librans work well anywhere where there are pleasant surroundings that are well ordered.

associations: *colour*—blues and pinks; *flowers*—bluebells, large roses; *gemstone*—sapphire; *trees*—ash, apple; *food*—cereals, most fruits and spices.

sign: SCORPIO ♏

dates: 24 October to 22 November

origin and glyph: the origin of the scorpion is unknown, although it appears in numerous guises in ancient history. The glyph symbolizes a serpent's coil and is linked with the male genitalia.

ruling planet and groupings: Pluto; feminine, fixed and water.

typical traits: Scorpians can show rather a mix of behaviour and character, on the one hand being very determined and strong-willed, and on the other being obsessive, awkward and arrogant. Once committed to something, whether a person or an ideal, they will be very faithful, although they are susceptible to being melodramatic, and when emotions become involved logic suffers. They are usually energetic, wanting the most out of life, whether at work or play, and will not relinquish their goal easily. Although they are perfectly capable of sacrificing others, they do hold on to what is right and will exhibit a strong sense of fair play and reason.

family: the Scorpian's desire to stay with a relationship holds good for partnerships, although their energy may need to be channelled if it is not to prove disruptive. They prefer people who are equally strong-willed but, despite outward appearances, may themselves be weaker than they look. They are certainly prone to depression, from which they find it hard to emerge, and this may contribute to the apparent extremes in marriage—some are very good, others less so.

As parents they will do their utmost for their offspring, but they can push a little too much and should consciously develop a balanced approach to parenthood, allowing their children some freedom.

Some children are often very affectionate but equally prone to sudden tempers. They should be helped to talk over problems to avoid depressed silences, and their emotional energies should be diverted into productive occupations.

business: when running a business, a Scorpian will work to his or her very limit to help ensure success and, to a certain extent, they welcome challenges and problems. They can employ charm when necessary but can also be hard and demanding at times. They also like financial security and are willing to work for it. Scorpians are well suited to being in the medical profession or in a profession where analysis and research are required.

wider aspects: the character of a Scorpian is built up of a fine balance of attributes, which, in a positive sense, can yield a tremendous achiever but conversely may produce someone riven with jealousy.

associations: *colour*—deep red; *flowers*—dark red flowers such as geraniums; *gemstone*—opal; *trees*—thorn-bearing varieties; *food*—foods with strong flavours.

sign: SAGITTARIUS ♐

dates: 23 November to 21 December

origin and glyph: the origin is unknown, but the glyph, represents the arrow of the Centaur.

ruling planet and groupings: Jupiter, masculine, mutable and fire.

typical traits: Sagittarians are essentially gregarious, friendly and enthusiastic, with a desire to achieve all goals that are set. They are rarely beset by depression, but their inborn enthusiasm can sometimes take them too far, and they may take risks. Although they are versatile and intelligent, their desire to jump from the task in hand to the next may result in some tasks being unfinished. In excess, their good qualities can become a nuisance, leading to tactless, hurtful comments (without the intent to hurt) and jokes that go too far.

family: freedom is important to Sagittarians, so much so that it may inhibit long-term relationships. After settling down, however, they are good in the family context, and their enthusiasm can help lift boredom or depression. Sagittarians will enjoy a friendship or partnership more if they are given a loose rein to enable them to do what they want. Often their ultimate goal is not materialistic but more spiritual.

As parents, this approach to life means that they encourage their children to be outgoing, and this is fine providing a child is not nervous or shy. The natural enthusiasm of Sagittarian children should be guided to productive ends, and their instinctive dislike of rules should be dealt with diplomatically. There is considerable potential in the child who has a gentle guiding hand upon him or her.

business: Sagittarians are not interested primarily in material gain and because they are particularly interested in education and travel, that is where money may be spent. Work of a varied nature is preferred, but care should be taken to make sure details are not omitted in the race to move on to something new. There is a natural desire to help others, which may manifest itself in a career in teaching, counselling, lecturing, the Church, law, and publishing.

wider aspects: when both mind and body have a certain degree of freedom, Sagittarians are at their best and will then employ their versatility and intellectual strengths to the full.

associations: *colour*—purple, deep blue; *flowers*—carnations; *gemstone*—topaz; *trees*—oak, ash, and birch; *food*—good food is enjoyed but overindulgence should be avoided. Specifically currants and the onion family.

sign: CAPRICORN ♑

dates: 22 December to 20 January

origin and glyph: it may have originated with a mythical sea-goat from ancient Babylon. The glyph, is said to represent a goat's head and a fish's tail.

ruling planet and groupings: Saturn, feminine, cardinal and earth.

typical traits: it is said that there are two types of Capricornian, one of which has greater and higher hopes of life. In general, they are patient, practical and can be very shy, preferring to stay in the background—but, they are strong-willed and can stand up for themselves. Capricornians have a reputation for being mean, ambitious and rather hard people. A mean streak may often be directed at the self, and ambition, if tempered with realism and humour, can be positive. Usually the character is enhanced by other elements of the chart to produce a warmer personality.

family: Capricornians make good partners, although they may come late to marriage to ensure a career has been established and that the correct choice is being made. Once set up, they are likely to be happy and to provide well, if economically, for the family. This aspect of caring can extend well outside the immediate family, and although there may be a lack of confidence, a Capricorn subject will not allow him or herself to be pushed around.

As parents, they can be too strict. However, they encourage their children and will make sacrifices to assist their child's progress.

Capricorn children may be a little slow to develop but usually come into their own eventually. They are very loyal and benefit from a secure background, which offers discipline, but at the same time they should be helped to build up their self-confidence.

business: although they make very good back-room people, Capricornians can make good leaders and do well in their own businesses. Many have an affinity for scientific work and pay attention to detail. They work well with people, although they tend to have an isolationist attitude, taking advice only grudgingly. One might well find them in local government, finance, publishing, building or politics.

wider aspects: those with Capricorn as their Sun sign are generally happy alone in leisure pursuits and therefore enjoy music, reading, etc.

associations: *colour*—dark colours; *flowers*—pansy, ivy; *gemstone*—amethyst; *trees*—pine, willow; *food*—starchy foods, meat.

sign: AQUARIUS ♒

dates: 21 January to 18 February

origin and glyph: there are several links with the water carrier, and the glyph clearly resembles water waves, although the similarity to serpents has also been noticed.

ruling planet and groupings: Uranus; masculine, fixed and air.

typical traits: Aquarians are renowned for their independence and the fact that they like to operate according to their own rules. This can lead to them becoming very stubborn, but they can be inspiring because they do not easily lose hope. Aquarians are friendly, although they may not be totally reliable when circumstances become difficult, and highly creative in terms of ideas. However, they are not necessarily sufficiently practical to see through the ideas. Overall, they may be a little perverse or paradoxical, but beneath it all is a gregariousness and a real wish to help.

family: because of their independence, Aquarians may find it difficult to establish an emotional tie. However, providing they find the right type, who is not weak but capable and sensible, personal relationships can be very successful. They are usually totally faithful.

With children, they are supportive but may find it difficult to cope with emotional problems. Children may be a little unconventional, and some school environments may not be conducive to the full development of their potential. On the positive side, children will be originators, naturally friendly, and show the Aquarian traits of creativity and an affinity for science. The natural friendliness should not, however, be allowed to develop into a trust of anyone, particularly strangers.

business: not surprisingly, Aquarians like the freedom to do whatever they want, and they tend not to heed anyone who tries to boss them around. They are highly inventive and are generally good with any subject of a technical nature. They are also highly competent at practicalities. This makes for a considerable range of occupations, and Aquarians often turn their hand to science, communications, teaching, social work and general administration.

wider aspects: Aquarians are by their very nature a little out on a limb and unconventional, but their very positive qualities make this an interesting Sun sign.

associations: *colour*—electric blue; *flowers*—orchid; *gemstone*—aquamarine; *trees*—fruit trees; *food*—a light diet is best, including fruits.

sign: PISCES ♓
dates: 19 February to 20 March
origin and glyph: there are numerous links between the two fishes and various deities from history, including Jesus Christ. The glyph represents two fish, linked, but also refers to the physical and spiritual side of the person.
ruling planet and groupings: Neptune; feminine, mutable and water.
typical traits: the Piscean person is really quite sensitive but above all is a highly sympathetic and caring person who invariably puts other people first, especially the family. They have great intuition and are good at understanding the needs of other people and make very good, kind friends. Sometimes they can take their idealistic and self-effacing stance too far, resulting in an unwillingness to face decisions,

and sometimes they will rely on other, stronger, characters to lead for them. They are usually always tactful but should beware that helping others and becoming involved emotionally is not always a good thing.

family: in partnerships, Pisceans can be a little difficult to cope with, but with the right partner will help to build a welcoming home. They like visitors and to visit others, and their self-sacrificing attitude means that they will usually go a little bit further to make people happy, or an occasion just right. It is important that their lack of strong will is not exploited by a stronger character.

Pisceans love children and make very good parents providing they are not too 'soft'. They do have an inner strength, and can be very tough and resourceful if the occasion demands it and when they rise to the challenge. Children often take second place to others and may need some help with their self-confidence. However, they can be very good in science and with parental encouragement can be good achievers.

business: it is not surprising, with their caring instincts, that Pisceans make good teachers and members of the health and related professions. They tend not to be particularly ambitious but can have extremely good business minds. Success is usually more likely if they have a supportive business partner. Other professions that often attract Pisceans include acting, the ministry, and anything linked with the sea.

wider aspects: Pisceans have to be careful that in helping and caring for others they tend to ignore their own pursuits or problems.

associations: *colour*—sea green; *flowers*—water lily; *gemstone*—moonstone; *trees*—willow; *food*—excesses should be avoided, salad foods are very suitable.

The Birth Chart

All the foregoing is background information that helps in the interpretation of a birth chart or horoscope. A typical blank chart is shown below. The solid central line represents the horizon and the numbered segments are the houses, as described previously. On this chart are plotted the positions of the Sun, Moon and planets.

To begin with, the following information about the subject is required:
—the date of birth,
—the time of birth and whether it was British Summer Time or not, and
—the place of birth and the appropriate latitude and longitude.

From this information, the position of the ascendant and midheaven can be plotted, followed by the planets' positions. As each planet is placed on the chart there will be certain angular positions developed between them, and when these form specific angles they are called *aspects*. These aspects have considerable influence on the chart and therefore on its subject.

In addition to these factors, there are further interpretive factors depending on the placing of the planets in the various signs and the positions of that same planet in one of the twelve houses.

There are numerous books that show how to construct a chart and

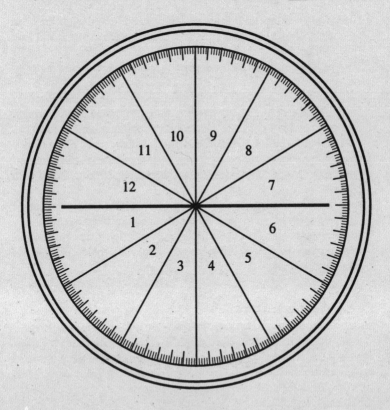

The Birth Chart

begin the quite complicated task of interpretation. There are also computer programs that make the task a little easier. There is not the space to develop this part of th esubject here, although all th information provided does give an insight into the character of the individual and the interesting approach offered by astrology.

Clairvoyance and Crystal Gazing

Among the many methods of divination, the most popular is that of crystal gazing, said to be convenient, consistently reliable and quick and is perhaps less distressing to the clairvoyant than many other methods.

This mode of divination has been practised from very early times with the aid of a crystal globe, a pool of water, a mirror, or indeed any transparent object. Divinations by means of water, ink, and such substances are also known by the name of hydromancy. Crystal gazing could be a very simple or a very elaborate performance, according to the period in history in which it was practised, but in every case the object is to induce in the clairvoyant a form of hypnosis, so that he or she may see visions in the crystal. The 'crystal' most in favour among modern crystal gazers is a spherical or oval globe, about four inches in diameter, and preferably a genuine crystal; but as a crystal of this size and shape is necessarily expensive, a sphere of glass is frequently substituted, and with very good results. It must, however, be a perfect sphere or flawless oval, highly polished, and held in an ebony or boxwood stand.

Among the Hindus, a cup of treacle or a pool of ink served the same purpose.

Precious stones were very commonly used by crystallomancers in the past, the favourite stone being the beryl in pale sea green or reddish tints.

By the ancients, crystallomancy was practised with a view to the invocation of spirits, and very elaborate preparations and ceremonials were considered necessary. The early practitioners had to be of pure life and religious disposition. For the few days immediately preceding the inspection of the crystal, the fortune-teller washed frequently, and was subject to strict religious discipline, with prayer and fasting.

The crystal, as well as the stand on which it rested, had to be inscribed with sacred characters, as had the floor of the room where the invocation was to take place. Then, and now, a quiet place is suggested for the purpose, where the clairvoyant is free from all distraction and disturbance.

As well as these states of solitude and cleanliness, there is the question of the mental attitude to be considered, and this is no less important than the material preparations. A perfect faith was considered to be an essential condition of success. If the clairvoyant was to be accompanied by one or two of his friends or observers they also had to conform to the same rules and be guided by the same principles.

The time of the invocation was chosen according to the position of the heavens of the various planets, all preparations having been made during the increase of the moon. All the instruments and accessories used in the performance—the sword, rod and compasses, the fire and the perfume to be burned on it, as well as the crystal itself—were consecrated prior to the actual ceremony taking place.

During the process of invocation, the clairvoyant faced the east and summoned from the crystal the spirit desired. Magic circles previously were drawn on the floor, and it was desirable that the crystallomancer remain within these for some little time after the spirit has been dismissed. It was thought to be essential that no part of the ceremonial be omitted, otherwise the event would be a failure.

Later, the view was developed that all such elaborate ceremonies were unnecessary, and that the *magnes microcosmi*, the magnetic principle in man, was in itself sufficient to achieve the desired object. In due course, though the ceremonial was not abolished, it became decidedly less imposing. If the person on whose behalf the divination was to be performed was not himself gifted with the clairvoyant faculty, he looked for a suitable medium, the best for the purpose being a young boy or girl, perfectly pure and innocent. Prayers and magical words were pronounced prior to the ceremony, and incense and perfumes were burned. Sometimes the child's forehead was anointed, and provided with suitable clothing for the impressive nature of the ceremony. Some writers mention a formula of prayers, known as *the Call*, which preceded the inspection of the crystal. Finally, it was handled over the medium. The first indication of the clairvoyant vision was the appearance of a mist or cloud in the crystal. This gradually cleared away, and the vision made its appearance.

Modern crystal gazing is carried on in much the same manner, though the preparations are simpler. The crystal is spherical and of the size of an orange; when in use it may be held between the gazer's finger and thumb, or, if the end is slightly flattened, placed on the table; alternatively it may be held in the palm of the hand against a background of black cloth. The operation may be more easily carried out in subdued light. A medium or clairvoyant person acts as the seer and if the divination be made for anyone else it is advisable that he or she be allowed to hold the crystal for a few minutes before it is passed into the hands of the clairvoyant.

The object of crystal gazing is, as has been said, the induction of an hypnotic state giving rise to hallucinations, the reflection of light in the crystal forming focal points for such hallucinations. The value of elaborate ceremonials and impressive rituals lies in their potency to affect the mind and imagination of the seer. So far, the mystery of the crystal vision is no mystery at all. But the remarkable frequency with which, according to reliable witnesses, visions seen in the crystal have tallied with events happening elsewhere at the same moment, or even with future events, is a fact for which science has not yet found an adequate explanation.

It has been suggested that if telepathy operates with greater freedom during the hypnotic state, so it may be also with the self-induced hypnosis of crystal gazing. And this, though it cannot be said to cover the entire ground, is perhaps, on the whole, the best explanation on offer. There are many well-attested cases where the crystal has been successfully used for the purpose of tracing criminals, or recovering lost or stolen property. The telepathic theory, however, will hardly apply to these instances where events have been witnessed in the crystal before their actual occurrence. Such mysteries as these must be left to the art of the psychical researcher to unravel.

Clairvoyance

Clairvoyance, originally a French word, means the ability to see clearly. The reason so few people possess this extraordinary psychic faculty, is because many human beings seem incredibly blind, deaf, and insensitive to anything beyond the ordinary emotions.

The power of prophecy and acute intuition is a sixth sense which most of us have in a slight degree which often remains dormant and uncultivated.

Clairvoyance has often been mistaken for superstition or wilfully imposed and cunning deceptions, and it is difficult for many people to believe that it is founded on science and truth.

It has stood firm through the ages in spite of the quackery of wizards, the paraphernalia of sorcerers (used to inspire fear and awe in the un-initiated), the sneers of those of material minds. All of us at some time or other have felt the control of that still small voice, potent and penetrating as conscience, which comes, unaccompanied by earthquake or fire, to instil us with awe, joy, extreme sadness, or warning at some critical juncture of our lives; often anticipating, with power greater than speech can convey, some event that concerns our wellbeing.

Why this power should be deemed more extraordinary or mysterious than the senses of sight, hearing, smell, and touch which, even to those thoroughly familiar with the anatomy of the human body, remain steeped in mystery, it is difficult to say.

Science teaches that a million delicate sounds escape the ear and brain, and as many minute exquisitely fashioned atoms escape the eye.

A magnifying glass reveals the marvellous structure of insects and microbes invisible to the naked eye, and it is only by means of a telescope that the beauty of the stars is discerned; in this way the developed power of clairvoyance can be called the magnifying lens of the soul.

It is perhaps because this lens is dull and misty that we fail to see.

The history of ages and a great deal of our most cherished literature prove its existence.

Many of the stories and prophecies of the Bible are founded on clairvoyance. People were simpler and more trusting then; for this reason it is said that visions and clear sight were granted to them.

Pilate's disregard of the warning conveyed in his wife's dream, affected the whole course of Christianity, and the Bible abounds with examples of the disasters that befell those who disobeyed the spiritual promptings sent to them.

Colour and character

Clairvoyance teaches that everybody has a distinctive colour, which conveys more of character and personality than any word or action. The shades of these colours vary according to temperament, and are as much concealed from untrained vision as the million tints composing the gold purple and green bands of the rainbow.

- Optimistic people give out a pale blue aura.
- Large minded progressive people have a pale green aura.
- Pessimistic worried people have an aura which is grey.
- Ill-health in mind or body gives a dark green aura.
- Kindly benevolent, humane people have a pink aura
- The thinker and scholar will have an aura of deep blue.
- The degraded have a brown aura.
- The passionate and bad-tempered have an aura which is red.
- The ambitious will be surrounded by an orange aura.

• The lover of beauty in art has an aura which is yellow.

These colours, however, although providing the key to the character, are subject to constant changes. Our moods sway and change our thoughts according to the happenings that affect us.

For example, bereavement or anxiety has power to transform the blue aura of the optimistic temperament to grey, and this temporary change of colour studied alone may puzzle the clairvoyant, and lead to a false diagnosis of character.

In order to prevent this, the seer should request some article constantly worn by the inquirer to be made available; the older and shabbier it is the better. A glove, an everyday tie or a ring constantly worn are equally valuable by which to discriminate between the temporary and habitual aura peculiar to temperament.

For example, when a man's glove emits a pale blue aura, in contradiction to the grey of his own personality, the deduction is that he is naturally of a hopeful and cheerful tendency, but that some mental anxiety or bereavement causes the grey, deep or pale, according to the depth of emotion dominating him.

The reason for this difference of colours is that the glove is, as it were, saturated with the essence of his normal disposition, while the colour of his character has been changed by circumstances or environment.

People of erratic temperament possess an aura of many and constantly changing colours, but those whose calm never varies maintain only one.

A few people are aware of the tones of their aura, and are therefore keenly sensitive to the influence of their surroundings.

They will be quite miserable if the paper on their walls, or the materials of their clothes, clashes in colour with that of their character; while they are at their best and happiest surrounded by the tints that blend or contrast harmoniously.

The clairvoyant and the crystal

The clairvoyant will possess six key qualities:–
1. The power of magnetism.
2. Mental health and influence.
3. Physical health and cleanliness.
4. Moderation in food and drink.
5. The power of discerning the aura and
   interpreting its colours.
6. Freedom from all bad habits.

In advanced clairvoyance the use of the crystal for vision is designated by many seers as 'claptrap' thought to be a vulgar 'playing to the gallery.' It is known to be bad for the eyes to gaze at any shining article for too long a period, yet in clairvoyance there is no doubt that it aids the concentration of sight and thought.

By means of crystal gazing the seer creates and becomes subject to the influence of auto hypnosis—that is, the ability to become entranced which veils his or her own personality forming a link to the client.

The surface of the crystal gradually reflects images, and subconscious impressions conveyed by and vital to the individual whose past, present, and future are being revealed.

Sympathy and intuition merge the gazer's aura with the temperamental colouring of the client. The seer's magnetic force creates further powers, while the sixth sense is the nucleus about which these are bound.

No student of clairvoyance can be successful in discerning character and personal emanations of colour unless disciplined by simple rules which should govern his or her life.

The clairvoyant should be approached in the same way in which one visits a doctor or solicitor, and there must be no determined reserve to conceal thoughts and character in the mind.

Clairvoyance in a room full of people is extremely difficult—indeed impossible, unless the onlookers can keep perfectly quiet.

It is always better to be alone with the inquirer in a small room where traffic noises do not penetrate, provided only with the necessary furniture, kept clean and fresh, airy, and well lighted.

The crystal should never be touched by any one except the clairvoyant, and must be kept free from spots and smudges. A black silk handkerchief round its globe will be a help to divination by preventing the reflection of lights.

The processes that occur in crystal-gazing are thought transference and telepathy. A communication of ideas is set up between the prophet and client, and the mirror-like surface of the crystal is the medium by means of which innate thoughts are reflected.

As far as possible, the clairvoyant submerges his or her own personality in that of the inquirer, putting himself in his or her place. Profound silence brings about the sense of atmosphere and aura, and by these means, and an intent gazing into the crystal, visions originate.

The crystal is supposed to be the magic bridge which gulfs the chasm fixed between itself and the spiritual world. In the iron it contains are situated the collective and culminating forces.

Mists of white, green, blue, and violet tints are symbols of good fortune and happiness; black, yellow, and red are warnings of disaster.

When the mists disperse and gradually ascend to the surface, the clairvoyant may reply to any question in the affirmative; mists that descend to the bottom are negative signs.

Images that develop to the left of the clairvoyant are real; those on the right are purely symbolical.

Chanting and controlling the mind

Words repeated over and over again have a mysterious power of isolating the sixth sense from the rest. For example, the word AUM is extraordinarily symbolical. It stands for three influences:–

A = the objective.

U = the subjective.

M = the eternal.

These are the kingdoms in the heart of man.

The objective, being the natural surroundings of objects and events which we all can feel and see.

The subjective, being the realm of influences the degree of which is felt according to the perception and training of our spiritual forces; too often vague and illusive, because most of us ignore its existence.

The eternal world, being that state to which the subjective world, in its highest state of development, leads this word repeated, slowly and steadily at first, and then at great speed, to have a marvellous power to create as it were a vacuum between the spirit and body of the prophet.

The mind dwells on its meaning; the vibration of the different letters acts on the mind, and the gazer is carried by gentle stages to the very seat of his spiritual being.

It is when the seer attains this full development that large, clear, and deep perceptions of the client's character are granted, and it is possible to reveal facts concerning the client which in a normal state would be absolutely impossible

The sensation experienced is that of being plunged into space in which the senses of sight, hearing, and touch are transmuted to the brain and spirit.

The student will most probably be discouraged at first at an inability to produce this state, but it should be remembered that hard work and perseverance are the attributes which all must give to attain perfection in any learning, art, or science.

One destined to become a great mathematician often stumbles in childhood with despair over the first addition sum, and the most distinguished musician has to do battle with the rudiments of music.

So it is in clairvoyance. Seemingly insuperable difficulties surround the novice who has never learnt to recognise the value and power of the sixth sense. Patience, a tranquil, determined mind, and not a little courage, are necessary in this branch of science. Time and growth work wonders in the persistent mind, and it will be seen that the obstacles gradually move aside, the curtain is lifted, and the strenuous seeker reaches that mature vision which he has formerly imagined dimly, if at all.

It is a good plan for the novice to ponder on his or her own name, and, shut away from all distractions, repeat it again and again aloud. The seer will gradually feel a sense of deepest mystery, for in that name is concentrated the riddle of existence. The blending of spiritual and material kingdoms lies behind it, and the material slips rapidly into obscurity.

Only when the heart is pure and worthy will the vision be granted — the clouds of bitterness, envy, hatred, and malice, which generally hide the precious jewel from the light, and render brilliance impossible, are discarded.

Everyone knows how difficult it is to control the mind, and keep it from mean and uncharitable thoughts. It is more rebellious even than the body, and influences it for good or evil.

Before all else, the clairvoyant must learn to discipline and constrain his or her thoughts.

A humble outlook, a longing for purity and singleness of purpose are needed to bring about the most noble qualities, and here it is that proper treatment of the body is invaluable.

Simple diet, early rising, daily exercise, constant isolation, and cultivation of good habits create the orbit for the higher faculties. These are the elementary rudiments of clairvoyance, and, unless they are mastered, the clairvoyant, no matter how diligent and persevering he or she may be in study and labour, will not succeed.

Fortune Telling by Numbers

We all have 'lucky numbers'—but what are they and where did they come from? Numbers have a major part to play in our lives. They are everywhere! There are quite simple ways of identifying the special number that brings you luck on a certain day.

That a certain amount of character and fortune may be revealed by means of figures is a fact that can be tested for itself. The results achieved by this method of divination are truly astonishing, and can be very rewarding to the mathematician in the attempt to solve the riddle of human nature.

Certain groups of figures stand for different qualities. Those given in the table following are only a small portion of the whole, but they are sufficient for the beginner. Each letter of the alphabet has its accompanying digit, and each digit has its abstract condition:-

A	1	Passion, ambition, design
B	2	Destruction, death
C	3	Religion, destiny, the soul
D	4	Solidity, sagacity, power
E	5	The stars, happiness, graces, marriage
F	6	Perfect labour
G	7	Course of life, repose, liberty, success
H	8	Justice, preservation
I	9	Imperfection, grief, pain, expectation
J	600	Perfection
K	10	Success, reason, future happiness
L	20	Austerity, sadness
M	30	Fame, a wedding
N	40	Fetes, a wedding
O	50	Pardon, liberty
P	60	Widowhood
Q	70	Science, the graces
R	80	A cure
S	90	Blindness, error, affliction

T	100	Divine favour
U	200	Irresolution
V	700	Strength
W	1400	Perfection of strength
X	300	Safety, belief, philosophy
Y	400	Long and wearisome journey
Z	500	Holiness
	800	Empire
	900	War, combats, struggles

The first thing to ask is the name of the subject. He writes it on a slip of paper, and next to each letter its accompanying figure. Here is the name, Dick James Smith:–

D	4	J	600	S	90
I	9	A	1	M	30
C	3	M	30	I	9
K	10	E	5	T	100
		S	90	H	8

Now they are added separately:–

Dick = 26   James = 726   Smith = 237

Add the three totals together:-

Dick	26
James	726
Smith	237
	989

The interpretation:–

900	War, combats, struggles
80	A cure
9	Imperfection, grief, pain, expectation.

The deduction being that Dick James Smith is endowed with a quarrelsome, headstrong nature, optimism, and inefficient willpower, which are destined to cause him trouble, loss, and misery.

Should the total of the names reach beyond 1390, the first digit must be subtracted, for example as in the name, Johannah Christine Whiting:–

J	600	C	3	W	1400
O	50	H	8	H	8
H	8	R	80	I	9
A	1	I	9	T	100
N	40	S	90	I	9
N	40	T	100	N	40
A	1	I	9	G	7
H	8	N	40		
		E	5		
	748		**344**		**1573**

Total = 2665, take away the first figure, leaves 665.

600	Perfection
60	Widowhood.
5	The stars, happiness, graces, marriage.

The analysis showing that Johannah Christine Whiting's life will be a mixture of joy and sorrow, the latter borne by a courageous and tranquil spirit. Her integrity and attractiveness of character will, no doubt, bring her much love and friends.

If the fortune-teller has a good memory, the table of qualities can be memorised, and a great aid to this is to practise with it perhaps analysing an author, statesman, or friend.

The fortune-teller's own name should reveal the fundamental truths of this method, and the analysis of people from history will show the distinguishing traits that have made them famous. For example, take Florence Nightingale:-

F	6	N	40
L	20	I	9
O	50	G	7
R	80	H	8
E	5	T	100
N	40	I	9
C	3	N	40
E	5	G	7
		A	1
		L	20
		E	5
	209		**246**

Total = 455

400	Long and wearisome voyage
50	Pardon and liberty
5	The stars, happiness, graces

The numbers of the alphabet

1	2	3	4	5	6	7	8	9
A	B	C	D	E	F	G	H	I
J	K	L	M	N	O	P	Q	R
S	T	U	V	W	X	Y	Z	

Now suppose your name is Gladys Templeton, write it downwards, like this:

G —	7		T —	2
L —	3		E —	5
A —	1		M —	4
D —	4		P —	7
Y —	7		L —	3
S —	1		E —	5
			T —	2
			O —	6
			N —	5

Total = 62

You have added to each letter the number that stands for it. Their total value added together is 62. These two numbers add up to 8. You may bank on the importance of this 8, though there are some numerologists who would add to it certain mystic numbers which represent the day on which you make the calculation. The above is simple and it works out, strange to say, with striking results!

Finding your lucky number

Suppose you were born on the 16th June 1971:

Take the date of the month	=	16
Add the figures together	1 + 6 =	7
June is the sixth month, so add		6
Add the year of your birth		1971
		1984

Add these figures together:–

$(1 + 9 + 8 + 4) = 22$ and

22 (*ie.* 2 and 2) = 4

You will find that the figure 4 will turn out well for you; also any figures or any number in which it appears; or any of its multiples 8, 12, 16, as well as 49, 48, 94, 84; and especially 40, for the 0 intensifies any figure which it comes after.

Note that number 4 itself is not a very good number, although it will be favourable for you. People whose number is 4 suffer from 'temper'— their own, as well as that of other people! To live in a house that is Number 4, to get a bus or train or theatre ticket in which 4 appears, more especially if the whole adds up to 4 or to a multiple of 4—this means happy travelling, auspicious enterprises. Wednesday being the fourth day of the week, will be lucky; April, the fourth month in the year also, especially if these be the day or the month of your birth.

But should you particularly dislike this number 4, it is up to you to change it. Some people add the day of the week's number to those given, Sunday being number 1, Monday number 2, and so on. This plan, if you adopt it, gives you a different number. You may work them both together, using one for business and the other for personal luck. But do not change entirely from 4, if this number is serving you well.

The Tarot

Introduction

The Tarot pack is a set of illustrated cards which may be used for predicting future events or for answering almost any kind of question put to it through someone familiar with its symbolism. As a divination technique, it offers possibilities not contained in any other system and it is the only predictive method that is possible for anyone to understand and use after only a few weeks of study and practice. As with all arts, only years of experience will bring full proficiency, but mastering the Tarot does not require the unleashing of dark, supernatural forces or the invoking of ghostly spirits, as many would think, but rather requires an openness to impressions coming from the unconscious mind. We all have this ability—it manifests itself in precognitive dreams, feelings of foreboding, good or bad impressions of people we meet—but we usually ignore these feelings, dismissing them as irrational. Tarot reading is a way of harnessing these intuitive feelings and using them for personal guidance.

History of the tarot

There is little agreement on when and where the Tarot originated. The earliest cards used in Europe bear some similarity to cards used much earlier in Egypt, India and China, but there is little evidence of a direct link. One theory suggests that gypsies brought the cards with them from the east, but while it is true that travelling people have used them for centuries in fortune-telling, it is unlikely that they invented them. Another theory is that the cards are named after the River Taro in the north of Italy and that the cards were invented in the area around there. For many centuries cards similar in design to those in use today could be found in wealthy European households. These cards were more likely to be for playing games than for purposes of divination, and their popularity rose and fell depending on the fashion of the day. When they were in vogue, draughtsmen and printers, unfamiliar with the Tarot, would rush out new sets of cards to satisfy demand. This inevitably led to the designs being altered as each new set had some small detail added or left out.

It was not until the eighteenth century that people started taking the Tarot more seriously. This was the Age of Enlightenment and there was a great deal of interest in the customs, religious beliefs and ideas of ancient civilizations. Antoine Court de Gébelin, an archaeologist and amateur occult scholar from the south of France, wrote a series of books on a diverse range of esoteric subjects and claimed that the Tarot had its origins in an ancient Egyptian text called *The Book of Thoth*. That de Gébelin's theories were so readily accepted can be attributed to the widespread passion for 'Egyptiana' at the time in European society. Hieroglyphic writing, years before the discovery of the Rosetta Stone, frustrated antiquarians, and it became fashionable to suggest that the apparently indecipherable symbols could provide answers to questions that had plagued mankind since the earliest times. De Gébelin followed this trend and made a connection between the Tarot and Egypt, which was popular but which had no basis in fact.

Nevertheless, many writers took up de Gébelin's theories and attempted to expand on them. But when the hieroglyphics were finally deciphered and it was discovered that there was little or no connection between them and the Tarot, those seeking a mystic source had to look elsewhere. Alphonse Louis Constant, writing as Eliphas Lévi, eventually came up with a connection to ancient Hebrew beliefs in two books published in 1855 and 1856. This featured the Jewish mystical system of the Cabbala, which linked letters of the Hebrew alphabet to numbers. He devised a new system of Tarot, which more correctly reflected his theories, but again no hard evidence was offered as to the origins of the cards.

Today we do not know much more than in de Gébelin or Lévi's time. There has been a great deal of speculation and many claims for the source of the Tarot—other writers have linked it with Sufi and Cabbalistic origins or found connections with Greek mythology and pre-Christian religions—but so little evidence to substantiate any claim has been forthcoming that it would appear that the true origins of the Tarot are forever going to remain a mystery.

Reading the cards

The Tarot pack most commonly used today is based on an Italian form known as the Venetian or Piedmontese Tarot which became the standard version in that country by the beginning of the sixteenth century. There are 78 cards in this pack, divided into two parts: the Major Arcana (22 cards) and the Minor Arcana (56 cards). 'Arcana' means secrets or mysteries.

The Major Arcana cards, also known as the Trump cards, display mysterious, esoteric imagery which appears to be have been influenced by pagan traditions. From pack to pack there may be differences in style, position of the figure, dress and other similar details, but there is a strong common symbolism and their interpretation remains more or less constant.

The Minor Arcana features 56 cards that are divided into four suits, each suit having ten Pip cards and four Court cards. This is a similar arrangement to a normal pack of playing cards, except for the Knight cards in each suit. The Tarot suits correspond to playing card suits but they have different names: Wands (also known as Batons or Rods) correspond to Clubs; Cups correspond to Hearts; Swords to Spades and Pentacles (also known as Coins or Discs) to Diamonds.

Selecting your cards

Before one can embark on a reading of the Tarot it is important that you are happy with the cards that you intend to use. Tarot convention decrees that effective readings can only be obtained if the reader uses cards which they feel comfortable and familiar with—using someone else's cards, therefore, is seriously frowned upon. This is because everyone has a different psychic energy and cards owned and used by one person will have a unique psychic identity impressed on them. Cards should also be wrapped in a piece of silk and kept in a wooden box when not in use. Again, this is so the cards do not become tainted by another person's psychic energy.

The importance of ritual

Although there are many who hold with elaborate rituals and ceremonies when preparing a reading, it is generally recognized that such customs are not absolutely necessary. Formality of some kind is important, however, for two reasons. Firstly, a reading requires that the unconscious mind be brought to the fore, and this can only be done in a state of relaxation and quiet. If the reader or the person receiving the reading is overexcited, restless or nervous, then the intuitive, hidden parts of the mind will not be adequately prepared. In order to achieve the right conditions, small rituals and routines are invaluable—shuffling the cards in a certain order, for example, or lighting incense and saying a small prayer—calm the mind and create a better atmosphere. Secondly, Tarot combines random or chance factors with elements that are rigid and fixed, and in order to make sense of these properties there needs to be a solid framework to work within.

Environment

A Tarot reading should not be considered a spectator sport. Distractions, such as people talking or laughing, can turn a reading into a farce. Although it may be difficult to refuse giving a reading at a party or among a group of friends, the best results are always obtained by two people in a quiet room where they are able to concentrate their minds fully.

Selecting a spread

If you have little or no previous experience of the Tarot it is important to begin with a spread that you are comfortable with and fully understand. In the following chapter the Celtic Cross Spread is explained. This is a fairly easy one to follow and many first time users of the Tarot find it very useful. Experience in handling the cards will build the necessary confidence to attempt more complex spreads, but it is always best to master one before tackling another.

Using a spread provides a framework that enables the reader to relate cards to specific areas of the enquirer's life. This means that each card in each position relates to a specific aspect of the enquirer's life. Often it may seem that a card has no relevance to the area indicated by its position in the spread. In such cases the general meaning of the card should be adapted to suit the position in which it appears in the spread. Thus a card that suggests difficulty in a relationship may, in a position where career matters are indicated, be taken as referring to difficulties in a working relationship.

Shuffling and cutting

Before shuffling the cards, it is often suggested that a Significator be selected. This is a card that represents the person seeking a reading or the situation about which the advice is being sought. If the Significator is to represent a person then it should be chosen by the similarities in hair and eye colouring between that person and the card. If the Significator is to represent a situation then it should be a card which broadly describes the situation. If you do decide to use a Significator then it should be removed from the deck before shuffling and placed face up on the table.

The cards should be well shuffled before beginning the reading. If you intend to use reverse meanings then half the cards should be turned around and well dispersed through the pack. It is important that once the reversed cards are shuffled in the pack by the reader that they are not reversed again or the reading given will be upside down. Once shuffled by the reader the cards should be handed to the person seeking the reading for them to shuffle. The cards should then be handed back to the reader—all the time both parties taking care not to turn the pack around.

Selecting the cards

There are two methods of selecting cards. One is for the reader to ask the other person to cut the deck twice using their left hand. Each time the top of the cut should be placed to the left of the bottom of the cut so that three piles are made. The three piles are then collected so that the cards originally on top go to the bottom. The reader then lays out the cards from the top of the pack in the chosen spread.

The second way is for the entire pack to be fanned out, face down across the table. The person seeking the reading should then select their cards, being careful to keep them in order. The first card should always remain on top of the pile of selected cards as this way it is easier to remember the order in which they were chosen.

Laying out the cards

Once the cards are selected they should be laid out face down in their correct positions in the spread. Only when they are all correctly laid out should they be turned over—when turning them over it should be from side to side, not from end to end, as doing this will reverse the meanings. When interpreting the spread, the cards should be regarded as upright or reversed from the reader's point of view.

Before looking at each card individually it is a good idea to take some time to get an overall picture of the spread. If there is a predominance of Court cards or of cards from one suit then this can be significant. If there are a lot of Cups, then relationships and matters of the heart will probably be a dominant theme in the reading. Wands indicate that careers or other enterprises are likely to be important, Swords suggest some form of conflict or struggle, and Pentacles indicate practical affairs. A lot of Court cards together can mean that factors outwith the enquirer's control will shape their destiny and that the actions of other people will have an important influence on their lives.

Looking at the spread as a whole also makes it easier to relate cards to each other. This is an aspect of reading the Tarot which improves with experience and it can often be simpler for a beginner to wait until the end of a reading to make summing up remarks. In some spreads there are very obvious connections when certain cards next to each other develop one theme. For example, three cards in a row may mean 'the way forward', and are therefore intended to be interpreted together. Other cards may modify the meaning of the cards next to them, and more time and thought is required when interpreting them. The ability to assess relationships between cards comes with experience and familiarity, however, and the beginner cannot be expected to see in a spread all the things a more experienced reader may see.

The Celtic Cross spread

The popular Celtic Cross Spread is most useful for obtaining an answer to a specific question. To begin, the reader selects a card to represent the person seeking the reading or which best describes the matter about which an enquiry is being made. This card is commonly called the Significator. If the Significator is to represent the enquirer then the card should be one which corresponds in some way to his or her personal description. A Knight should be chosen if the enquirer is a man aged over forty; a King should be chosen if the man is under that age; a Queen if it is a woman over forty; and a Page for a younger female.

The four Court cards in Wands represent very fair people, with blond or auburn hair, fair complexion and blue eyes. The Court cards in Cups signify people with light brown or dull fair hair and grey or blue eyes. Those in Swords stand for people having hazel or grey eyes, dark brown hair and dull complexion. Lastly the Court cards in Pentacles refer to persons with very dark brown or black hair, dark eyes and sallow complexions. These allocations are not absolutely rigid, however, and you should also be guided by the temperament of the enquirer; a dark person may be exceptionally outgoing and gregarious and would, therefore, be better represented by a Sword card than a Pentacle. On the other hand, a very fair subject who is quite easy-going and relaxed should be referred to by Cups rather than Wands.

If it is decided that it is better to make the Significator refer to the matter being asked into then the card which is most closely associated with that area should be chosen. For example, if the question is to do with the success of a legal dispute, then the Justice card should be made the Significator.

Having selected the appropriate Significator, place it on the table, face upwards. Then shuffle and cut the rest of the pack in the normal Tarot manner, that is, three times, keeping the face of the cards downwards.

Turn up the top or **first card** of the pack and cover the Significator with it, saying, 'This covers him'. This card indicates the influence that is affecting the person or matter of the inquiry and gives an idea of the direction of the reading as a whole.

Turn up the **second card** and lay it across the first, saying, 'This crosses him'. This indicates the nature of the obstacles in the matter. If it is a favourable card, the opposing forces will not be serious, or it may indicate that something good in itself may not be productive of good in that particular connection.

Turn up the **third card** and place it above the Significator card, saying, 'This crowns him'. This card represents (a) the enquirer's aim or ideal or (b) the best that can be hoped for under the circumstances.

Turn up the **fourth card** and place it below the Significator and say, 'This is beneath him'. It shows the foundation or basis of the matter, that which has already happened and the relationship of the enquirer to that event.

Turn up the **fifth card** and place it on the side of the Significator from which he is looking. If the Significator is not a Court card and cannot, therefore, be said to be facing any particular way, then the reader must beforehand select the direction in which the card is said to be looking. Placing the card, say, 'This is beside him'. This indicates an influence which has passed or is passing away.

Turn up the **sixth card** and place it on the side that the Significator is facing and say, 'This is before him'. It shows an influence that is coming into action and will operate in the near future.

The cards are now disposed in the form of a cross, the Significator—covered by the first card—being in the centre.

The next four cards are turned up in succession and placed one above the other in a line on the right-hand side of the cross.

The first of these, or the **seventh card**, signifies the Significator—whether a person or a thing—and shows its position or attitude in the circumstances.

The **eighth card** signifies his house, that is, his environment and the tendencies at work therein which have an effect on the matter—for instance, his position in life, the influence of close friends, and so forth.

The **ninth card** gives his hopes or fears in the matter.

The **tenth card** is what will come, the final result, the culmination which is brought about by the influences shown by the other cards that have been shown in the reading.

It is on this card that the reader should concentrate all their intuitive faculties, taking into account all the divinatory meanings attached to it. In theory, this card should embody all else that has been gathered from the interpretations of the other cards.

The reading is now complete; but should the last card have not given up any conclusion then it might be worthwhile to repeat the operation, taking the tenth card as a Significator.

It is significant if in any reading the tenth card is a Court card. This indicates that the subject of the reading will be greatly influenced by the person represented by that card, and the outcome of anything troubling the enquirer may be dependent on his or her actions. If this is the case then more can be learned if the Court card is taken as the Significator in a fresh reading.

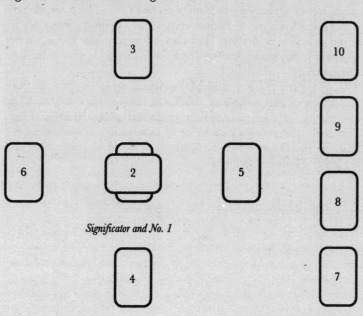

Significator and No. 1

The Significator

1	What covers him.	6	What is before him.
2	What crosses him.	7	Himself.
3	What crowns him.	8	His house.
4	What is beneath him.	9	His hopes or fears.
5	What is behind him.	10	What will come.

The Major Arcana

The Trumps

The twenty-two cards of the Major Arcana, also known as the Trump cards, signify underlying influences on one's life. These are circumstances which are out of human control and are more commonly referred to as fate or destiny. They also represent things which are not apparent in day-to-day life but which are hidden from view in the subconscious.

Many experts also see in the Major Arcana the journey of life, from the innocence and wonder of childhood, through tests and hardships to maturity, and then on to old age, death and spiritual transcendence. The cards reflect such a path in life by using universal symbolism. For example, the Empress and the Emperor as the protective mother and the guiding father respectively.

The Fool

This card shows an attractive young man in a carefree pose standing at the edge of a precipice. He often has his belongings on a stick over his shoulder and a dog by his side.

The Fool represents a carefree, relaxed and open attitude. It suggests the ability to live day by day without worrying about the future. The Fool also signifies childlike qualities such as trust and spontaneity.

Reversed Childishness and irresponsibility are indicated when the card appears reversed. It can therefore be taken as a warning to be more responsible and to have more thought for the consequences of one's actions.

The Magician

This card depicts a practitioner of the magical arts. A lemniscate, the symbol of infinity, is usually shown above his head.

One hand of the figure, gripping a wand, is pointing upwards to the heavens and the other is pointing down, signifying the drawing of power from a higher source and directing it towards practical, earthly matters. As well as signifying skill in directing energies, this card also indicates charm, articulacy and the ability to lead others.

Reversed The inability to turn thought into action is indicated here. This is due to poor leadership and communication skills and a lack of experience and confidence.

The High Priestess

The Priestess sits between two pillars that represent the pillars of Jerusalem, Boaz and Jakin. One is black, signifying the feminine characteristics of intuition and mystery, and the other white, representing the masculine principle of reason.

This card signifies guidance and wisdom of a spiritual or moral nature which comes from unconscious sources—intuition, dreams and fantasies.

Reversed The card can suggest a lack of inner harmony resulting from the suppression of feelings and the failure to acknowledge unconscious guidance. In a man's spread this reversed card signifies negative feelings towards women or that feminine qualities in himself are being ignored.

The Empress

This card shows a woman, often pregnant, sitting in a rich, fertile environment.

Unlike the High Priestess, who is virginal, the Empress represents motherhood and fertility. She also signifies physical and spiritual security and contentment in domestic situations and personal relationships. The benefits of this are generosity, kindness and the enjoyment of other people's company.

Reversed The Empress can also mean dissatisfaction with personal circumstances and a lack of material and emotional comfort. There could also be difficulties with physical health, particularly related to pregnancy and childbirth.

The Emperor

In contrast to the Empress, the Emperor sits in a hard and cold environment with a stern expression on his face.

This card represents masculine power and fatherly responsibility. In a reading it may indicate a connection to a position or figure of authority and could suggest that there is an opportunity to take control over others.

Reversed This indicates a problem connected with control, perhaps a dispute with a father or domineering husband or some other difficulty in a personal relationship. It also indicates a hostile attitude to authority and governance which may be nurturing resentment and rebellion.

The Hierophant

A Hierophant was an initiating priest in ancient Greece. He is depicted as giving advice to two figures in the foreground under his authority.

Originally this card signified the seeking of religious guidance, but in this secular age it represents all forms of guidance where the person giving advice is in a position of authority. Such authority figures include doctors, lawyers, professional counsellors, teachers and tutors. The card indicates that the advice given from such sources will be reliable and useful.

Reversed This indicates that advice given may not be reliable or that the nature of the problem is such that the advice is inappropriate.

The Lovers

Adam and Eve in the Garden of Eden are shown in this card with an angel looking down on them.

This card is not so much about love itself as about decision-making and commitment. The two lovers have their hands open and this signifies that the right decision will be made if there is careful thought and consultation. This applies to any major decision, such as getting married, moving house or changing job.

Reversed This is a warning against making a hasty decision or not making a decision at all and letting important issues go unresolved.

The Chariot

This card shows an upright warrior figure in a chariot with two sphinxes, one black, one white, in the foreground.

The rider represents self-determination and control. The sphinxes represent the opposing forces within human nature which have to be mastered before progress can be made. In a reading the card implies that with enough strength of purpose ambitions can be realized and obstacles overcome.

Reversed This is a warning against losing control and letting one of the two sphinxes gain dominance, thus pulling the rider off course. In order to regain control one has to be rational, assess the situation, and attempt to balance conflicting impulses.

Strength

This card shows a young woman taming a lion. She has a garland in her hair and around her waist.

The lion represents strong, negative emotions such as anger or jealousy and the woman moral strength and self-control. Together they show the importance of balance between these factors. A calm and rational approach in a situation where strong emotions may be aroused is urged.

Reversed Lack of self-belief, despair, and feelings of powerlessness are signified by the reversed card. These feelings can be overcome, however, if strong emotions are correctly channelled.

The Hermit

The Hermit is portrayed as an old man dressed in a habit and carrying a lantern. The barren background signifies isolation.

As the hermit has withdrawn from society, so the card signifies a need to withdraw and contemplate life. It also indicates a need to be more self-reliant and in control of events. This is especially true during times of worry or crisis. Help from others is unwelcome, however, as it is only through contemplation of one's own self that the strength to make progress can be found.

Reversed This indicates loneliness and self-pity. Instead of living in the past the card urges one to look forward and seek solutions to problems.

Wheel of Fortune

The Wheel of Fortune is shown being turned by a sphinx, the symbol of feminine wisdom. Various animals are shown around the wheel, representing the Living Creatures of Ezekiel.

This card indicates fate and events beyond human control.

In the upright position it indicates good luck or the optimistic outlook that things will work out for the best. This can also mean that one has a fatalistic outlook on life, leaving too much to chance and failing to make decisions.

Reversed Usually this indicates bad luck and events out of one's control. It can also signify that leaving things to chance will be damaging.

Justice

Justice is depicted as a woman on a throne with a sword in one hand and a set of scales in the other.

This card signifies a legal matter and concern that justice be done. If the card appears upright in a reading then reason and justice will prevail and the issue will be resolved fairly without recourse to heated, emotional argument.

Reversed In this position the card indicates unfairness, bias and injustice. It may also indicate that in a situation where there is deadlock a completely new approach is required in order to make progress.

The Hanged Man

Although the sight of a man hanging by one foot from a tree can be a little alarming, this card is not a bad omen.

The strange hanging figure represents self-sacrifice and dedication to a cause. Often those virtues are criticized and ridiculed by others who cannot see the end purpose. It can also mean a change in attitude or direction that is personally rewarding but misunderstood by others.

Reversed This signifies lack of purpose and apathy, often coming about through the misguided pursuit of illusory goals and the neglect of one's spiritual wellbeing. It is a call, therefore, to re-order one's priorities and pursue that which is truly rewarding.

Death

The skeleton on horseback is often seen as gruesome and frightening by those unfamiliar with the Tarot. Usually, however, this card signifies change rather than actual death, and the flag being carried aloft and the shining sun in the background are symbols of new life.

More specifically, the card indicates radical change and renewal with one phase of life ending and a new one beginning. With change there is also some grief for things that are lost, and this has to be faced up to and overcome.

Reversed This signifies resistance to change and fear of the future. It may be that changes made in one's life are more traumatic the more one holds on to the past.

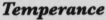

Temperance

This card depicts a winged figure pouring liquid from one chalice to another. One foot is on land while the other is in water, symbolizing equilibrium and balance in nature.

Temperance in a reading signifies good self-control and a balanced personality. It also suggests that balance and caution may be required in a situation, particularly if that situation involves arbitrating between two other parties.

Reversed Imbalance and uncertainty are indicated by this card. This brings unhappiness, mood swings and self-doubt, and in dealings with other people this emotional instability means inconsistency and clumsiness.

The Devil

A card that is often misinterpreted. The Devil figure does *not* mean evil, lust and demonic possession. Rather it signifies unpleasant emotions, which all of us experience from time to time, such as anger, frustration and bitterness.

The figures chained to the plinth symbolize being stuck in an uncomfortable situation. The card suggests that feelings of helplessness can be defeated, however, and that possibly there may be solutions to the situation that have not yet been explored.

Reversed This means much the same as the upright card, although it can also mean that a bad situation has been allowed to go unchallenged for too long.

The Tower

This card depicts a tower being destroyed by a thunderbolt and the inhabitants falling to earth. A crown is usually shown being blown off the top of the flaming tower.

This card represents an unexpected blow to the ego or pride, which at first can seem humiliating and damaging. In the long term, however, it proves to be a useful experience from which lessons can be learned. It can also mean a physical injury, which, again, is not as damaging as it first appears.

Reversed This signifies some misfortune or unpleasant event, which could have been avoided or which has been allowed to develop over a period of time. In a sense, therefore, the resultant injury is self-inflicted.

The Star

The Goddess of the Stars appears naked, pouring two jugs of water, one on the earth and one into a pool. The setting is serene and peaceful, and the sky is filled with one large star and seven smaller ones.

This card indicates peace, contentment and wellbeing. This can come after a period of turmoil and so represents a return to physical and spiritual health. New beginnings and fresh experiences may be ahead.

Reversed This indicates the opportunity for rest and repair, an opportunity that may not yet be realized. The reversed card, therefore, is a sign of hope and an encouragement to someone feeling anxiety or self-doubt.

THE MOON .

THE SUN .

The Moon

This card shows a dog and a wolf howling at a moon which has a female profile within. A path leads from the sea, between two dark towers, to the horizon. A lobster is seen emerging from the sea.

This card represents confusion and lack of direction. The lobster symbolizes unconscious fears of failure and despair, and the dog and wolf represent aspects of our animal nature that may do us harm. The woman's face on the moon is associated with delusion and deception.

Reversed Morbid fantasizing and feelings of utter despair may have become a serious problem—it is time to confide in a friend and seek support.

The Sun

This card depicts a small boy riding a white horse while the sun, with a masculine face, gazes down.

The Sun symbolizes success, happiness and personal achievement. In a reading this card indicates the possession of energy, optimism and high ideals, and it bodes well for the eventual fulfilment of ambitions. There is also a sense given of enjoyment and fun in the pursuit of one's goals.

Reversed This indicates a gap between personal plans and ambitions and the present reality. More effort, planning and dedication are needed. At the same time it is important to guard against feelings of despondency.

Judgement

This card depicts the dead rising from their graves at the call of an angel's trumpet, in Biblical terms, the Day of Judgement.

This card signifies self-assessment. In the upright position it is a positive appraisal and there is an acceptance of the past and a sense of satisfaction and achievement. The future can therefore be faced openly and without fear.

Reversed The card still signifies change, except that when looking back there is regret and remorse and a feeling of dissatisfaction with the way things turned out. This self-condemnation is damaging and usually unwarranted. It is far better to accept what has happened and move on.

The World

This card features a dancing woman surrounded by a laurel wreath in the centre and an angel, a bull, an eagle and a lion in the four corners.

This card represents the successful completion of a project or the happy conclusion of a phase in life. As well as a sense of fulfilment and contentment, there is a much deeper, spiritual sense of self-awareness and understanding.

Reversed In this position the card indicates a circle of frustration and boredom. A new approach is needed to break free of the cycle. It can also signify delays to the completion of a project or phase in life which may be frustrating and holding back personal development.

The Minor Arcana

The fifty-six cards of the Minor Arcana consist of four suits: Wands, Cups, Swords and Pentacles. There are 40 numbered, or 'Pip' cards, and 16 Court cards. The four suits represent the elements: the suit of Wands is associated with fire, Cups with water, Swords with air, and Pentacles with earth. The meanings of each card relate to the qualities displayed by each of these elements.

The Pip Cards

Unlike the cards of the Major Arcana, which relate to spiritual matters, the Pip cards represent everyday circumstances and events and how people feel about them.

For ease of reference the cards have been grouped by their numerical values rather then by their suits. The significance of the numbers is outlined below:

The Aces

The Aces represent two things. As a whole, they signify singularity or the unity of several components; individually they represent the elements of fire (Wands), water (Cups), air (Swords) and earth (Pentacles).

The Twos

The Twos represent the relationship between two entities. This can be a personal relationship or the relationship between two loyalties, emotions or impulses.

The Threes

The Threes represent the concept of creation and symbolize the product that results from some form of union, for example, a child. They also represent the link between two opposing forces and are associated with fate and divinity.

The Fours

Four is the number of the material world, representing the four elements and the four dimensions. As it is strongly associated with nature and matter it indicates stability and order.

The Fives

The stability and order of four is disrupted by the addition of one to make five. It is the number of disorder and confusion and indicates the arrival of difficult times.

The Sixes

Six is the number of days in the Creation so it represents completion and fulfilment. It also indicates reward for efforts and justice.

The Sevens

Seven is considered to be a magical or lucky number and is associated with virtue and wisdom.

The Eights

As four and two are the most stable numbers, their multiplication to give eight means that number indicates success, progress and personal development.

The Nines

Nine is three times three, so it contains the creative force of that number tripled. It also indicates the final stages of creation and the reaping of rewards.

The Tens

Ten represents a new stage in development as well as being the number of completion. It can also be seen as 'just enough', where one more brings in destruction or decadence.

The Court Cards

The Court cards in the Minor Arcana usually consist of a Page, a Knight, a Queen and a King. These cards are generally thought to represent particular individuals and can be seen as the person having the reading, people known to them, or people they are going to meet.

Each kind of Court card represents a particular kind of person, and the suit they appear in indicates what distinctive personality traits they have:

The Pages

A Page represents a child, either a boy or a girl, or a young woman. All the Pages are associated with the earth element, signifying practical matters, organization and planning.

The Knights

Usually depicted on horseback, the Knights represent youth, progress and energy. All the Knights correspond to the element of fire and the fiery spirit is present to some degree in all of them.

The Queens

The Queens represent mature women. If the person consulting the cards is female, however, it can often refer to them. The associated element is water, indicating gentleness and other traditionally feminine qualities.

The Kings

The Kings represent mature men. As with the Queens, if the person consulting the cards is male it can often refer to them. The element associated with Kings is air, which indicates authority, rationality, and other traditionally male qualities.

Ace of Wands

This card shows a hand appearing from a cloud, gripping a stout club.

It is a strongly masculine image indicating creativity, virility, enthusiasm, excitement, personal growth and ambition. It is a particularly promising card to receive if starting out on a new venture as it shows that the ability and creativity are there to make it a success.

Reversed A misdirection of energies is indicated, and there are feelings of frustration, weakness and apathy. However, some of the elements of the upright reading are still present, and things could be turned around with self-discipline and organization.

Ace of Cups

An open hand is shown in this card holding a chalice from which four streams of water are falling. There is also a dove descending to place a wafer in the chalice.

This card represents the feminine element of water and is associated with love, relationships and emotional growth. It shows that there is openness, contentment, and fulfilment in a relationship. Specifically, it could indicate a marriage or a pregnancy.

Reversed This indicates sadness and despondency. The water represents tears brought about by feelings of loneliness and a lack of security. There may also be an end to, or a disappointment within, a relationship.

Ace of Swords

This card shows a hand gripping a sword, the point of which is encircled by a crown.

This is a card of great forcefulness and represents the ability to think clearly and rationally. It also stands for justice and authority and can signify legal matters or some other dispute where clear thinking and decision making is required.

Specifically, it could mean that there is a sense of fulfilment when a correct decision has been made or when there has been a favourable outcome to some dispute.

Reversed This indicates feelings of frustration with what is felt to be an unfair decision or situation.

Ace of Pentacles

A hand from the clouds holds a pentacle in this card. Beneath there is a garden scene and a mountain can be seen through a gap in the hedge.

This card stands for fulfilment and stability in personal, physical, or material terms and a sense of total contentment with one's present situation.

Reversed This can indicate an unhealthy preoccupation with material gain, a poor home life, unstable relationships, bad health, or worry about financial matters. It may also show that for some reason there is a lack of enjoyment of life and an inability to see the good aspects of one's situation.

Two of Wands

A man is shown in this card with a globe in one hand and a staff in the other. He looks out to sea from a battlement which has a second staff fixed to it.

Wands are associated with careers, ambition and creative energy. This card indicates that some kind of crossroads has been reached and that a decision is called for. It suggests that this may be the time for assessment and planning.

Reversed This indicates some loss of momentum brought about by self-doubt and a feeling that personal achievements have not been as valuable as had previously been thought. There may also be a sense of anticlimax and a falling out with work colleagues.

Two of Cups

The couple shown in this card are pledging one another and above their raised chalices there is a lion's head supported by a pair of giant wings.

This card represents a love affair, a marriage, a business partnership, or a close friendship, and indicates that this relationship is of particular importance as there may be a need for support during a difficult time.

Reversed This represents problems in a once close relationship. This could mean an argument or conflict of some kind or it could mean distrust and a sense of betrayal. It also indicates that decisions regarding the long-term future of a relationship are best left for a time.

Two of Swords

In this card a blindfolded woman balances two very long swords on her shoulders.

This indicates that there is some sort of power struggle going on or the breakdown of a once close relationship and that there is a need for a balanced and rational approach to the problem. Self-restraint and caution against making rash decisions is indicated.

Reversed This card represents a tense situation which has become intolerable. Either one or both sides in the dispute are now venting their true feelings and there is little hope for reconciliation while both parties remain in this frame of mind.

Two of Pentacles

This card shows a young man dancing with a pentacle in each hand. The two pentacles are linked by an endless cord.

A balanced and progressive attitude towards the practical matters of everyday life is indicated here. Any problems which come up are easily dealt with and any setbacks which occur are soon forgotten. There is a general feeling of contentment and optimism.

Reversed A lack of balance is indicated and there is likely to be inconstancy and impatience in one's actions, mood swings, uncertainty, and periods of self-doubt which impede progress on many levels. There is also a recklessness and immaturity in some behaviour which is damaging.

Three of Wands

This card shows a male figure with his back turned standing between three staffs. He is looking out over a sea view and ships can be seen passing by.

Some form of creative initiative is indicated here. It may be related to a business venture, but it could also apply to a new career or lifestyle. Progress is very much dependent on luck, although there has been a good start made and there is every reason to be optimistic for the future.

Reversed This card indicates indecision, lack of confidence, and procrastination. No progress is being made and good opportunities which may not come again are being missed.

Three of Cups

Three cheerful young women are shown in this card lifting their chalices to each other. Around their feet lie different vegetables and fruits.

A creative force within the emotional realm is indicated as being very much to the fore by this card. This may signify a new relationship, a marriage, or the birth of a child. Alternatively, it could mean a period of spiritual, psychic, or artistic growth.

Reversed Intolerance and selfishness in a relationship are indicated by this card and a potentially good situation is being spoiled as a result. Divorce, domestic problems, argument and exploitation of another's goodwill are all indicated here.

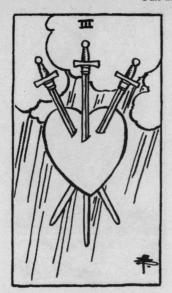 

Three of Swords

This card shows three swords piercing a heart. Storm clouds are gathered in the background.

Three may sometimes be an unfortunate number as it can mean conflict, aggression and the escalation of problems. There are also similarities with the Death card of the Major Arcana in that changes which may be good in the long term are very painful and difficult to face up to in the short term.

Reversed This indicates that a difficult and painful period of transition is likely to have lasted for a long time. This has led to conflict, argument and destructive practices being entered into out of a sense of frustration.

Three of Pentacles

A sculptor is shown at work here in a monastery while a monk and another hooded figure look on.

This card represents creativity, hard work and long-term rewards. There is a feeling that one's efforts and energies are being meaningfully employed and are helping other people. This is recognized and appreciated, which is also very satisfying.

Reversed This indicates that there is frustration because hard work and effort are not being recognized or rewarded as much as they should be. Often there is criticism and this further undermines confidence in personal ability and leaves a feeling of being taken for granted.

Four of Wands

In this card four staves hold aloft a garland. Two female figures stand in the background with nosegays in their hands and behind them is a castle and a bridge going over a moat.

Artistic expression and creative impulses being pursued in a calculated, methodical way in a stable and secure environment are indicated here. It can also indicate a rewarding holiday or a change in environment that bring new experiences and broaden the mind.

Reversed This indicates a situation where there are restrictions on creativity and self-expression in the form of rules and regulations. This is causing unhappiness and resentment.

Four of Cups

An unhappy young man sits beneath a tree in this card. He is contemplating three cups laid before him while a fourth is offered by a hand appearing from a cloud.

An underlying feeling of being in a rut is indicated, and there is little value placed in the good things one actually has. New experiences and situations are craved, which will stimulate and excite.

Reversed This indicates that boredom has become overly indulgent self-pity. It is possible that there are problems with reliance on alcohol, drugs or food. If so, then help must be sought to overcome the problem.

Four of Swords

This card shows a knight lying upon his tomb. Three swords are on the wall and one by his side.

This indicates a period of recovery from an illness or a period of contemplation after a difficult time, perhaps after a bereavement. It can also simply mean that it is time to 'get away from it all' and enjoy a well-earned holiday.

Reversed Feelings of being isolated and ignored are indicated by this card. This may result from illness or because friends have moved away or distanced themselves in some other way. It could also mean that a certain situation has been left behind but feelings of regret or resentment remain.

Four of Pentacles

This card shows a crowned figure gripping one pentacle tightly and resting his feet on two more. A fourth pentacle rests on his crown.

A very solid domestic situation is indicated. There is great resistance to any form of change, which can be very good if it follows a period of hardship and struggle. It can also be very limiting, as after a time the situation may become too predictable and safe.

Reversed This is often said to be the miser's card, as it indicates a reluctance to give anything up. This can apply to a relationship, career, or any other aspect of life. A fear of failure is probably the root cause and this should be addressed.

Five of Wands

This card shows five youths playfully brandishing staves in mimic warfare.

Optimism and energy are indicated here. Little annoyances and minor setbacks are also indicated, but these should be regarded as interesting challenges to be met and overcome. This can actually be very satisfying for the enquirer, adding excitement to his or her life.

Reversed This indicates that the obstacles and setbacks are more serious in nature and that there is very little enjoyment to be had from them. There is also likely to be conflict and argument, possibly with one person who aims to disrupt another's plans.

Five of Cups

A dark, cloaked figure dominates this card. He is looking sideways at three prone cups. Two more cups stand upright behind him.

This card indicates unhappiness with the way some event has gone and a feeling of missed opportunity. Dwelling on what might have been is a futile exercise, however, and it is far better to accept things and move on.

Reversed The feelings of loss indicated by this card are more serious. It may be that someone or something very important has gone. This could mean an actual bereavement, in which case these feelings will persist until one comes to term with the loss.

Five of Swords

This card shows a young man with a disdainful look on his face gathering up swords. Two other dejected figures are shown retreating from the field.

A sense of humiliation and defeat is indicated here. A personal weakness may have been revealed, or there may have been a conflict with a domineering person, which has resulted in exposure to ridicule. This is only a minor setback as it is probably only pride that has been hurt.

Reversed This indicates that more lasting damage has been done and that some form of betrayal, dishonesty or trickery has been involved. It may be that one person has been the cause of this upset, who is too powerful to be challenged.

Five of Pentacles

Two pathetic-looking figures, poorly dressed and apparently homeless, are shown on this card. Snow lies on the ground around them as they pass by a stained glass window.

Unemployment, financial difficulties, or the absence of love or security are indicated here. The problem may be alleviated, however, by the support of another party, perhaps a close friend.

Reversed This indicates an acute awareness of a bad situation. Poverty, domestic insecurity or unemployment may be signified, or there may be a general feeling of insecurity stemming from a lack of love or companionship. Things will only get worse if help is not sought to remedy the situation.

Six of Wands

This card shows a horseman with a staff in his hand which is adorned with a laurel crown. Footmen bearing staves are at his side.

Success and achievement in some enterprise is indicated here. A lot of energy and effort has probably been directed towards some end result and now that that commitment has paid off, it is time for celebrating and enjoying the fruits of one's labour.

Reversed This indicates that the completion of some project has been delayed or has gone without the proper recognition. Expected news may also have been delayed due to some misunderstanding or lack of proper communication.

Six of Cups

Two children are shown here, innocently playing in an old garden. They have filled six cups with flowers.

This is a card of the past and memories. It can indicate reward for past efforts and recognition for acts of kindness. It may also mean that reminiscing about the past will bring pleasure or that perhaps an old friend or lover will return unexpectedly to pay back a kindness or lend a hand in time of need.

Reversed This indicates being haunted by an unhappy past to the extent that the present cannot be fully enjoyed. It can also signify a reluctance to face up to changes in a relationship or in a domestic situation.

Six of Swords

This card shows a ferryman carrying passengers in his punt across calm waters.

Getting away from a bad situation is the theme of this card. This may be a slow and difficult process, and should be planned far in advance and adequately prepared for. It can also indicate a holiday or a move to a new job or home.

Reversed This indicates that a solution to some problem is only temporary and that a permanent solution has been avoided. Taking the easy way out may suffice in the short term, but eventually the problem will resurface and might be even more difficult to deal with.

Six of Pentacles

A well-dressed merchant is shown here weighing money in a pair of scales and distributing it to two beggars.

Fairness and balance with regard to money and possessions are indicated by this card. This may indicate charitable feelings and the need to 'put something back' into society. Generally, the enquirer is likely to be generous by nature and a person who gets pleasure from helping others.

Reversed This indicates a feeling of being taken for granted and not getting proper recognition. The situation may seem unfair, as if one person has been doing all the giving and another all the taking. It may also indicate theft of money or possessions.

Seven of Wands

This card shows a young man balanced on a craggy eminence brandishing a staff, apparently in self-defence.

This card signifies great personal ability, determination and energy. A test that calls for a supreme effort is indicated, perhaps an interview for a job or an examination of some sort. There is nothing to indicate failure, and there will probably be satisfaction in being able to handle such a situation well.

Reversed A challenge may prove to be too much, although it is more likely through lack of confidence than of ability that they will fail. Self-doubt is holding back the true expression of ability and that needs to be addressed.

Seven of Cups

In this card a silhouetted figure contemplates seven strange visions that have appeared before him.

This card suggests that choices have to be made carefully with regard to future goals and ideals. There may be a tendency to fantasize about future achievements. Those that are unrealistic must be separated from those worth pursuing—a process that calls for rational analysis.

Reversed Confusion and uncertainty are indicated by this card. There may be too many choices and possibilities for an easy decision to be made. Deluding oneself with unrealistic and unattainable dreams and fantasies is also indicated.

Seven of Swords

This card shows a young man apparently in the act of stealing five swords. Two more swords remain in the ground and a camp is nearby.

The chance to use one's intelligence to deal with a problem in a clever and skilful way is indicated. There may be some tricky opposition to face, but with cunning and guile they will be defeated. An unorthodox and unusual approach will often pay off.

Reversed This card indicates a reluctance to take chances or make pre-emptive moves to solve a problem or break a deadlock. Timidity, conventionalism, and fear of ridicule and failure only serve to prolong difficulties however.

Seven of Pentacles

The young man in this card rests his head and looks intently at seven pentacles attached to a clump of greenery.

This card indicates that sustained effort will bring the results hoped for. There is also the suggestion that a stroke of luck will progress matters.

Reversed This indicates a feeling of despondency and an inclination to abandon a project which is not progressing. It may be that mistakes have been made along the way which have put the end hoped for in jeopardy and which cannot be rectified. It is probably best to accept defeat and move on to something new.

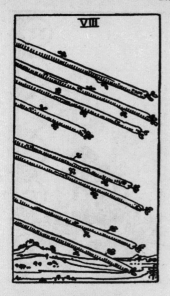 

Eight of Wands

This card shows eight staffs in flight across open country.

Progress towards a satisfactory conclusion of any matter at hand is indicated here. There will be no more delays or hold-ups and things which have long been hoped for will start to happen.

Reversed This indicates that there is confusion and uncertainty as things are not going the way they are supposed to. Lack of organization and planning, and an inability to cope with a complex situation, mean that although there is much activity and effort, little is actually achieved.

Eight of Cups

A dejected-looking man is shown in this card walking away from two rows of cups.

This card indicates that something very important is missing from one's life. There may be a good degree of emotional and material stability in the present situation, but a need to find a deeper level of contentment is constantly nagging. A drastic change in lifestyle may be called for to satisfy this longing.

Reversed This indicates uncertainty with future plans and a need to give things some serious thought. It may be that there is dissatisfaction with the present situation but very little idea of what one can do to change things.

Eight of Swords

This card portrays a young woman, bound and blindfolded, surrounded by upright swords.

A desire to make changes and improve certain aspects of one's life is indicated here.

For the time being, however, only small improvements are likely to succeed. This may be frustrating, but effort and perseverence will pay off in the future.

Reversed Feelings of being hemmed in and held back are stronger when the card is reversed. However, the situation is unlikely to get any worse, and if some small changes can be initiated now then later developments may be more kind.

Eight of Pentacles

This card shows a young stonemason at his work, the results of which he exhibits in the form of trophies.

Prosperity and personal satisfaction are indicated here, and there is a strong sense of achievement and pride derived from the exercise of one's own particular skills. This feeling may come from work well done or from some hobby or sporting achievement.

Reversed A problem with long-term goals and the frustration of personal ambitions are indicated here. Worries about money and short term security mean that too much time is spent on small and transitory gains that detract from working towards bigger goals.

Nine of Wands

This card shows a young man with an expectant look on his face leaning upon his staff. Eight other staffs are lined up behind him.

Rewards and benefits stemming from past deeds are indicated here. Hardships and struggles in the past, which have built resilience and character, are now being acknowledged. A more balanced, cautious and mature approach to life's problems has also developed.

Reversed This indicates a stubborness and defensiveness stemming from bad experiences in the past. This undermines any attempt to progress with something new or different, and it is a problem that needs to be addressed.

Nine of Cups

A well-contented man resting after a feast is central in this card. Behind him, a counter holds nine cups, which are probably full of wine.

A general feeling of wellbeing and contentment in domestic affairs is indicated by this card. Generosity and unselfishness abound, and sharing this happiness with friends and family brings a great deal of satisfaction.

Reversed This card indicates complacency, false optimism, and poor judgement. Everything may not be as it seems—situations may not be as secure or friendships as close as assumed.

Nine of Swords

In this card a figure sits upright in bed, head in hands. Nine swords hover menacingly above the bed.

A preoccupation with past experiences, particularly those that were painful, is indicated here. There is anxiety about what other people think and say about you. There is also a fear of the future and an inability to relax, which may cause sleeplessness and depression.

Reversed This card indicates that the depression is more intense and persistent. There is also suspicion of other people being unfair or cruel. In such a situation help from others is required and may be the only way to improve matters.

Nine of Pentacles

A young woman is shown here standing among an abundance of grapevines. A bird rests on her wrist.

This card indicates that the pursuit of some goal has been successful and the fruits of one's labours can now be enjoyed. The pursuit may not have been easy, however, and this makes the final outcome all the more enjoyable. This card also indicates someone who lives alone and who enjoys his or her personal achievements in solitude.

Reversed This indicates insecurity and fear that achievements may be undermined by past deeds. It also suggests a dependency on another person and a sharing of the credit for some achievement.

Ten of Wands

A man struggling to carry the ten staves held in his arms is shown here.

This card indicates over-burdening with responsibilities and commitments. There is a sense of oppression, which is causing unhappiness and distress. It may be that pride is standing in the way of delegation, but if the workload is not shared then everything may prove to be too much.

Reversed This indicates that more may have been taken on than can be handled. This has led to tiredness, confusion and an increasing inefficiency. It is time to re-evaluate the situation and prioritize commitments, perhaps giving up some responsibilities.

Ten of Cups

This card shows a man and woman standing in awe of a rainbow, which holds the ten cups. Two children are playing happily by their side.

This card indicates fulfilment and contentment within the context of a family or group of close friends. There may also be the less favourable interpretation that one of the group or family is not as happy as the others.

Reversed This indicates that someone or something is disrupting an otherwise idyllic situation. If it is a person then it may not necessarily be his or her fault. It could be that the other members of the group or family are neglecting them and not paying attention to his or her needs.

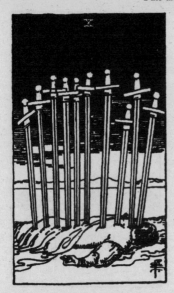 

Ten of Swords

A prostrate figure is shown here, pierced by all the swords of the card.

This card indicates that caution should be shown when getting involved in a new venture, especially if it means trusting people whom you don't know. It also signifies the conclusion of something that has caused a great deal of pain and suffering. In a business venture or relationship this may mean that the crisis point has been reached and that things can only improve.

Reversed This indicates that the crisis point has not yet been reached, so preparations should be made for further trouble. Again, caution should be shown when dealing with a group of people.

Ten of Pentacles

This card shows a man and woman standing under an archway with a child by their side. Two dogs are also seen in the foreground being petted by an old man.

This card stands for family support—in both an emotional and a financial sense. Everyone benefits from this system of support if everyone plays an equal role and gives as much as he or she takes. Financial benefits from family connections are also indicated, perhaps an inheritance.

Reversed This card indicates that family and friends may be more of a hindrance than a help, stifling individuality and giving advice that has not been sought. There may also be problems with an inheritance.

Page of Wands

Personality

This card shows a confident, up-right, young man surveying the land around him.

An energetic, lively, and resourceful personality is indicated. He or she is a good and reliable friend, and may also be the bearer of good news.

Reversed A self-centred personality with a tendency to gossip and spread hurtful rumours is indicated. He or she cannot be trusted with a secret.

Situation

This card indicates involvement in new and challenging ventures. A high level of enthusiasm and commitment is called for.

Reversed Bad news, or the delay of good news is indicated. Apathy and a lack of energy or ideas may also be signified.

Page of Cups

Personality

The young man in this card intently studies a fish rising from his chalice.

This indicates an imaginative and studious personality with a good deal of charm and a natural modesty.

Reversed A lazy, wasteful person lacking in direction and willpower is indicated.

Situation

This signifies that there are hidden talents which are now being discovered. Study and reflection are also indicated as being beneficial at this time.

Reversed Certain talents and skills are underutilized, and good opportunities for self-improvement may be being ignored or missed.

Page of Swords

Personality

This card shows a lively young man holding a sword in an upright position.

An intelligent and capable personality is indicated. He or she is thorough about things and may also at times be cautious and mistrustful.

Reversed This indicates a very cunning and manipulative person who uses other people and situations to advantage.

Situation

Clear thinking and caution are called for. All proposals should be carefully considered before a decision is made.

Reversed This indicates an environment of suspicion , which cannot be allowed to persist. A problem needs to be tackled head-on.

Page of Pentacles

Personality

The youthful figure in this card looks intently at the pentacle that hovers above his outstretched hands.

This card indicates a steady and dependable personality with qualities that can always be relied upon. He or she could be a student or an apprentice.

Reversed A pompous and dull person is indicated who can frequently be obstructive and unhelpful.

Situation

This card indicates a working environment with a fixed routine that is very boring. It may only be temporary.

Reversed This card indicates unhappiness and frustration caused by a tedious and dull job or lifestyle.

KNIGHT of WANDS.

KNIGHT of CUPS.

Knight of Wands

Personality

This card shows a confident young man astride a fast-moving horse.

This indicates an attractive, adventurous personality, although there may be a tendency towards wild and unpredictable behaviour.

Reversed A reckless, unreliable personality, always stirring up trouble and disrupting things. Also impatient, never finishing anything of worth.

Situation

This card indicates involvement in new and challenging ventures. Holidays, adventures and lifestyle changes are likely.

Reversed A difficult and stressful time is indicated. A disastrous holiday or an unwise career move may be signified.

Knight of Cups

Personality

A graceful young man on a well-controlled horse is shown in this card.

A sensitive and imaginative personality is indicated here. There may be a tendency, however, to indulge in fantasy rather than apply ideas practically.

Reversed This indicates a personality who is not as pleasant as he or she first appears and may have something to hide.

Situation

Love, romance, and new relationships are indicated. There may also be opportunities for artistic expression.

Reversed Indicates unforeseen difficulties in a seemingly favourable situation.

Knight of Swords

Personality

A determined young man rides into battle in this card.

This indicates an intelligent, courageous, loyal and trustworthy personality. He or she is very capable in demanding situations and makes a strong ally.

Reversed This indicates an aggressive, impatient personality, often in conflict with others, who wastes energies and creates problems.

Situation

A period of some difficulty is indicated. The outcome will be favourable if a firm line is taken.

Reversed This indicates that in the difficult times ahead a hot-headed approach will only cause greater problems.

Knight of Pentacles

Personality

The young rider in this card sits astride a heavy horse and surveys what is ahead.

A practical and dependable personality is indicated. He or she will always work hard to get what is wanted.

Reversed A very conservative, dull and plodding character is indicated who frequently displays great stubborness.

Situation

The time has come to slow down and relax. Steady progress will still be made.

Reversed Little progress is being made towards what is desired and that the situation has become stagnant and boring. A change in approach is needed.

Queen of Wands

This card shows a confident, capable woman with an open outlook.

A sociable, active and resourceful woman who can direct her energies in several directions effectively is indicated. Outgoing and generous, she is a good wife and mother, and has many friends and interests. She will also have a good family life and be successful in business.

Reversed This card represents someone who thinks she is efficient and organized and who likes to be in control. This may be mistaken for arrogance, however, by those who resent her domineering and interfering attitude. She may think that others cannot manage without her.

Queen of Cups

The woman shown here appears rather self-absorbed as she contemplates a very elaborate chalice.

A quiet, reserved woman who keeps a lot concealed and so has an air of mystery about her is indicated. She is attractive and makes friends easily, but at times her personality may be hard to fathom. She is kind, intuitive and sympathetic, and her artistic and psychic skills are likely to be very highly developed.

Reversed This card indicates an impractical, frivolous woman, much given to self-deception and fantasizing. She may be rather vain and self-interested, with few real friends to count on in times of need.

Queen of Swords

With a rather stern expression on her face, this woman raises her weapon in her right hand and rests the hilt on the arm of her throne.

This card represents an intelligent, independent and strong-willed person who may be very ambitious. Traditionally a widow, she can also be a woman living alone who is divorced or separated. Despite her strength and independence, however, there is a degree of loneliness and a need for companionship.

Reversed This indicates a very cold and domineering woman. Her hard exterior conceals an inner loneliness, however, and she uses her coldness as a form of self-defence.

Queen of Pentacles

This card shows a reflective woman sitting on a throne in a very fertile and nurturing environment.

A loving, sensuous, open-hearted woman who likes to create a good atmosphere around herself is indicated. She is a good wife and mother who enjoys her domestic security and likes to share what she has with others. She also appreciates beautiful things and loves nature and animals.

Reversed This card indicates a woman who is obsessed with material worth. She is often suspicious and jealous of others. Underneath the unpleasant exterior, however, there may be a very insecure person who craves love and attention.

King of Wands

This card shows an alert and capable man sitting on a throne decorated with lion motifs.

An intelligent, fair-minded man who is able to see other people's point of view is indicated here. He is good at giving advice and resolving disputes amicably. A considerate husband and father, he is generous to others, dependable and affectionate.

Reversed This represents an intolerant man who can be very narrow-minded and critical of others. He always believes that he knows best and is often accused of being patronizing. He appears to be incapable of listening to anyone else's point of view and as a result is often accused of being insensitive and unsympathetic.

King of Cups

The figure in this card sits on a throne surrounded by the sea. A dolphin is leaping out of the water on one side and a ship passes by on the other.

This card indicates a cultured, sophisticated, well-educated man. He may be rather difficult to fathom at times, but a cool and competent exterior could be hiding emotional difficulties. He may be afraid of intimacy and, although supportive of those close to him, be slow to demonstrate affection.

Reversed This card represents someone who cannot be trusted, especially in business. He may use his superior education and privileged social contacts to take advantage of others and deceive people who thought themselves friends.

KING of SWORDS.

KING of PENTACLES.

King of Swords

This figure appears to be sitting in judgement. His sword is held aloft, and a stern expression suggests a cold efficiency.

A powerful, strong-willed man who is well suited to a position of authority is indicated. He is fiercely independent, does not like being constrained in any way, and enjoys trying out new ideas and innovations. His rationality and ambition take him to the top of his profession.

Reversed This represents a very unpleasant character who can be dangerous to know and is best avoided in all walks of life. He is intelligent and independent but also a bully, cruel and unkind to those around him and exploitative of those weaker than himself.

King of Pentacles

This card shows a relaxed and confident man sitting on his throne in a flourishing garden.

A good, honest, hard-working man who has achieved stability and security through his own efforts is indicated. He may be well off, but money has never been an important motive for his actions. His tastes are simple, and he enjoys the good things in life. He may be skilled with his hands and has a talent for solving practical problems.

Reversed This represents a weak person who pursues, but cannot find pleasure or satisfaction in, material things. He may take out his frustrations on other people.

Key Words

The Trumps

The Fool	*Upright*: innocence, trust, openness
	Reversed: recklessness, irresponsibility
The Magician	*Upright*: ability, confidence, communication
	Reversed: lack of ability, poor communication
The Empress	*Upright*: fulfilment, contentment, motherhood
	Reversed: insecurity, discomfort, hardship
The Emperor	*Upright*: authority, responsibility
	Reversed: inferiority, resentment, frustration
The Hierophant	*Upright*: advice, learning, teaching
	Reversed: misinformation, bad advice
The Lovers	*Upright*: commitment, decision, choice
	Reversed: procrastination, bad decision
The Chariot	*Upright*: empowerment, drive, ambition
	Reversed: conflict, misdirection
Justice	*Upright*: reason, fairness
	Reversed: injustice, bias, unfairness
The Hermit	*Upright*: solitariness, independence
	Reversed: exclusion, self-pity
Wheel of Fortune	*Upright*: chance, luck, optimism
	Reversed: misfortune, pessimism
Strength	*Upright*: inner balance, strength, control
	Reversed: helplessness, imbalance
The Hanged Man	*Upright*: perseverance, sacrifice
	Reversed: apathy, dissatisfaction
Death	*Upright*: change, renewal, rebirth
	Reversed: delay, indecision
Temperance	*Upright*: balance, caution, arbitration
	Reversed: clumsiness, uncertainty
The Devil	*Upright*: anger, resentment, helplessness
	Reversed: suffering, despair
The Tower	*Upright*: misfortune, accident, humiliation
	Reversed: procrastination, self-injury
The Star	*Upright*: calm, healing, renewal, recovery

	Reversed: delay, prolongation
The Moon	*Upright*: confusion, turmoil, deception
	Reversed: fear, despair, helplessness
The Sun	*Upright*: optimism, ambition, success
	Reversed: impatience, frustration
Judgement	*Upright*: self-assessment, progression
	Reversed: regret, remorse, dissatisfaction
The World	*Upright*: completion, fulfilment
	Reversed: delay, frustration

Wands

Ace of Wands	*Upright*: creativity, energy, ambition
	Reversed: frustration, apathy
Two of Wands	*Upright*: assessment, planning, decision
	Reversed: self-doubt, anti-climax, conflict
Three of Wands	*Upright*: beginnings, optimism, luck
	Reversed: delay, indecision, procrastination
Four of Wands	*Upright*: creativity, openness, adventure
	Reversed: frustration, resentment
Five of Wands	*Upright*: challenge, growth, satisfaction
	Reversed: setbacks, conflict, argument
Six of Wands	*Upright*: good fortune, reward, satisfaction
	Reversed: delay, misunderstanding
Seven of Wands	*Upright*: effort, success, fulfilment
	Reversed: failure, self-doubt
Eight of Wands	*Upright*: progress, completion, fulfilment
	Reversed: confusion, misdirection
Nine of Wands	*Upright*: resilience, reward
	Reversed: reluctance, failure, conflict
Ten of Wands	*Upright*: responsibility, commitment
	Reversed: exhaustion, confusion
Page of Wands	*Upright*: energy, vigour, new beginnings
	Reversed: apathy, mistrust, suspicion
Knight of Wands	*Upright*: excitement, unpreditability
	Reversed: stress, impatience, recklessness
Queen of Wands	*Upright*: energy, ability, purpose
	Reversed: interference, arrogance
King of Wands	*Upright*: intelligence, generosity
	Reversed: intolerence, narrow-mindedness

Cups

Ace of Cups	*Upright*: love, emotion, growth
	Reversed: sadness, loneliness, disappointment
Two of Cups	*Upright*: support, trust, friendship
	Reversed: conflict, betrayal, separation
Three of Cups	*Upright*: optimism, growth
	Reversed: selfishness, exploitation
Four of Cups	*Upright*: boredom, apathy
	Reversed: self-pity, indulgence
Five of Cups	*Upright*: unhappiness, regret, loss
	Reversed: remorse, sadness
Six of Cups	*Upright*: reminiscing, rewards
	Reversed: nostalgia, delay
Seven of Cups	*Upright*: illusion, choice
	Reversed: delusion, fantasy
Eight of Cups	*Upright*: development, sacrifice, growth
	Reversed: uncertainty, change
Nine of Cups	*Upright*: happiness, optimism, generosity
	Reversed: complacency, superficiality
Ten of Cups	*Upright*: fulfilment, contentment
	Reversed: disruption, unhappiness
Page of Cups	*Upright*: sensitivity, modesty
	Reversed: dissatisfaction, apathy
Knight of Cups	*Upright*: idealism, originality, optimism
	Reversed: deception, concealment
Queen of Cups	*Upright*: sensitivity, kindness
	Reversed: vanity, selfishness
King of Cups	*Upright*: sophistication, coldness
	Reversed: deception, manipulation

Swords

Ace of Swords	*Upright*: intellect, reason, fairness
	Reversed: injustice, bias, frustration
Two of Swords	*Upright*: argument, breakdown
	Reversed: conflict, aggression
Three of Swords	*Upright*: conflict, change
	Reversed: suffering, frustration
Four of Swords	*Upright*: recovery, renewal
	Reversed: isolation, loneliness

Five of Swords	*Upright*: humiliation, defeat
	Reversed: dishonesty, trickery
Six of Swords	*Upright*: renewal, rebirth
	Reversed: delay, postponement
Seven of Swords	*Upright*: intelligence, unorthodoxy
	Reversed: timidity, conservatism, fear
Eight of Swords	*Upright*: delay, obstruction
	Reversed: helplessness, frustration
Nine of Swords	*Upright*: anxiety, worry, suspicion
	Reversed: depression, isolation
Ten of Swords	*Upright*: caution, progress
	Reversed: conflict, difficulty
Page of Swords	*Upright*: caution, tact, wariness
	Reversed: mistrust, suspicion
Knight of Swords	*Upright*: courage, conviction, strength
	Reversed: aggression, impatience
Queen of Swords	*Upright*: independence, ambition
	Reversed: lonelinesss, coldness
King of Swords	*Upright*: authority, power, innovation
	Reversed: cruelty, exploitation

Pentacles

Ace of Pentacles	*Upright*: stability, security, contentment
	Reversed: instability, anxiety
Two of Pentacles	*Upright*: contentment, optimism
	Reversed: impatience, recklessness
Three of Pentacles	*Upright*: reward, satisfaction
	Reversed: frustration, criticism
Four of Pentacles	*Upright*: security, predictability
	Reversed: reluctance, resistance
Five of Pentacles	*Upright*: difficulty, insecurity
	Reversed: isolation, helplessness
Six of Pentacles	*Upright*: fairness, generosity
	Reversed: unhappiness, carelessness
Seven of Pentacles	*Upright*: perseverence, effort, luck
	Reversed: defeat, acceptance
Eight of Pentacles	*Upright*: progress, prosperity, pride
	Reversed: frustration, worry
Nine of Pentacles	*Upright*: achievement, security, solitude
	Reversed: insecurity, dependency

Ten of Pentacles	*Upright*: security, support
	Reversed: interference, hindrance
Page of Pentacles	*Upright*: dependability, security
	Reversed: frustration, unhappiness
Knight of Pentacles	*Upright*: practicality, dependability
	Reversed: stagnation, boredom
Queen of Pentacles	*Upright*: openness, sensitivity, generosity
	Reversed: materialism, insecurity
King of Pentacles	*Upright*: honesty, practicality, security
	Reversed: greed, weakness

The I Ching

The first step in this is to translate the results of the casting of coins, or the more traditional yarrow stalks, into patterns of broken and unbroken lines of the same length. If casting coins, heads will be assigned a solid line and tails a broken line. The outcome is two six-line figures called hexagrams. There is a system of sixty-four possible hexagrams. (Each hexagram is composed of two three-line figures called trigrams. There is a system of eight possible trigrams.) The first of the two hexagrams will offer an answer to a question as it affects your present situation; the second hexagram offers advice pertaining to future conditions. The I Ching provides a system of analysis and commentaries for every hexagram.

Nature of the I Ching

The I Ching translates literally into English as *The Book of Changes*. Its theme is change—paradoxically the only constant and dependable thing in life—and regeneration, i.e., how one should respond to or deal with the changes one will inevitably face in life.

In the context of a specific consultation of the I Ching, one of three possible kinds of fundamental change that affect any situation is uncovered: either non-change, cyclical change or sequential change. A non-change situation does not mean that there is no forward movement in time, no change—that would be impossible, but that things change only within the existing framework or system of things, which itself is not subject to change for the time being. Cyclical change happens in the same way as seasonal change. And sequential change is progressive change, as when one generation is superseded by the next, younger generation, in the nature of cause and effect. The I Ching also focuses on the role and the meaning of significant coincidences in relation to change.

The I Ching does not specifically predict or prescribe what the future outcome of any present situation will be. Rather, it indicates what it believes are suitable courses of action to take in any particular situation, and in so doing invites us to consider its suggestions, giving them careful thought before we come to our final decision about which course to take and which choice to make.

The basis of the I Ching

The underlying philosophy of the I Ching, is the belief that chance events are in fact are not random or accidental, meaningless or trivial occurrences, but are significant and meaningful. Seemingly random occurrences are actually fundamentally and meaningfully connected to everything else that occurs at the same moment of time as they do; that is, simultaneous events have a connection above and beyond the basic fact that they are contemporaneous, and this connection has nothing to do with notions of cause and effect. Therefore, says the I Ching, it is possible to gain insight into the underlying forces that are influencing change in our lives by properly interpreting the significance and meaning of apparently chance events. These enable a link or an influence to be divined or perceived between the state of our subjective psychic and spiritual lives and the principles of change that are affecting us. The role of the I Ching is to interpret the significance of these chance events.

History

How, when and where did the text and method of the I Ching originate? It all began with the trigrams, which are reputed to have been the life's work of the first Chinese Emperor Fu Hsi. He was also a teacher and scholar and his formulation of the trigrams is said to have been the culmination of life-long study dedicated to discovering the underlying principles of the universe. The inspiration of the lines that form the trigrams was supposedly the patterns in the shell of a tortoise.

The origin of the trigrams is described in the form of a 'creation-myth' involving the essential opposing energies or principles of yin and yang, which are the basis of all things, everything in the universe being generated from their polarity. Yin is feminine and has passive power; yang is masculine and has active power. Paradoxically, yin and yang are both opposing and complementary, as can be seen from the symbol which represents them.

Yin and yang are light and dark, night and day, masculine and feminine, positive and negative, and all other fundamental and creative polarities. In terms of cosmology yin is related to the moon and controls the earth, yang is related to the sun and controls the heavens.

The I Ching states that Great Primal Beginning created the two primary principles of yin and yang and two primary trigrams. These then generated four images which in turn generated the eight founding trigrams of the I Ching.

Fu Hsi's original trigrams were expanded in a later period of early Chinese history by a feudal lord called King Wen and his son, the Duke of Chou. Shortly before 1,000 years BC they developed the three-line trigrams into six-line figures and created a system of sixty-four hexagrams. Each hexagram was given a distinctive name and a commentary was provided for each one which explained it and gave advice. In the I Ching this is known as the T'uan or the Judgement. There is also a commentary on the Judgement and the individual lines of each hexagram, which is known as Hsiang Chuan or the Image. It is believed that the text of the I Ching attributed to King Wen and his son includes material which in fact originates from multiple authors beginning centuries before their time. So the I Ching incorporates aspects of ancient Chinese culture, many thousands of years old, in the form of oracular systems, ancient historical writings and poems.

Some centuries later, about the beginning of the fifth century BC, a further series of commentaries were written about the text of King Wen and added to the I Ching. These are known the T'uan Chuan or the Ten Wings and are attributed to the legendary Chinese philosopher and sage, Confucius, who was a great student of the I Ching. His contribution to the I Ching led it to become even more popular in China as a system of oracular divination.

The I Ching survived a barbaric period in Chinese history which was catastrophic for other texts, when in 213 BC the Emperor Ch'in Shih Huang Ti of the Chin dynasty (221-206 BC) ordered a massive book-burning. Many ancient and important works of Chinese literature and culture were disastrously destroyed, including many copies of the I Ching. Fortunately, enough copies survived.

As one of the few texts of Chinese culture that were left after the barbaric book-burning (at this period, like other texts prior to the invention of paper, the I Ching would have been written on strips of wood or bamboo), the I Ching became the object of even more scholarly devotion. Further commentaries and text were added by the adherents of Taoist philosophy as well as those by Confucianists and other schools of thought during the civilized and creative Han dynasty (202 BC-220 AD) which followed the barbarous Chin period. By the end of the second century AD imperial edict had ensured that the I Ching and four other classic texts associated with Confucianism were engraved in stone so that their wisdom would never be lost to humankind.

During later periods in Chinese history further commentaries continued to be added to the I Ching, most notably by the philosopher Chu Hsi during the Sung dynasty (960-1279). It is reported that by the early eighteenth century the I Ching included commentaries by over two hundred different scholars, dating back to the second century BC.

The original translated versions of the I Ching were faithful renditions of the full I Ching and the same is true of most modern editions. This, though, causes difficulties for the contemporary novice reader of the I Ching, who invariably has problems following and understanding the text. The language, even in a good translation, can seem frustratingly enigmatic and arcane, with obscure passages of poetry and puzzling metaphor. Many aspects of the text can only be understood with a knowledge of their historical context. The order of the various sections of the unabridged I Ching can also present problems.

Consequently it is usual, and more sensible, for novice readers of the I Ching to begin with an introductory text that serves as a bridge to the full I Ching.

If you do find any of the discussions of the philosophy and method of the I Ching heavy-going, then skip them and carry on with the basic consultation of the hexagrams. The discussions of method and philosophy are important and relevant, but you can always come back to these sections later and read and ponder them at your leisure.

Consulting the I Ching

The first thing that has to be done is to decide what you want to consult the I Ching about. Remember, it should not be a trivial or frivolous matter, but concern something of real importance for the course of your life. Having chosen a subject for the consultation, you then have to frame this correctly as a specific question that the I Ching will be able to answer. This is crucial. It is fruitless and pointless to approach the I Ching with questions seeking a yes/no answer or an answer that will absolve you or remove the onus from you of involvement in making your own decisions. Also, avoid vague or generalized questions along the lines of, 'What should I do about my job/relationship/life?' Instead, compose specific questions like: 'What will happen if I leave this job?'; or, 'How will marriage affect our relationship?'; or, 'What will be the outcome if I decide to live abroad?'. You should formulate your question so that it will have a specific answer rather than a number of possibilities. Take your time, if necessary, over the wording of your question. Write it down if it helps to make the process easier.

There are two main ways of doing a consultation: the more traditional but time-consuming method using fifty yarrow sticks, which takes between half an hour and an hour; or the quicker and easier way using three coins.

Coin method

Any three coins will do. For the purposes of the throw, the 'heads' side of the coin is the yang side, and the 'tails' side of the coin is the yin side. Take the three coins and shake them in your hand, then throw them onto a flat surface. Then record which side of the coins are uppermost. There are four possible combinations in which the coins can land:

1. heads   heads   heads
2. tails   tails   tails
3. heads   tails   tails
4. tails   heads   heads

Each of these possible combinations is assigned a yin or yang line-value. Yin is represented by a broken line and yang by a solid line. At this point, reference must be made to what are known as 'moving lines', and also to 'old' and 'young' lines. But it would complicate matters too much at this initial stage to take into account 'moving lines' etc. They will be discussed later. For the time being we will follow the procedure of drawing two hexagrams for each consultation: the first will present an answer to a question as it applies to the circumstances of the present; the second will offer advice concerning future conditions.

The line values which are assigned to each of the four possible heads and tails combinations depend on whether it is the hexagram of the present or the hexagram of the future. The following table gives the line values for the present and future hexagrams.

Coin Combination	Present Hexagram	Future Hexagram
1. heads heads heads	solid line (yang)	broken line (yin)
2. tails tails tails	broken line (yin)	solid line (yang)
3. heads tails tails	solid line (yang)	solid line (yang)
4. tails heads heads	broken line (yin)	broken line (yin)

In order to construct your two hexagrams—the first for the present, the second for the future—you must throw the coins six times and record the result of each throw as yin or yang line values for the present hexagram and for the future hexagram. The following example shows what this might look like, depending on the outcome of your throws.

Coin Combination	Present Hexagram	Future Hexagram
1. tails heads heads	yin (bottom line)	yin (bottom line)
2. heads tails tails	yang (second line)	yang (second line)
3. tails heads heads	yin (third line)	yin (third line)
4. heads heads heads	yang (fourth line)	yin (fourth line)
5. heads tails tails	yang (fifth line)	yang (fifth line)
6. heads tails tails	yang (top line)	yang (top line)

Build each six-line hexagram from the bottom line up, beginning with the line values for your first throw, the second line will be from the line values of your second throw, and so on as shown in the table above. The following two hexagrams are built from the results of the throws recorded above.

Present Hexagram   *Future Hexagram*

Generating hexagrams in this way is relatively quick and uncomplicated. There are other reasons, though, why some prefer using the casting of yarrow sticks to build the hexagrams.

Yarrow stick method

The yarrow sticks method uses a bundle of fifty sticks of the same length. Stalks from the yarrow plant (Achillea millefolium) were used because, according to legend, the yarrow plant grew on the grave of Confucius. Traditionally, though, the sticks used were of bamboo or any suitable wood.

The traditional method of beginning to consult the I Ching using yarrow sticks is to face south and place the text of the I Ching in front of you, with the yarrow sticks and a burning incense-candle by your right side. Take the yarrow sticks in your right hand and, keeping them horizontal, pass them through the smoke of the burning incense in a circular, clockwise movement. This is held to help with the formulation of the question. Place the sticks down and remove one stick from the bundle with your right hand and put it aside. This stick will not be used in the procedure, the remaining forty-nine sticks only being used.

You divide them randomly into two piles and place them right and left. Take a stick from the right-hand pile and place it between the little finger and the ring finger of the left hand. Then the left-hand pile is placed in your left hand, and with your right hand you take from it bundles of four sticks at a time and lay them aside. You will end with a final group of four sticks or less. These should now be placed between the ring finger and the middle finger of the left hand. You then count through the right-hand pile in groups of four, laying them aside, and place the final group of four or less between the middle and index finger of the left hand. You will now have a total of either five or nine sticks held in the fingers of your left hand. (The various possible combinations are: 1+4+4, or 1+3+1, or 1+2+2, or 1+1+3. It can be seen, therefore, that the number 5 is more likely to be obtained than the number 9). Lay these sticks to one side for the time being.

Put all the remaining sticks together in one pile and then divide randomly again into two piles. Repeat the above process, beginning by taking a stick from the right-hand pile and placing it between the ring finger and the little finger of the left hand. When you have finished, lay aside the pile of sticks you have placed in your left hand—you will have either four or eight sticks in total.(The possible combinations this time are: 1+4+3, or 1+3+4, or 1+1+2, or 1+2+1. It can be seen that there is a fifty-fifty chance of producing totals of either four or eight).

Then begin the whole process for a third time with the sticks that are remaining. The number of sticks in your left hand when you finish will again be either four or eight.

You will now have three small piles of sticks. Count the number of sticks in each pile. A pile of four or five sticks is assigned a value of 3. A pile of eight or nine sticks is assigned a value of 2. You then total the combined values of your three piles. You will finish with one of four possible numbers, from four possible combinations, in the following way:

Values	Total Value
2+2+2 =	6
3+3+2 =	8
2+2+3 =	7

The possible total values correspond to either yin or yang lines in the Present and Future hexagrams in the following way

Total Values	Present Hexagram	Future Hexagram
9	yang line	yin line
6	yin line	yang line
8	yin line	yin line
7	yang line	yang line

At this stage in your casting of the yarrow sticks you have derived a single number value from your counting of the numbers of sticks and this has been translated into yin or yang line values for the bottom line of your present and future hexagrams. To get the remaining five lines for each of your hexagrams repeat the whole procedure five times.

Certain questions are provoked by the yarrow stalks procedure of consulting the I Ching. The first obvious one is: 'If only forty-nine sticks are going to be used, then why begin with fifty?' It would, indeed, seem illogical not to begin with forty-nine sticks in the first place. Logic has nothing to do with this initial procedure or with the whole procedure of I Ching. I Ching proceeds deliberately by the illogical. In the realms of

the non-logical, the symbolic and the metaphorical other kinds of meaning, other kinds of perception of reality are possible which are not open
to the exclusively logical and rational.

The removal of one stick from the fifty is held to generate symbolic
significance and meaning, as well as mystical power. Firstly, the forty-
nine sticks left have a mystical significance and power, as forty-nine is
the number seven squared and seven, in many traditional and ancient
systems of belief and oracular divination, is regarded as a highly significant number in terms of its mystical power. (The mystical significance
of numbers will not be dealt with especially in this text. There are,
though, many texts on the subject of numerology if you are interested
in finding out more.) Secondly, there is a symbolic aspect to beginning
with fifty and then taking one away, that emulates the complementary
polarities of yin and yang, the energies or principles which generate all
meaning, all things. Beginning with the whole and then making it less
than whole, creates a difference, a change between what was whole
and what is now not whole. Difference is the moment of the birth of
perception, hence of possibility and the future of creation. All change is
the outcome of difference, deriving from that essential difference between yin and yang, and change is the source of all meaning, all life.
Thus removing the stick is a highly auspicious thing to do, symbolically
emulating the all-generating, mutually influencing opposition of yin
and yang.

Some prefer the yarrow sticks method for the opportunity it allows
for meditation and reflection during the period it takes to build the
hexagrams. To many, though, it is simply the sense of symbolic and
mystical power that the yarrow stick method generates that makes it
the preferred method.

There are other traditional methods of consulting the I Ching which
have been used by the Chinese; for example, using grains of rice or
using marked 'wands'. The latter has some similarities with the yarrow
stick method as the wands are sticks of the same length, but only six are
used and they are painted black with a white bar across one side. The
bundle of wands is thrown onto the ground. Then, beginning with the
nearest, they are picked up in turn. If the white bar is uppermost then
that signifies a yin line otherwise they signify a yang line. And the order
in which they are picked up is the order of the lines in the hexagram,
beginning as always with the bottom line. One disadvantage with this
method is that it does not incorporate a means of providing lines for
two hexagrams—for the present and the future.

Whichever of the two main methods you decide to use, the outcome will be that you have drawn two six-line hexagrams, building them up from the bottom line. This way of constructing the hexagrams probably derives from the Chinese system of writing characters, but it is likely it is also intended to symbolize or emulate the direction of most natural growth: from the earth to the sun.

Some practice in drawing a hexagram would be useful. Initially, we will use the coin method, and concentrate on drawing a present hexagram only. We will assume that you have thrown the coins and have obtained the following results:

first throw—two heads and one tail
second throw—two heads and one tail
third throw—one heads and two tails
fourth throw—three tails
fifth throw—two heads and one tail
sixth throw—three heads.

Now look at the hexagram. Start from the bottom line, which is your first throw, and work your way up, as follows:

The sixth throw gives a solid yang line.
The fifth throw gives a broken yin line.
The fourth throw gives a broken yin line.
The third throw gives a solid yang line.
The second gives you broken yin line.
The first throw gives you a broken yin line.

Hexagram 52
Ken—The Mountain

The methods described so far will enable you to begin immediately consulting the individual hexagrams in the hexagram system, reading the commentaries and pondering the meanings in relation to the questions you pose. However, it is now time to bring in the significance of what was referred to in passing earlier—'moving lines'. Their role in creating a 'future' hexagram as well as one for the present has to be explored and explained.

Moving lines method

The aspect of the hexagram lines we will be looking at here is whether they are what is known as 'moving lines'. For individual lines this means they are referred to in one of four possible ways: 'old yang' and 'old yin'; or 'young yang' and 'young yin'. The moving lines are the lines that are not fixed. So, young yin and young yang are the lines in their unchanging form, confirmed in their polar positions of yin and yang, respectively. But old yin and old yang are in the process of changing into their polar opposite. When the yin or yang power attains its zenith, it becomes 'old'. At which point it changes to its polar opposite.

An old yin line in a hexagram is shown as a broken line with an 'x' in the centre, as follows: ━━x━━

And an old yang line is drawn as an unbroken line with a small circle in the centre, as follows: ━━o━━

So an old yin line is in the process of moving from yin to yang and will become a yang line; and similarly, an old yang line is in the process of moving from yang to yin and will become a yin line.

Earlier, in the descriptions of the coin and yarrow stick methods, we looked at how to translate the throws of the coins or yarrow sticks into yin or yang values in order to draw the lines of the hexagram. The translation method used was different in the yarrow sticks method as it assigned numeric values to heads and tails. This is also the method used if one wishes to build hexagrams which explicitly incorporate moving lines; and it can be used with coins as well as yarrow sticks.

When using the three coins, throws them as before and note how they fall in combinations of heads and tails, with the heads side still being the yang side, and the tails side still being the yin side. This time though, the yang (heads) side is assigned the numeric value of 3; and the yin (tails) side is assigned the numeric value of 2. Count the value of each coin on this numeric basis, and then add these values together. Each throw of the coins will yield one of four possible values: six, seven, eight or nine. The hexagram lines for each value are drawn below:

━━o━━	9
━━ ━━	8
━━━━	7
━━x━━	6

The top line is old yang and has a value of 9.

The broken line below is young yin and has a value of 8.

The solid line in second position is young yang and has a value of 7.

The bottom line is old yin and has a value of 6.

It is possible when you cast your coins, or yarrow sticks, to have no moving lines, because you have values of 8 or 7 for every throw and so you have a hexagram composed only of young yin and young yang lines. If so you would only draw one hexagram as this one refers to a situation that is static or ending.

It is more than likely, though, that when you cast the coins you will indeed get a moving line, which is a 6 or 9. 6 is old yin and the 9 is old yang. In this case you would draw the hexagram incorporating the moving lines. You would then draw a second hexagram, the same as the first except for the moving lines, which are changed into their 'young' opposites, i.e.: old yang becomes a broken yin line, and old yin becomes a solid yang line.

Six throws of the coins have obtained the following hexagrams:
first throw—two 3s and a 2 = line value of 8
second throw—three 2s = line value of 6 (moving line)
third throw—three 3s = line value of 9 (moving line)
fourth throw—two 2s and a 3 = line value of 7
fifth throw—two 3s and a 2 = line value of 8
sixth throw—two 2s and a 3 = line value of 7

The first hexagram, incorporating moving lines: the second line is old yin (6) and the third line (9) is old yang. *The second hexagram, with moving lines changed into opposite values: the second line is young yang, and the third line is young yin.*

You then have to read both hexagrams, by looking them up in the hexagram system. You will also have to read the meanings of the moving lines, but for the first hexagram only. You only need to take the line readings into account when you have moving lines in a hexagram. You will look at the reading for the line number where you have a moving line. The moving lines highlight areas of change and aspects of significant note. The moving lines indicate that the whole situation is unbalanced, being either too positive or too negative, and so is open to change. The second hexagram represents the change that will occur in the future.

Regarding the second or 'future' hexagram, it is appropriate here to take note of what James Legge said on this matter in the introduction to his translation of the I Ching: "The object of the divination . . . was not to discover future events absolutely, as if they could be known beforehand, but to ascertain whether certain schemes, and conditions of events contemplated by the consulter, would turn out luckily or unluckily."

The intention of the I Ching was never to give authoritative predictions about what was going to occur in the future, but to indicate whether plans and actions initiated in the present were likely to turn out favourably. This is more in the nature of what is called a prognosis, meaning a plausible and valid assessment of the probability of a present situation having one future outcome as opposed to another.

Whatever method you use to generate hexagrams it is important to realize and remember that each hexagram is composed of an upper and lower trigram. The trigrams were the origin of the I Ching and each of the eight has a name and commentary assigned to it. Each possible individual line in a trigram has a name and associated commentary.

The trigrams

The origins of the trigrams were single yin and yang lines which were used as oracles. In ancient times, oracles were a common feature of all cultures. (For example, in ancient Greece, there was famously the oracle of Apollo at Delphi). The oldest oracles committed themselves to simple yes or no answers to the questions they were posed. This type of oracular declaration was the origin of the lines of the trigram (and hence of the hexagrams and the I Ching). 'Yes' was indicated by an unbroken (yang) line: ——————; and 'no' was a broken (yin) line: —— —— . At some point though, it was felt necessary to have a greater degree of differentiation, and so the single lines were combined in pairs, which resulted in four possibilities:

Later, a third line was added to these four combinations, thus producing the system of eight trigrams. These trigrams were thought of as symbols or images that comprised everything that happens in heaven and earth. They were also regarded as being in a state of continual transition, one trigram changing into another.

The eight trigrams are symbols that represent transitional states. They are images that are always in the process of changing into another image. So in terms of how they relate to phenomena in the real world, the focus is not on things as they are, on their fixed nature; the concentration is not on an analysis of what the constituent parts are of any phenomenon, what causes and effects brought it into existence. The trigrams do not represent things in themselves, but the tendencies of these things in movement.

Each of the trigrams is assigned a specific name which corresponds to different processes in the natural world

Ch'ien
(Heaven / Sky)

K'un
(Earth)

Chen
(Thunder)

K'an
(Water)

Ken
(Mountain)

Sun
(Wind)

Tui
(Marsh / Lake)

Li
(Fire)

These are further classified into what are known as major and minor trigrams, according to their combination of strong yang lines and yielding yin lines. Their English names are as follows:

> Major yang trigrams: Heaven and Marsh
> Minor yin trigrams: Thunder and Fire
> Major yin trigrams: Earth and Mountain
> Minor yang trigrams: Water and Wind.

Each of the trigrams has a main attribute. For example: Heaven is the Creative, which is strong (yang); and Earth is the Receptive, which is yielding (yin). Each trigram also has different meanings and associations corresponding to different classes of phenomena in the natural, animal and human worlds. For example, there are different trigrams for the different functions associated with the family roles of mother, father, three sons and three daughters. To clarify this by example: the sons represent the different stages of the principle of movement: start of movement; danger in movement; and culmination of movement, rest. The daughters signify the different stages of devotedness: gently penetrating or spreading; clarity and adaptability; and tranquil joy.

The following table lists the trigrams, with their names, main attributes and key associations for each .

Name	Ch'ien	K'un	Chen	K'an	Ken	Sun	Li	Tui
Signifies	heaven	earth	thunder	water	mountain	wind	fire	marsh
Attribute	creative/ strong	receptive/ yielding	arousing/ moving	abyss/ danger	unmoving/ resting	gentle/ penetrating	separate/ clarifying	happy/ joyful
Animal	horse	cow	dragon	pig	dog	cat	bird	sheep
Season	early winter	early autumn	spring	winter	early spring	early summer	summer	autumn
Polarity	yang	yin	yang	yang	yang	yin	yin	yin
Element	metal	soil	grass	wood	stone	air	fire	flesh
Direction	north west	south west	east	north	north east	south east	south	west
Family member	father	mother	first son	middle son	third son	first daughter	second daughter	third daughter
Colour	purple	black	orange	red	green	white	yellow	blue
Body part	head	solar plexus	foot	ear	hand	thighs	eye	mouth

Ch'ien signifies supreme creative inspiration. Its three unbroken lines represent strength, vitality and good fortune. It also signifies completeness, coldness, power and forcefulness.

K'un is the opposite of Ch'ien. It is feminine and passive. It relates to yielding and nurturing, kindness, devotion and loyalty.

Chen is to do with movement and speed. It relates to expansion and growth, impulsiveness and experimenting.

K'an signifies danger. It relates to depth of thought and concentration.

Ken represents completeness and stillness. It has to do with caution, thoroughness and inevitability.

Sun relates to fauna and growth, flexibility and separateness.

Li represents clarity, beauty and enlightenment. It also relates to clinging and resolution.

Tui signifies delight and joy, sensual pleasure and magical achievement, growth and success.

These then are the primary trigrams which in combination make up the sixty-four hexagrams of the I Ching. As well as the upper and lower primary trigrams of a hexagram, the original authors also took into consideration what is called a hexagram's nuclear trigrams. These consist of the lower nuclear trigram, made up of the second, third and fourth lines of the hexagram; and the upper nuclear trigram, made up of the third, fourth and fifth lines. Both primary trigrams and nuclear trigrams are indicated in the hexagram below.

Upper primary trigram: Sun {lines 4,5,6}
Upper nuclear trigram: Ken {lines 3,4,5}
Lower nuclear trigram: Chen {lines 2,3,4}
Lower primary trigram: Tui {lines 1, 2,3}

The I Ching's system of sixty-four hexagrams is entirely composed of the core system of primary trigrams in all their possible combinations. The combined associations of the two primary trigrams makes up the particular properties of a hexagram. The table that follows provides a key to all the possible hexagrams, with the upper and lower primary trigrams that make up each hexagram. You can locate a hexagram in the table by finding its upper and lower trigrams and hence the number of the hexagram.

Key to the hexagrams

UPPER TRIGRAMS / LOWER TRIGRAMS	Chi'en	K'un	Chen	K'an	Ken	Sun	Tui	Li
Chi'en	1	11	34	5	26	9	43	14
K'un	12	2	16	8	23	20	45	35
Chen	25	24	51	3	27	42	17	21
K'an	6	7	40	29	4	59	47	64
Ken	33	15	62	39	52	53	31	56
Sun	44	46	32	48	18	57	28	50
Tui	10	19	54	60	41	61	58	38
Li	13	36	55	63	22	37	49	30

The hexagrams

This section deals with the sixty-four hexagrams of the I Ching. They are listed in numerical order, and an extensive textual commentary and interpretation accompanies each drawn hexagram. The significance of the hexagrams lies in their representative or symbolic nature. Each of the hexagrams symbolizes a transitional state in human life, and the hexagram system as a whole is the symbolic representation of a series of situations in human life. The hexagrams consist of six lines, and all the sixty-four possible hexagrams are derived from the core system of eight three-line trigrams, which themselves are derived from combinations of the basic solid yang line and broken yin line. Within the hexagram it is the 'movements' of these individual yang and yin lines (i.e., the 'moving lines' that were discussed earlier) that change one hexagram into another, thus signifying the change of one situation into another. Of course, as we have seen above, when a hexagram has no moving lines it means that, for the time being, there is no movement within the situation that it represents: it is not in the process of changing into another situation, and thus another hexagram. In this case, when reading the textual commentaries, only the meaning of the hexagram as a whole has to be considered, and not the individual lines.

Each hexagram has a Chinese name, with an English translation. The analysis and discussion of each hexagram covers three main areas: the Judgement (the Tuan of King Wen); the Image and Line Readings (the Hsiang Chuan of King Wen's son, the Duke of Chou); and the Interpretation (based on the T'uan Chuan, or Ten Wings, which is mainly attributed to Confucius and his followers).

The Judgement identifies the overall theme and the meaning of the hexagram, including its auspicious or inauspicious nature. The Image concentrates on discussion of the hexagram's symbolic content and analysis of individual lines. (Keep in mind that the only individual lines that are of importance are the moving lines; these are the lines that you will go to the line analysis for. The other, non-moving, lines in a hexagram have a purely functional role in constructing the hexagram). The Interpretation is based on the explanatory comments on the Judgement and the Image, called the T'uan Chuan; but it is used here give an interpretative account of the Judgement and also the structure of the hexagram.

At the head, though, of each section of discussion on a hexagram, you will find the 'Commentary'. This is a paragraph which is intended to collate or bring together in a convenient and readily understood form the import and meaning of the hexagram. It incorporates elements from all the other discussions and interpretations of the hexagram.

Timing

The crucial factor in using the I Ching to help one intervene successfully in one's fate, was timing. The earlier one intervened in a situation with the correct action, the more likely it was that you would be able to shape it to your wishes—wishes that would be in concordance with the morally correct motives and actions advocated by the I Ching. Identifying this germinal phase of a situation is the key; and this is the key function of the I Ching. If situations are in their early stages then they can be controlled. Taking the appropriate action at this time will enable one to decisively influence outcomes. But if a situation is allowed to develop to its full consequences before we try to intervene in it—then it is too late. By this time the situation has an overwhelming momentum of its own and the only moral choice left is how to accommodate oneself to it, how to accommodate it in one's life.

The power of the I Ching

The I Ching, with the combined power of the hexagrams and the accompanying text, now had the power and the ability to divine, and put one who consults it in touch with, the forces of movement and change that influenced human life. The hexagrams and their lines, with their movements and changes, were able to represent the movements and changes of the underlying or creative powers of the universe. And the I Ching allowed an individual to have an influence on these controlling influences.

The casting of the yarrow stalks which enabled an individual to 'tap into' the fundamental governing forces of his life had a two-fold significance. Its use of chance was a route into the non-logical, unconscious aspects of himself, which were at a profound level in tune with, in concordance with, the life-forces of the universe. And the yarrow-stalk itself was, literally, a divining rod. As a humble form of plant life it was a direct link to, and was a physical manifestation of, the life-force; and as a sacred plant it had a link with the fundamental spiritual principles of life.

The use of coins is also a good means of tapping into the revelatory power of chance, as the opposite sides are directly symbolic of the basic polarities which are the basis of the universe: yin and yang. Also, in their actual use, as well as being physical objects, coins are also symbolic objects, and so provide or represent that link between the physical and the spiritual which is at the heart of the process of consulting the I Ching.

The philosophy of the I Ching

The moral dimension, then, became an integral and fundamental aspect of the I Ching. The I Ching also had the avowed ability to divine or perceive the fundamental movements and changes of the universe and reproduce them, in the form of the hexagrams and their text, for the moral and spiritual benefit of those who consulted it. Thus was the I Ching established as an authoritative and revered book of wisdom. It was perceived and used as such by philosophers such as Lao-Tse, the founder of the philosophy and religion of Taoism. His thought and teaching were imbued with the wisdom of the I Ching, and it inspired him to some of his profoundest aphorisms. The ancient Chinese philosopher Confucius was also influenced and inspired by the I Ching. His famous aphorisms and proverbial sayings were collected by his disciples and pupils in a text called the *Analects for the Benefit of Posterity*. Both of these sage philosophers studied the lore and wisdom of the I Ching and used it in their philosophies. Confucius in particular is reputed to have developed a close and profound relationship with the I Ching in his latter years, and legend has it that he said if he was allowed another fifty years of life he would devote them to the study of the I Ching.

As an ancient book of wisdom, then, which inspired the most famous of Chinese philosophers and the enduring philosophies of Taoism and Confucianism, the philosophy that underpins or informs the I Ching is obviously important. It can be formulated as consisting of three main concepts or themes. The fundamental and basic idea that underpins everything else is the idea of change, the second fundamental theme is the theory of images, and the third crucial aspect of the I Ching are the Judgements.

Change

Change is the basis of the I Ching and of the universe. Confucius famously compared life and the process of change to a constantly flowing river. If one looks into a river one cannot fix one's attention on a fixed piece of river that stays the same and does not change. The river only exists as a constantly moving flow. So it is with time and change. One who is concerned with the meaning and significance of change does not focus his attention on individual things or situations, which are merely transitory. One concentrates on the river, on the eternal and unchanging principle that creates all change. This principle or law is the Tao of the philosopher Lao-Tse. The Tao is the one path, the way of all things. Everything is part of the one way. For this one way to come into being and influence it had to have a founding principle, a fixed point from which everything flows. This founding concept is called the 't'ai chi', originally meaning the ridge-pole. The ridge-pole or single line in itself represents oneness; but from this oneness all duality comes, for the single line also creates an above and a below, a right and a left, a front and a back. In other words we have the principle of opposition and a universe of opposites, from which all things and all meaning are created.

The originating polar opposites are known as the principles of yin and yang. They are also represented as the complementary light and dark parts of a circle.

Yin and yang are the two alternating primal states of being, their constant flowing into and changing into one another creating all the oppositions and all change in the universe. Change consists partly of the continuous transformation of one force into another, and partly as a cycle of change of pairs of complementary opposites in the world, such as night and day, summer and winter, heat and cold etc. All change is governed and given meaning by the universal law of the Tao.

Images, ideas and the senses

The second fundamental theme of the I Ching is the theory of images or underlying ideas. The eight founding and core trigrams of the I Ching are images of states of change, not of fixed situations or things. This is associated with the idea that all occurrences in the physical, known world are the representations or expressions of an original 'image' or 'idea' in the unknown, unseen world that underlies, and gives rise to, all know and perceived reality. (This is similar to, but not the same as, the Greek philosopher Plato's *Theory of Forms or Ideas*).

So everything that happens in this physical and visible world is just a representation of a 'real' event in the unseen and unknown world that lies beyond us and to which we, ordinarily, have no access. Also, the representation in this world which we perceive as an event in time, happens later in time that the 'real' event or idea; so the 'real' event is the origin in both the sense of 'being' and the sense of time.

Not everyone is denied access to this originating world beyond the ken of our ordinary senses. Holy men and wise men—sages—can gain entry to this mysterious and sacred realm or dimension. They are in direct contact with the higher sphere of the 'ideas' through the powers of their intuition; and from this perspective of insight and illumination they are in a position to intervene with authority and a wise decisiveness in human affairs. So wise men become not only mediators between heaven and earth, the two primal forces of yang and yin, they become like a third primal force in their ability and power to govern and shape events.

The I Ching, therefore, is in the position and function of a holy man or 'wise man', offering the benefits of its insight and wisdom to those who consult it. The I Ching, in its trigrams and hexagrams, is able to delineate the underlying states of change and show them through its images; it is also able to show the beginnings or birth of new and unfolding situations and events. This allows those who consult the I Ching to intervene with foresight and sagacity in the changing situations in their lives.

The Judgements

The third founding principle of the I Ching are the Judgements. The Judgements give expression in language to the images. They are able to articulate with prescient foreknowledge whether a given action in the present will have a future outcome that will be auspicious or inauspicious, bring good fortune or misfortune. The Judgements allow someone who consults the I Ching to make the decision to refrain from a course of action that seems favourable in the present but is liable to lead to future misfortune. So the consulter is not at the mercy of fate, not always the passive and suffering victim of its tyrannical whims and caprices.

The Judgements of the I Ching, along with the commentaries on them and interpretations of them, present to the interested and reflective reader a rich fund of ancient yet still relevant Chinese wisdom. In their breadth and depth the Judgements also allow the sagacious reader to consider and ponder the rich variety of human experience—to his own potential enrichment. Ideally, learning from his reading of the Judgements, the 'wise reader' will develop his own intuitive judgement and free will. These discerning and discriminating powers will help the 'wise reader' to mould the path of his life towards that of the one true path of the Tao. And thus the I Ching will have fulfilled its role and function as a book of wisdom.

Final points on the text

The quotations from the I Ching which are used in the text that accompanies each of the following hexagrams are taken from the Legge translation. In a few places the language has been modified to clarify its meaning; but otherwise the flavour and idiom of the original translation is preserved.

The Hsiang Chuan, or Image, of the Duke of Chou uses the recurring symbol of 'the dragon' in its analysis of the individual lines of each hexagram. Legge provides this interpretation of the symbolism of 'the dragon': "'The dragon' is the symbol employed by the Duke of Chou to represent 'the superior man' and especially 'the great man' exhibiting the virtues or attributes characteristic of heaven [. . .] It has been from the earliest time the emblem with the Chinese of the highest dignity and wisdom, of sovereignty and sagehood, the combination of which constitutes 'the great man'".

The 'dragon' or 'superior man', 'great man' or 'wise man' are analogous terms for an idealized state of perfect wisdom and moral behaviour to which the 'ordinary man' must at all times aspire. Each in his own way and to a different extent must try to exemplify the virtues and moral strength of the 'wise man'. Either as a more or less enduring part of his character or as an aspect of his attitude and conduct in a specific situation, the ordinary man can strive to emulate, to attain and demonstrate, some at least of the attributes and qualities of the 'wise man'—which will include also accepting the responsibilities of such a position and role. So that the ordinary man following a path of virtue and honour can aspire to share at least temporarily in the respect and honour accorded to the 'wise man'.

In the quotations from the Image and its line readings, the symbolism and terminology of 'the dragon' has been replaced here by such phrases as 'the wise man' or the 'creative power' in order to make the sense slightly more prosaic and referential than the original symbolism. The intention being, simply, to make it easier for the new and uninitiated reader to understand and grasp the meanings and concepts that are being referred to.

As you read through and become acquainted with the text in the hexagram system, please keep in mind that this book is a guide to the I Ching—an accessible and useful means, it is hoped, to forming an initial acquaintance with a text that can be fairly daunting for a newcomer to it. This introductory text, though, is not intended to be a substitute for the original full text of the I Ching. If reading the unabridged version of the I Ching, one would ponder the meaning of the text in the light of one's own situation and decide whether to accept that it has a relevance and practical meaning for that particular situation. Even more so for this guide, then. The modern and occasionally simplified readings and interpretations of the quoted parts of the I Ching should not be taken as gospel, or the last word on the subject. Feel free to disagree with or dispute them in the light of your own reading and understanding of the quoted sections of the I Ching. Conversely, you should also be open to the possibility that the commentaries and interpretations of the hexagrams are saying something meaningful and relevant about you and your situation. You don't have to be afraid that having an open mind is the same as having a gullible mind. You will see, as you work through the texts of the hexagrams, that the I Ching makes it a cardinal virtue that at all times one retains one's integrity of mind and feeling.

When you have familiarized yourself sufficiently with this guide, you will then be in a position to do what was referred to in the introduction: make up your own mind as to the value of this text and by extension, the I Ching itself. At that point you can also make the decision whether to move on from this introductory text to a full and unabridged version of the I Ching. Whatever you decide it is hoped that this text will have adequately fulfilled its own limited remit and responsibility as a reliable guide.

Before you begin the process of consulting specific hexagrams for an answer to a specific question you have posed, read or skim through the whole chapter first, in order to familiarize yourself with the hexagrams and the style and format of the analysis and discussion of each hexagram. Remember: when you do consult the hexagrams properly for the first time, make sure that the two hexagrams you have drawn have been correctly built from the bottom line upwards.

Hexagram 1
Ch'ien—The creative

Component trigrams
Primary: Ch'ien—Heaven, creative (upper and lower). Nuclear: Ch'ien—Heaven, creative (upper and lower).

Keywords
Heaven, energy, creativity, action, perseverance, masculinity.

Commentary
This is an auspicious situation. A worthy goal is attained through the correct deployment of moral and spiritual energies. Continue with your intentions, as you will succeed because you have the energy, the desire and the resolve to do so. Your perseverance towards an outcome that will be right for you will ensure that things will unfold as you wish them. Beware of failure being snatched from the jaws of victory, though, because of overconfidence or trying to force the issue. Remain in patient harmony with your creativity and time will reward you by delivering your desired goal.

Judgement
The primary power is that which is great and originating, penetrating, advantageous, correct and firm.

Submit to the flow and let things take place in their own time. When anything ends something new begins, as the cycle of creativity continues.

Interpretation

The hexagram is complete and perfect yang with no yin lines. It is composed entirely of the Ch'ien trigram which represents heaven, creativity and energy; and in combination in upper and lower trigrams it signifies working in harmony with the pure energy and creativity of the universe

To achieve success in something worthwhile and morally good. Ch'ien also contains the concept of ceaseless movement and continual change, a never-ending process of evolution. The theme of the hexagram is change and transformation and this is embodied in the way that its six yang lines transform into their polar opposite in the six yin lines of K'un, Hexagram Two. Where Ch'ien is energy, K'un is form and the two together—like yin and yang—are necessary for creativity. Creativity and the form in which it manifests itself are inseparable.

Image

Heaven, in its motion: strength. The wise man nerves himself to ceaseless activity.

Learn to develop, always move positively into the future. Stay strong and persevere and the help of 'heaven' and the power of creativity will bring you success.

Line readings

Line 1: *The creative power is lying hidden in the deep. It is not the time for active doing.*

Wait patiently and wisely for the right moment to commit yourself to action, to your plans. You will know it when it arrives. Don't try to anticipate it.

Line 2: *The creative power appears in the field. It will be advantageous to meet the great man.*

Things are beginning to happen. Look out for someone who can help you achieve your goal. A partnership at this time would be fruitful.

Line 3: *The wise man is active and vigilant all the day, and in the evening still careful and apprehensive. The position is dangerous, but there will be no mistake.*

Success and power also confer responsibilities. Behave prudently and maturely. Don't react to envy and don't get overconfident. Be aware of yourself and the effects of your influence but don't let this bring you down or make you anxious.

Line 4: *The creative power stirs and prepares to move, but remains hidden in the deep. There will be no mistake.*

Assess the situation for yourself and take the responsibility of deciding correctly whether it is the right time to move forward.

Line 5: *The creative power aligns with heaven. It will be advantageous to meet with the great man.*

Work in harmony with the power of change and creativity and you will become influential and attract other people of influence, to your benefit.

Line 6: *The creative power exceeds the proper limits. There will be occasion for repentance.*

Don't isolate yourself from others, become aloof in your time of success. Neither should you overreach yourself, entertain grandiose ideas about yourself or your ability. If you don't conduct yourself prudently and modestly you will bring on failure.

Hexagram 2
K'un—The receptive

Component Trigrams
Primary: K'un—receptive, earth (upper and lower). Nuclear: K'un—receptive, earth (upper and lower).

Keywords
Earth, form, yielding, gentleness, giving, obedience, femininity.

Commentary
The future holds promise for you but it may depend on others. Submit yourself to those you trust and who have your interests at heart. Be responsive to sound advice and follow it by acting appropriately. Have the necessary faith and strength to wait for your good fortune, but remain ready and responsive. Don't loose patience or become impulsive and seek to take the initiative or promote yourself and your interests. Adopt a quiet and patient resolution and be confident in the assurance that things will happen as you want them in time.

Judgement
The yielding power is that which is great and originating, penetrating, advantageous, correct and having the firmness of the mare. When the superior man has to make any movement, if he take the initiative, he will go astray; if he follow, he will find his proper lord. The advantageousness will be seen in his getting friends in the south-west, and losing friends in the north-east. If he rest in correctness and firmness, there will be good fortune.

The best, the wisest course at this time is to submit yourself to the influence and lead of trusted and respected others. This is passive strength. To take the initiative yourself would be rash and invite failure and confusion because of inexperience.

Interpretation

This hexagram is all yin, with no yang lines. It signifies subordination to the way of others, the wisdom of being passive and receptive; but it also indicates action and movement inspired by meditation and receptiveness to the currents of creative energy. Solitary meditation and communing with your inner nature will lead to change and a new beginning. The hexagram is concerned with notions of physical space and acceptance of responsibility. This is demonstrated in the way it yields its own space by its own structure: the six yin lines change inevitably and naturally into the six yang lines of Ch'ien. This embodies the concept that creativity and the form in which it expresses itself are one.

Image

The earth is capacious and sustaining. The wise man, with his great virtue, supports men and things.

As you should live in harmony with the sustaining and protecting strength and power of the earth, so you should live in harmony with others and rely on their strength and support.

Line readings

Line 1: *One treads on hoarfrost. The strong ice will come soon.*

The supportive power of yin will soon help you if you keep going, but beware of being misled by unreliable or deceptive support.

Line 2: *Be true, calm and great; naturally done, it will be in every respect advantageous.*

Adopt the classic yin strengths and virtues of honesty, obedience to right authority, and calm perseverance. Don't succumb to transient doubt or misgiving.

Line 3: *Keep one's excellence under restraint, but firmly maintain it. If one should have occasion to engage in the king's service, one will not claim the success, but will bring affairs to a good issue.*

Quietly confident, you can continue in your chosen course without being deflected by the temptation to act prematurely. You can learn from other's example without feeling the need to attract attention to yourself or seek accolades.

Line 4: *Be like a tied sack. There will be no ground for blame or for praise.*

Protect yourself from harm by behaving prudently and cautiously. Keep your own counsel and maintain a quiet reserve.

Line 5: *Show a genuine humility. There will be great good fortune.*

Maintaining self-possession and a quiet decorum is the best and most fitting way to conduct yourself.

Line 6: *One tries to rule but only finds strife.*

By remaining wisely passive, and showing genuineness, loyalty and due obedience to wise and supportive sources of authority and help, you will be worthy of the benefits that will come your way. Don't be presumptuous or dismissive, otherwise you will only find failure. Be receptive to the ideas of others and welcoming of change.

Hexagram 3
Chun—Initial adversity

Component Trigrams

Primary: K'an—water (upper). Chen—thunder (lower). Nuclear: Ken—mountain (upper), K'un—earth (below).

Keywords

Water, thunder, beginnings, immaturity, youth, inexperience.

Commentary

Possible opportunities can also be possible dangers. Be wary and remain alert. Trust and confidence in yourself and your chosen course, along with strength and determination, will be required to ensure that you will survive any potential hazards and initial difficulties. Then you can successfully move forward. Accept help if it is offered. Don't try to push things to a quick and successful conclusion: you could be running into a pit of failure. Take time to look, listen and learn.

Judgement

There will be great progress and success, and the advantage will come from being correct and firm. Any movement in advance should not be lightly undertaken. There will be advantage in appointing assistants.

Be prepared for setbacks at the start of something new. These are only to be expected. Don't give up. Enlist the support and help of others. Eventually, you will come out on the other side and find all is running smoothly.

Interpretation

This is a time of difficulty and danger, of chaotic circumstances and confusion. Thunder is a harbinger of dangerous conditions and water can also be hazardous to those who don't know the art of using it to support them, who can't swim to safety. There is tension in the air but this can also be an opportunity to learn and grow.

Image

Clouds and thunder. The wise man adjusts his measure of government as in sorting the threads of the warp and woof.

By maintaining a sense of balance and clear-sightedness during a period of disorder and confusion, being prepared to be flexible and resourceful also, you will guide yourself towards a haven of peace and good order.

Line readings

Line 1: *There is difficulty in advancing. It will be advantageous to remain correct and firm. Rule by serving will bring favour.*

Keep the faith and your patience even when you seem to be going nowhere. Things will change. Be wise in the use of your time and energy. Avoid conflict with others and seek their support. Think about what you are doing but don't let this deflect you from your goal.

Line 2: *The young lady is distressed and obliged to return; even the horses of her chariot seem to be retreating. But she is not assailed by a lascivious man but by one who seeks her to be his wife. The young lady maintains her firm correctness, and declines a union. After ten years she will be united, and have children.*

Respond correctly and carefully to a tense, stressful situation. You should be in control of your destiny and have given thought to what you are doing and where you are going. Even genuine sources and offers of help should be treated with caution and care, as they may lead to situations where things get out of hand, especially out of your hands.

Line 3: *One follows the deer without the guidance of the forester, and finds oneself in the middle of the forest. The wise man, acquainted with the secret risks, thinks it better to give up the chase. If one goes forward, one will regret.*

Trust and rely on your own instincts and judgement. If it seems foolish or risky to proceed, then don't.

Line 4: *The lady retreats with her horses and chariot. She seeks, however, the help of the one who seeks her to be his wife. Advance will be fortunate; all will turn out advantageously.*

Seize the day. Act when the moment seems ripe. Seek out partnerships to help you if any are available. Success will be yours.

Line 5: *There are difficulties in the way of dispensing the rich favours that are expected of one. With firmness and correctness there will be good fortune in small things. In great things there will be misfortune.*

Be alert to how you are affecting others, but don't let others' influence take over. Take time to explain yourself. Don't brush others or their misunderstandings aside. Take them on board and move forward slowly until things are better.

Line 6: *One is obliged to retreat, weeping tears of blood in streams.*

An important time of choice. Somehow resolve the impasse you face, or start something new. The situation you are in cannot be allowed to stagnate. Take the initiative, one way or another.

Hexagram 4
Meng—Innocence

Component Trigrams
Primary: Ken—The Mountain (upper). K'an—Water (lower). Nuclear: K'un—Earth (above), Chen—Thunder (below).

Keywords
Ignorance, youthful folly, mountains, water, fog, misapprehension, instruction.

Commentary
You are inexperienced and lack wisdom. Retain your enthusiasm but learn as you keep going. Only act after careful and sensible thought. Look back over everything you took for granted about the situation. The situation will become clearer, but this will only be achieved through your perseverance. Seek direction from someone more experienced, but don't forget help your own self-development. Deepen your self-knowledge and recognize your own folly.

Judgement
There will be progress and success. I do not go and seek the youthful and inexperienced, but he comes and seeks me. When he shows the sincerity that marks the first recourse to the oracle, I instruct him. If he apply a second and third time, that is troublesome; and I do not instruct the troublesome. There will be advantage in being firm and correct.

It is the role of the student to seek out the teacher, but the teacher will only respond to a respectful attitude and sensible questions. As a seeker of guidance you must give careful thought to your questions. This is the epitome of your position when you consult the I Ching.

Interpretation
This hexagram signifies youthful inexperience but also implies youthful success. For anyone engaged in something new it suggests 'beginner's luck'. Learn from others and from your own experience.

Image
A spring issuing forth from a mountain. The wise man strives to be resolute in his conduct and nourishes his virtue.

As you go on, strive to learn and to gain increased clarity of mind and understanding. With perception and foresight comes a calm assurance which will be valuable in the future.

Line readings

Line 1: *One has to dispel ignorance. It will be advantageous to use punishment for that purpose, and to remove the shackles from the mind. But going on in punishment will give occasion for regret.*

Sometimes one can only learn through committing errors and facing the criticism and rebukes of others. If the criticism is justified and fair, then it should be accepted and learned from. Develop your own powers of self-criticism and self-discipline but don't let them inhibit you or hold you back.

Line 2: *To exercise forbearance with the ignorant will bring good fortune.*

It will be to your credit and advantage to deal kindly and patiently with those who, like you, are inexperienced and lacking in knowledge.

Line 3: *When a woman sees a man of wealth she will not keep her person from him, and in no way will advantage come from her.*

Don't let your respect and admiration for another turn into a dangerous idolater. Never lose your sense of yourself and your own worth and the responsibilities you owe to yourself. Neither should you become closely associated with any individual you are not compatible with.

Line 4: *One is bound in chains of ignorance. There will be occasion for regret.*

Don't respond to difficulties arising from your inexperience by daydreams, compensatory fantasy and escapism. You will only make things more difficult for yourself. Dreams are for the sleeping mind; keep your waking mind on the real world.

Line 5: *One is a simple youth without experience. There will be good fortune.*

Sometimes good luck can attend innocence and simplicity. Youthful optimism should be retained, as well as a modest sense of one's limitations and abilities. An inflated sense of oneself should be deflated as soon as one perceives it.

Line 6: *One punishes the ignorant youth. But no advantage will come from doing him an injury. Advantage would come from warding off injury from him.*

Mistakes must be recognized and learned from, but there is no need to make an issue of them or to wallow in them—whether they belong to you or to another inexperienced person. This is a waste of time and energy, which creates difficulty and disorder. Deal sensibly with mistakes by accepting them as moments or opportunities of learning, then put them behind and move on.

Hexagram 5
Hsu—Waiting

Component Trigrams

Primary: K'an—Water (upper), Ch'ien—Heaven (lower). Nuclear: Li—Fire (above), Tui—Marshes (below).

Keywords

Sustenance, water, heaven, patience, nourishment, light, perseverance.

Commentary

Carry on honestly and sincerely with the tasks at hand, and be patient with regard to your attainment of your real goal. Wait for the most favourable moment before trying to advance your plans. In the meantime cultivate patience and self-control. If you concentrate on those areas of your life that offer the greatest possibility of continuity, then you will be doing the right thing. Don't expect others to help before the moment is right. Keep in good spirits—you will attain your goal.

Judgement

With sincerity, there will be brilliant success. With firmness there will be good fortune; and it will be advantageous to cross the great stream.

Remain committed to your course, but pause and take time out. Use it as an opportunity for a period of reflection and taking stock of yourself and your plans. Get things into a realistic perspective. Continue to have faith in yourself.

Interpretation

The K'an trigram represents danger, and this is an obstacle to the strength and creative energy of Ch'ien. Strength could confront this danger and struggle with it; but the best plan is to bide one's time and wait for the most propitious moment. This hexagram is about self-discipline. Calmness and self-restraint are the keys to success. There are streams which must be crossed but not now. You must have the strength to wait for the right moment to cross the stream.

Image

Clouds ascending to heaven. The wise man eats and drinks, feasts and enjoys himself as if there were nothing else to employ him.

Be content and happy with what you have in the present. Soon, new growth will be possible when the clouds deliver the nourishing rain. In the meantime enjoy the moment for what it has.

Line readings

Line 1: *One waits in the distant border. It will be well for one to constantly maintain the purpose thus shown, in which case there will be no error.*

Keep your mind calmly on the present moment while you wait for some trouble to arrive. Its shape and timing is outside your control so concentrate on what is in your control, but remain ready to deal with whatever comes. You will know it when it arrives and with self-possession and calmness you will be able to cope successfully with whatever challenges it brings.

Line 2: *One waits on the sand of the mountain stream. One will suffer the small injury of being spoken against, but in the end there will be good fortune.*

You may be isolated as the scapegoat for something that goes wrong, and have to face general censure and disapproval. Let it wash over you and don't censure or blame those who find a convenient scapegoat in you. There may be upsetting gossip but do not respond to it. Keep your peace and your counsel. Eventually, things will turn out well for you.

Line 3: *One is in mud close by the stream. One thereby invites the approach of injury.*

Faced with worrying difficulty, your anxiety has caused you to act too soon and made the situation worse. Avoid any further complications and trouble by stopping where you are and being prudent and cautious while you wait.

Line 4: *One is waiting in the place of blood. But one will get out of the cavern.*

You can do absolutely nothing about a situation and so you feel trapped. Keep calm and try to accept that this as how it was meant to be.

Line 5: *One is waiting amidst the trappings of a feast. Through firmness and correction there will be good fortune.*

Take the opportunity of a brief distraction from your troubles and enjoy the pleasures that are on offer to you. But don't be tempted by them into forgetting that you have to continue in your journey. Use this time as a welcome respite that will allow you to gather strength for going on.

Line 6: *One is in the cavern. But there are three guests coming, without being urged, to one's help. If one receives them respectfully there will be good fortune in the end.*

Your may run into trouble in your direction towards your hoped-for goal. Have faith in other people and remain open to help from them. Things may not turn out as you wished but you will be able to move on with little loss.

Hexagram 6
Sung—Conflict

Component Trigrams

Primary: Ch'ien—Heaven (upper), K'an—Water (lower). Nuclear: Sun—Wind (above), Li—Fire (below).

Keywords

Strength, danger, stormy waters, obstruction, caution.

Commentary

You find your strength and your direction bringing you into a situation of conflict with others. Don't pour fuel onto the fire by trying to oppose and overcome the obstacles before you. If you fall into the temptation of seeking to win by using your strength and force this will only provoke the same force being used against you. Conflict is useless, a waste of time and energy. The urge to win is a false goal and a distraction. Withdraw and remain aloof from dispute and contention. It is the wise and politic thing to do. Seek compromise and accommodation with others. Listen to criticism and take advice.

Judgement

Though there is sincerity in one's contention, yet one will meet with opposition and obstruction; but if one cherish an apprehensive caution, there will be good fortune. If, though, one perseveres with the contention to the bitter end, there will be evil. It will be advantageous to see the great man; it will not be advantageous to cross the great stream.

You are stuck in a state of stagnant conflict through your insistence that everyone should always concede to the justness and rightness of your case; everyone else is wrong and you are always right. You have to concede that this is not the case and be prepared to meet others halfway. Follow the advice of an objective judge. In the meantime, it is not an auspicious time to start anything new.

Interpretation

In the structure of the hexagram, the upper primary trigram signifies strength and energy; the lower one denotes danger. There is a danger from outside is the suggestion, and this will lead to confrontation. The theme of the hexagram is conflict. Sometimes conflict cannot be avoided; but then it must be dealt with properly. Aggression will not solve things. Develop the ability to negotiate with others and seek a rapport with them. Pay heed and respect to sound and authoritative advice. Avoid getting involved in anything that takes you out of your depth.

145

Image

Heaven and water moving away from each other. The wise man, in the transaction of affairs, takes good counsel about his first steps.

Make this a period of inner communing and meditation about the imminent new beginning; but don't act on your intentions yet.

Line readings

Line 1: *One is not perpetuating the matter of contention. One will suffer the small injury of being spoken against, but the end will be fortunate.*

At the moment when it seems conflict is about to begin you should pull back and pull away from the other person. Don't worry about what is initially said regarding this action, as it will all come out right in the end.

Line 2: *One is unequal to the contention. One should retire; one will fall into no mistake.*

Your calm withdrawal from the situation will benefit everyone, but especially yourself.

Line 3: *Firmly correct, one keeps in the old place assigned for one's support. Perilous as the position is, there will be good fortune in the end. Should one engage in the king's business, one will not claim the merit of achievement.*

Continue learning the traditional wisdom that you have judiciously and successfully been acting upon. Let your old ways stay in the past. Don't take on any new work or responsibilities from your employer.

Line 4: *One is unequal to the contention. One returns to a study of heaven's ordinances, and rests in being firm and correct. There will be good fortune.*

Be firm but flexible, so that if your strength and purpose brings you up against someone who initiates conflict, you can calmly walk away. Be resolute in this and everything will turn out for the best.

Line 5: *One is contending, and with great good fortune.*

Put your faith in an objective third party to provide a fair assessment and good advice. If you are sincere and in the right then you will benefit.

Line 6: *One has the leather belt of reward conferred by the king, and thrice shall it be taken away in the morning.*

Don't get overconfident in the first flush of success. Where there has been one conflict there will be more.

Hexagram 7
Shih—The army

Component Trigrams

Primary: K'un—Earth (upper), K'an—Water (lower). Nuclear: K'un—Earth (above), Chen—Thunder (below)

Keywords

Earth, water, firmness, authority, group action, danger, dissension, devotion.

Commentary

There is a lack of harmony in your present situation, with contending forces causing confusion and unrest. But if you show firmness of purpose and keep your eye steadily on a goal which is worthy of attainment then you will succeed. Your exemplary action will transform aimless confusion into coordination and a worthwhile sense of direction. You will be an inspiration and a guide to others and will command their respect and admiration. With their help and support you will attain a position of distinction.

Judgement

With firmness and correctness and a leader of age and experience, there will be good fortune and no error.

A group of soldiers requires a steady and competent leader to unite them and keep them in good order. The leader must ensure that justice and peaceful concord prevail in the group. In and through this leadership he will command the respect, loyalty and love of his soldiers. The implication is that you should recruit the enthusiastic support of those around you to work together for a worthwhile common goal.

Interpretation

The only solid line in the hexagram is found in the middle line of the lower primary trigram. This gives the image of a general who is the commander of the broken yin lines. This hexagram is about proper discipline and legitimate and worthy power. It shows that an effective army requires effective soldiers and leadership. The good army remains in a state of prepared readiness until action is necessary, when it responds with spirit.

Image

Water in the midst of the earth. The wise ruler nourishes and educates the people and collects from among them the multitude of his army.

A ruler must instil a respect and desire for justice, good authority and harmony in his people by his own merits and example, commanding love and respect for his kindness, strength and unstinting support.

Line readings

Line 1: *The army goes forth according to the proper rules. If these not be good there will be misfortune.*

Success depends on the right motivation and the best preparation. Take a good and honest look at yourself.

Line 2: *The leader is in the middle of the army. There will be good fortune and no error. The king has thrice conveyed to him the orders of his favour.*

You are awarded a distinction which is merited by the respect those around you have for your good judgement and successful work. They share in the credit and honour, as you all work together in a situation of mutual respect.

Line 3: *The army may have many inefficient leaders. There will be misfortune.*

Be honest about your faults and weaknesses otherwise your endeavour will end in failure. Maintain a perceptive and judicious sense of authority and control over yourself and others.

Line 4: *The army is in retreat. There is no error.*

Now is the time to make a tactical retreat from a situation. You are not capitulating but surviving to fight again another day. Wait until a more advantageous time arrives. Be patient.

Line 5: *There are birds in the fields which it will be advantageous to seize and destroy. There will be no error. If the oldest son leads the army, and younger men idly occupy offices assigned to them, then however firm and correct he may be, there will be misfortune.*

Success requires maturity. You must compensate for the immaturity of yourself and your advisers by seeking out those who can give wise and mature guidance. Guard against the mistake of confusing age with wisdom.

Line 6: *The king gives his rewards, appointing some to be rulers of states, and others to undertake the headship of clans; but small men should not be employed.*

You have achieved success but don't bask in your moment of glory. You should take time to survey and assess the nature and merits of your attainment with a scrupulous honesty. Ask yourself if you are where you deserve to be and where you want to be, and whether you are better, morally and practically, than the person you have replaced. Be true to yourself.

Hexagram 8
Pi—Union

Component Trigrams

Primary: K'an—Water (upper), K'un— Earth (lower). Nuclear: Ken— The Mountain (above), K'un—Earth (below).

Keywords

Water, earth, cooperation, sound relationships, alliance, unity.

Commentary

You are in a favourable situation for strengthening the bonds you already have with your chosen associates, joining together for mutual support and benefit. Your success in achieving your goal depends on harmonious alliance and cooperative effort. You must be worthy, though, of others' commitment to your interests. Don't fall into the error of thinking that your status and power means that you can do what you like, in terms of yourself and other people. The best and fairest leader ensures the right forms of cooperative action to bring about creative progress in the community. That wise leader also knows that it is his honesty and sincerity which is the binding and decisive factor in the success of the situation, and is the true measure of his own success.

Judgement

In union there is good fortune. But let one re-examine oneself, as if consulting an oracle, and see whether one's virtue be great, unremitting and firm. If it be so, there will be no error. Those who have not rest will then come to one; and with those who are too late in coming it will be ill.

You must decide if you have the strength to enter into a long-term partnership with someone you have a common bond with. Your cannot dither over this decision or you risk it being summarily withdrawn.

Interpretation

In the structure of the trigrams, water lies on the earth. Water merges with the earth and they become one. The theme here is harmony. The hexagram emphasizes success deriving from harmonious and beneficial union. It has to be brought about by a leader who maintains a consistent virtue appropriate to his status and power. And this proper authority promotes union as it is communicated successively to those in responsible positions of power and influence. Anyone with whom you feel a strong bond is someone who will be able to give you help when you need it, but if your intuition does not support this then it is not the right time.

Image

Water flowing over the earth. The ancient kings established the various states and maintained an affectionate relation to their princes.

You should form close relationships with others in your group and make sure that your goals are their goals also, because only by working together for common aims will the group attain them.

Line readings

Line 1: *One seeks by sincerity to attain one's goal. There will be no error. Let the breast be full of sincerity as an earthenware vessel is of its contents, and it will in the end bring other advantages.*

Be sincere in all that you do and make sure you are in sympathy with others. Be prepared to be flexible and accommodating.

Line 2: *One moves towards union and attachment that comes from the inward mind. With firm correctness there will be good fortune.*

You must be true to yourself and others. Don't be false to your own self and direction just to try and remain in harmony with others.

Line 3: *One is seeking for union with such people as one ought not to be associated with.*

You are involved with a group that is wrong for you and must withdraw. Otherwise you will be unable to freely form other friendships in the future. Maintain some friendly contact with the group after you leave it if it makes the process easier.

Line 4: *One seeks for union with the one beyond oneself. With firm correctness there will be good fortune.*

You can freely reveal and express your thoughts and feelings, remembering to remain true to yourself and in touch with your own direction and goals.

Line 5: *The king urges the pursuit of the game in three directions only, and allows the escape of the animals before him. The people of his towns do not prevent it. There will be good fortune.*

Only those who chose to be a part of your group, should be. Coercing someone into to it, or to remain in it if they don't want to, is wrong.

Line 6: *One seeks union and attachment without having taken the first step towards such an end. There will be misfortune.*

Seize the day. Delay can be fatal. Decide what you want to do and do it straight away.

Hexagram 9
Hsiao Ch'u—Taming power

Component Trigrams
Primary: Sun—Wind (upper), Ch'ien— Heaven (lower). Nuclear: Li—Fire (above), Tui —Marsh (below).

Keywords
Restraining power of the small, wind, heaven, patience, strength, yielding.

Commentary
Tame any urge to force your way past obstacles in your path. Self-

control and restraint can be more formidable and effective than aggressive force. It is better at this time to cultivate your inner strengths and outer qualities. By so doing you will dissolve away or outlast your present obstacles. Be strong in yourself and be gentle and kind to others. With faith and trust in yourself you will be able to survive any temporary setbacks in good spirits. If you try to take short-term advantage of a situation, or if you act arrogantly with others, then you will bring trouble down upon yourself.

Judgement
There will be progress and success. We see dense clouds, but no rain coming from our borders in the west.

This hexagram concerns strength with gentleness. You will be able to move some temporary obstacles from your path by being congenial to others while remaining true to yourself and your aims.

Interpretation
The solitary broken line is in a position of great influence, and great power is being held under restraint. The humble and yielding element in the hexagram holds sway for the time being. You may not be going forward at the moment but everything is auspicious for success. This will be achieved by consolidating outward strengths of reciprocal respect and amicable relations with others while remaining steadfast to your inner self and goals.

Image
The wind moves in the sky. The wise man adorns the outward manifestation of his virtue.

Use this fallow period in the advancement of your plans as an opportunity to assess how you present yourself to others and how you behave towards them. This is the ideal opportunity to make any adjustments and improvements that you feel are necessary, so do not waste it.

Line readings
Line 1: *One returns and pursues one's own course. What mistake should one fall into? There will be good fortune.*

If you are unable to achieve your goals just now then it is best to walk away from the situation and wait for a much more opportune moment.
Line 2: *One returns to the proper course. There will be good fortune.*

Consider following the example of others who have retreated from similar goals to yours.
Line 3: *The supporting strap has been removed from the carriage. A husband and wife look on each other with averted eyes.*

Restrain your aggression and your forceful attempts to coerce people into your way of thinking. Continuing to try and push yourself forward against the obstacles that confront you will result in failure.

Line 4: *One is sincere. The danger of bloodshed is thereby averted, and the ground for apprehension dismissed. There will be no mistake.*

Follow the example of those prescient others who are aware that circumstances are changing: act now without delay.

Line 5: *One is sincere and draws others to unite around one. Rich in resources, one employs one's neighbours in the same cause as oneself.*

Your are well-matched with those you are in partnership with and this augurs well for the future. You are also fortunate in your friendships.

Line 6: *The rain has fallen, and it is time for the onward progress to stop. One values the fullness of one's achievement and virtue. But weakness that has achieved such a result, if it plumes itself upon it, will be in a position of peril and like the full moon, which must now wane. When the wise man attains his end, he remains in quiet.*

Be alert and wary when you are on the point of success. Take nothing for granted and be careful that you aren't getting into something that will feel like a trap.

Hexagram 10
Lu—Stepping

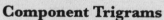

Component Trigrams
Primary: Ch'ien—Heaven (upper), Tui—Marsh (lower). Nuclear: Sun—Wind (above), Li—Fire (below).

Keywords
Sky, marsh, propriety, courtesy, purpose, degree, order, caution.

Commentary
Don't hold back, but move onward swiftly with confidence. This hexagram is about harmony between the small and the great. When you achieve good relationships with those above and below you then you ensure that anything is within your grasp. Remain correct in your dealings with others, showing due deference and generous forbearance where appropriate. Make sure that you have the support of influential people in your undertakings. This will be of more benefit in achieving your aims than any impetuous initiatives of your own. Beware of incurring the disfavour of someone in authority by behaving rashly.

Judgement

One treads on the tail of a tiger, which does not bite one. There will be progress and success.

Despite difficulties and possible dangers, your proper conduct towards others and your determination and inner strength will take you onwards to success.

Interpretation

This hexagram has joy below strength and indicates that there will be a fortunate ending to a period of danger and endurance. This is achieved through the observance of proper conduct in oneself and toward others. Learn to work harmoniously with others, despite disparities in status, and achieve success together. Others may have valuable experience and advice to share with you that you must be humble enough to accept with grace. Don't be aloof and rude to those to whom you should be generously offering your attention and support, behave with prudence and humility.

Image

Heaven above, the waters of the marsh below. The wise man discriminates between high and low, and gives settlement to the aims of the people.

Though some people are at higher levels in the hierarchy of power and influence they do not discriminate against those below them. There is mutual respect.

Line readings

Line 1: *One treads one's accustomed path. If one goes forward, there will be no error.*

You have the choice of accepting or rejecting favourable opportunities for your progress which will be offered to you.

Line 2: *One treads the path that is light and easy in quiet and solitude. If one is firm and correct, there will be good fortune.*

Your way is clear and untroubled, so don't be tempted to stray off your path into conflicts with others who are having troubles.

Line 3: *A one-eyed man thinks he can see. A lame man thinks he can walk well. One treads on the tail of a tiger and is bitten. All this indicates ill fortune. There is a mere braggart and fool acting the part of a great ruler.*

The imagery here denotes self delusion leading to a potentially dangerous situation. Don't be presumptuous or complacent about your situation, keep a sharp look-out. Do not overestimate what you are capable of or underestimate the capabilities of others, otherwise you will fail.

Line 4: *One treads on the tail of a tiger. One becomes full of apprehensive caution. In the end there will be good fortune.*

Although things may be difficult there is cause for hope and optimism. Remain cautious but determined and you will overcome the problems that you face.

Line 5: *One has a resolute tread. But though one is firm and correct, there will be peril.*

You should continue in your path with determination but with special care. Anticipate and be prepared for further difficulties along the way.

Line 6: *One should look at the whole course one has trodden, and examine what the evidence tells. If it be complete and without failure, there will be great good fortune.*

From your position of achievement it is now time to assess what you have done and compare it with what you set out to do. This is important as others will judge you by end results and how you achieved them, not by initial motives.

Hexagram 11
T'ai—Tranquility

Component Trigrams
Primary: K'un—Earth (upper), Ch'ien—Heaven (lower). Nuclear: Chen—Thunder (above), Tui—Marsh (below).

Keywords
Earth, heaven, harmony, union, cooperation, prosperity, beginnings.

Commentary
Everything in the situation is favourable. It is all going as it should for you. It is a good time for a successful new undertaking. Harmony and cooperation are the means to success. Join together with others in a shared endeavour to achieve a common goal. Your selfless aspirations will be supported and guided by worthwhile and influential people. But if you are selfish or insincere then you will fail. Having finally achieved success, you must then ready yourself for dangerous challenges and difficulties.

Judgement
We see the little gone and the great come. There will be good fortune, with progress and success.

It is possible for anyone to develop the strength of a calm demeanour if they want to. A sense of contentment then follows and everything is rendered harmonious.

Interpretation

This hexagram shows three yielding, yin lines leaving and three strong, yang lines approaching. This suggests the onset of a favourable and successful time. Your whole situation is harmonious and in good order. The calmness and strength within you is reflected by the benign peace around you.

Image

Heaven and earth in communication together. The wise ruler, in harmony with this, fashions and completes his regulations after the courses of the heavens and the earth, and assists the applications of the adaptations furnished by them, in order to benefit the people.

As the farmer works in harmony with the seasons to provide for his needs, so the wise and sensible person progresses by working with nature and not against it.

Line readings

Line 1: *When grass is pulled up it brings with it other stalks with whose roots it is connected. One's advance will be fortunate.*

Others with the same aims as you will want to join with you, and you should welcome them on board.

Line 2: *One is forbearing with the uncultivated; one can cross the river without a boat; one does not forget the distant; one has no selfish friendships. Thus does one prove oneself acting in accordance with the course of the due Mean. Forbearing; resolved; vigilant; impartial.*

Showing forbearance, being resourceful and determined, being vigilant, and being selfless and impartial in relations with others: these are the four principal ways of overcoming difficulties, which you should adopt for all undertakings in your life.

Line 3: *While there is no state of peace that is not liable to be disturbed, and no departure of evil men that will not be followed by their return, yet when one is firm and correct, and accepts that disorder may occur, one will commit no error. There is no occasion for sadness at the certainty of such recurring changes; and in this mood the happiness of the present may be long enjoyed.*

Things are always changing so you must expect bad fortune to follow good. Accept this as natural and you will be able to fully savour the present favourable moment.

Line 4: *One does not rely on one's own rich resources but goes down to meet one's neighbours. They all come, not because they have received warning, but in the sincerity of their hearts.*

You should have an inner confidence and contentment from your justified success, and therefore have no need to adopt vainglorious displays of conduct and behaviour in order to impress or intimidate others with your success. Be sincere and at ease with others.

Line 5: *The king's younger sister marries and humbly serves her husband. By such a course there is happiness and there will be great good fortune.*

Be modest and sincere.

Line 6: *The city wall falls into the moat. It is not the time to use the army. The ruler may announce his orders to the people of his own city; but however correct and firm he may be, he will have cause for regret.*

Because you have not integrated all aspects of your life into a strong and harmonious whole then the inevitable change is coming into your vulnerable life. You have no choice but to accept what happens. A passive, stoic patience is now required.

Hexagram 12
P'i—Stagnation

Component Trigrams
Primary: Ch'ien—Heaven (upper), K'un—Earth (lower). Nuclear: Sun—Wind (above), Ken—The Mountain (below).

Keywords
Standstill, obstruction, disharmony, disunion, lack of cooperation, lack of means, deterioration.

Commentary
This is not an auspicious time. You have been going in the wrong direction and now you are faced with a testing time of struggle and disorder. You may be cut-off from someone close or deprived of the pleasure of something in your life. There may be unworthy people in positions of influence who will take against you. Things will get worse before they get better. But eventually, better they will. In the meantime you should not begin anything new. You must wait patiently for favourable circumstances to return. Face and accept your fate with quiet fortitude and a firm resolve not to let it prevent you from finding your way back to your true path and moving forward again. If you remain steadfast in this way you will find the troubles will clear and you will be able to see a happier time approaching.

Judgement
There is a lack of good understanding between the different classes of men. This is unfavourable to the firm and correct course of the wise man. We see the great gone and the little come.

You are surrounded by disruption and confusion. Withdraw if necessary. The important thing now is to remain true to yourself. You may become the focus for malign intent by some. The only thing to do is stay out of their way.

Interpretation

Three strong yang lines are leaving, three yielding yin lines are approaching. The situation is the reverse of hexagram 11. It is not an auspicious time. There will be trouble and disorder. The favourable period of development has reached its climax and the forces of decline and dissolution are taking over.

Image

Heaven and earth are not in intercommunication. The wise man restrains the manifestation of his virtue, and avoids the calamities that threaten him. There is no opportunity of conferring on him the glory of reward.

Don't be lured into anything merely because you have been seduced by its glamorous appeal.

Line readings

Line 1: *Grass pulled up brings with it the other stalks with whose roots it is connected. With firm correctness there will be good fortune and progress.*

Sometimes you have to withdraw from an adverse situation in order to preserve your energies for better future circumstances and avoid creating much worse consequences. Have patience and determination and your time will come.""

Line 2: *Patience and obedience for the small man brings good fortune. If the great man is patient and obedient in the face of distress and obstruction, he will have success.*

Sometimes it is necessary to be involved with materialist people as long as you have successfully remained aloof from their influence and have been faithful to yourself. You should continue in this course.

Line 3: *One is ashamed of one's hidden purpose.*

Those who have prospered through unfair means cannot hide this fact from themselves and their guilt will finally catch up with them. If this refers to you then you should act accordingly on that shame and return to a truer path.

Line 4: *One acts in accordance with the command of heaven, and commits no error. One's companions will come and share in one's happiness.*

You must employ authority in order to proceed. Others will come to help you and share in your success.

Line 5: *One brings the distress and obstruction to a close. But continue to be cautious.*

As obstruction disappears and you begin to move forward you should be vigilant for unlooked-for and unexpected setbacks. Exercise caution, curb any tendency to complacency and presumption.

Line 6: *Distress and obstruction are removed. Now there will be joy.*

New progress is beginning, with some help from others. The outlook is promising.

Hexagram 13
T'ung jen—Fellowship

Component Trigrams

Primary: Ch'ien—Heaven (upper), Li—Fire. Nuclear: Ch'ien—Heaven (above), Sun—Wind (below).

Keywords

Heaven, fire, coherence, union, victory in numbers, like-mindedness.

Commentary

You should involve yourself in a union with others to achieve the worthiest of aims. Be guided by your intuition about the goals to aim for. Everyone should strive in their allotted tasks to achieve a mutually beneficial outcome, otherwise the undertaking will fail. You should commit yourself unselfishly and in the spirit of true kinship to this communal endeavour. If you are able to remain true to yourself and do not arrogantly insist you are right in the event of disputes arising, then you will gain great reward. Act with prudence and good judgement, and be respectful to the thoughts and feelings, and success will be yours.

Judgement

We see the union of men out in the open: progress and success. It will be advantageous to cross the great stream. It will be advantageous to maintain the firm correctness of the wise man.

Mutual success depends on your clear-sightedness, a firm commitment to your goal, and true kinship with others.

Interpretation

The hexagram has fire mounting upwards to the heavens which is an image which denotes that things are moving in the right direction. It is the yielding yin line in this hexagram which holds the seemingly stronger yang lines together. The hexagram is the complement of Shih or The Army. The union which is promoted here must be out in the open, clear and honest. It will be achieved and held together because of worthiness of character and not because of status or influence. A union

158

bonded with love and respect will be capable of withstanding the greatest of afflictions, but it will still require to exercise a due caution and circumspection.

Image

Heaven and fire. The wise man distinguishes things according to their kinds and classes.

Nothing can function without good order. If there is anything which needs putting into some kind of order then now is the time to do it. This could include looking at relationships.

Line readings

Line 1: *The union of men comes through an open gate. There will be no regret.*

Be open and honest with those you have bonded together with to achieve a common goal.

Line 2: *One joins in with one's kindred. There will be occasion for regret.*

You limit your potential by restricting yourself to a small circle of friends. Open up to a wider circle of companionship.

Line 3: *One stands on top of a high mound, and hides one's arms in the thick grass. But for three years one makes no demonstration.*

You are not yet fully and unselfishly committed to the aims and individuals of the group of which you are a member. This is the case with others as well. There is an awareness of all this which has resulted in mutual suspicion and a lack of honesty. It would be better for you to withdraw a little from the group and take a back seat. It will take much time for you and this group to accept one another.

Line 4: *One is mounted on the city wall; but does not proceed to make the attack that one has contemplated. There will be good fortune.*

Your belief that there was conflict in the group was false. You have misjudged the situation and the others in the group and are feeling suitably bitter towards you. This is a salutary experience as it imparts the lesson that you cannot always be right.

Line 5: *One first wails and cries out, and then laughs. The great army conquers, and men meet together.*

Although you sometimes feel isolated in the group you are a valuable member of what is a strong and coherent group with many common bonds. Don't brood, but simply accept the satisfying responsibilities of being a member and take pride in the part that you play .

Line 6: *One is in the suburbs. There will be no occasion for repentance.*

You should promote the case for a common humanity by seeking to create bonds with those different from you, trying to find common cause with them.

Hexagram 14
Ta Yu—Possessing plenty

Component Trigrams

Primary: Li—Fire (upper, Ch'ien—Heaven (lower). Nuclear: Tui—Marsh (above), Ch'ien—Heaven (below).

Keywords

Fire, heaven, abundance, prosperity, rectitude, supreme good fortune.

Commentary

It is a time of great achievement and prosperity for you when your circumstances will significantly improve. You will attain your goal with a surprising lack of difficulty. Your best qualities are made obvious to all, and your actions are characterized by an obvious integrity and worthiness. You are the fortunate beneficiary of support and help from powerful and influential people. Make sure you don't treat them or their help lightly or abuse it by failing to grasp the opportunities before you.

Judgement

There will be great progress and success.

When the ruler possesses the qualities of firmness, determination and strength, clear-sightedness and a sense of order, and they are combined in effective harmony, then he will be accorded honour.

Interpretation

Fire above the heavens: everything is now clear, evil is overwhelmed and the forces of good prosper and advance. This hexagram indicates, directly and positively, that this is an exceptionally auspicious time for you. All of the trigrams, both primary and nuclear, signify rising. It indicate a period of great prosperity and good fortune. The only thing that could possibly interfere with this is stupid self-pride and selfishness. In the hexagram a benevolent ruler is supported by able and willing helpers. His modesty and unselfishness enables him to see with clarity the need for harmony with others.

Image

Light in the heavens. The wise man represses what is evil and gives distinction to what is good, in sympathy with the excellent heaven-conferred nature.

We should all strive to emulate the wise man who conquers evil and establishes the power of good.

Line readings

Line 1: *There is no approach to what is injurious, and there is no error. Let there be a realization of the difficulty and danger of the position and there will be no error to the end.*

Guard against sacrificing your integrity for the sake of gaining power and possessions. Tendencies to arrogance and pomposity must be eliminated before you are faced with imminent difficulties. If you face the problem knowing your own strengths and weaknesses then the outcome will be favourable.

Line 2: *A large wagon carrying its load. In whatever direction advancement be made, there will be no error.*

You must show flexibility and not become a slave to your possessions. Be prepared to move if necessary and be open to the willing help of others.

Line 3: *A prince presents his offerings to heaven. A small man would be unequal to such a duty.*

To give is better than to receive. Hoarded wealth and possessions will stifle your potential and consequently bring you misfortune. You must willingly share your good fortune with others.

Line 4: *One keeps one's resources under restraint. There will be no error.*

Don't be envious of others and don't show-off to others. Be modest and composed within yourself.

Line 5: *One is sincere with others, who in return are sincere also. Let one display a proper majesty, and there will be good fortune.*

Don't let the sense of your own dignity blind you to others. Don't stand on your own self-importance but reciprocate others' unselfish offers of friendship. Your own displays of generosity and benevolence will be rewarded.

Line 6: *One is accorded help from heaven. There will be good fortune, advantage in every respect.*

A sincere, modest and honourable person has been duly rewarded by heaven for his faith and outstanding qualities. If you meet such a person share in his good fortune and learn from his example. Acting like this person will ultimately be to your own advantage.

Hexagram 15
Ch'ien—Humility

Component Trigrams

Primary: K'un—Earth (upper), Ken—The Mountain (lower). Nuclear: Chen—Thunder (above), K'an—Water (below).

Keywords

Earth, the mountain, compensation, obedience, sincerity, generosity.

Commentary

A favourable situation awaits you if remain modest and worthy. You must cultivate these virtues for their own sake and this will offset any possible faults you develop. Adopting this course will bring you to success. By respecting and honouring others you increase your strength and worthiness for success. To be humble, though, does not mean to be abject; you should be prepared to challenge and speak out against evil in others if you find it. Your prospects for enduring success are good but only if you attain the strength to be consistent and sincere in your humility.

Judgement

There will be progress and success. The wise man being humble will have a good outcome from his undertakings.

Those who brag about themselves and disdain others, those who scorn others and show disrespect towards them, will win no friends and gain no help and support. A good person, who is humble, honest and sincere in dealings with others, is a worthy person. Model yourself on the good person.

Interpretation

In the hexagram the single yang line—the third line— is strong but it humbles itself. The earth is raised to a superior position. You should cultivate the virtue of modesty in all sincerity, with no ulterior motives. Be humble in your relations and dealings with others. Thus will you overcome any tendencies towards pride and disrespect for others. Balance is required. The means is modesty and humility; their discipline is endless. You must ceaselessly strive to cultivate them if you wish to grow in strength and worthiness of character.

Image

A mountain in the midst of the earth. The wise man diminishes what is excessive in himself, and increases where there is any defect, bringing about an equality, according to the nature of the case, in his treatment of himself and others.

Balance and compromise, disdaining extremes, are the wise positions to attain.

Line readings

Line 1: *A wise man adds humility to humility. Even the great stream may be crossed with this, and there will be good fortune.*

If you are humble and sincere, and in harmony with others, then you can confidently tackle difficult undertakings, assured of success. But if you are in a situation of conflict then you should postpone any new endeavour.

Line 2: *Humility has become recognized. With firm correctness there will be good fortune.*

Only those who are valued for their modesty of character are entrusted with important tasks. Your inner self is shown by your outward conduct and behaviour, which is noted by others and judged accordingly.

Line 3: *The wise man of acknowledged merit will maintain his success to the end, and have good fortune.*

If you are successful you will attract attention. Do not allow this to turn your head and lead you into conceit and immodesty. If you retain modesty you will retain the loving regard and supportive friendship of others.

Line 4: *One whose action would in every way be advantageous, increases the more his humility.*

Don't shirk the work and responsibilities which are given to you, or look for the means of doing nothing with your time and energy. Others depend on you and you are responsible to them.

Line 5: *One, without being rich, is able to employ his neighbours. He may advantageously use the force of arms. All his movements will be advantageous.*

Modesty does not mean being ineffectual. Sometimes you have to be authoritative to get things done. But you must retain clarity and tact. You may be given responsibility for completing a task. It would be modest and wise to ask for guidance from another.

Line 6: *Humility that has made itself recognized. The humble man will with advantage put his troops in motion; but he will only punish his own towns and state.*

If you fall into immodesty then you will come into conflict with others, even those you are in close harmony with. You must look to yourself and correct your faults. Restore your harmonious relations with others by returning to the path of modesty and humility.

Hexagram 16
Yu—Enthusiasm

Component Trigrams

Primary: Chen—Thunder (upper), K'un—Earth (lower). Nuclear: K'an—Water (above), Ken—The Mountain (below).

Keywords

Thunder, earth, groups, harmony, joy, opportunity, caution, preparation.

Commentary

Some goal you have long planned for is now within reach. You must act boldly now if you want to achieve it. Involving those you have authority over in a well-devised and sound plan will increase your probability of success. Make sure, though, that you have left nothing to chance otherwise the consequences could be costly for you. If you take the correct action now with all the enthusiasm you can muster then you cannot fail and will be well rewarded.

Judgement

It is to one's advantage to set up princes as allies, and to put the army in motion.

Your enthusiasm will inspire those around you to combine with you in a joint endeavour which will achieve great success.

Interpretation

In the upper position of the hexagram is thunder and movement, in the lower is earth and obedience. These ideas combined give the concept of enthusiasm. The yang fourth line is regarded as the principal administrator of the ruler. With thunder comes movement and the earth obeys. Enthusiasm for action from within you, arouses and attracts the enthusiasm of others.

Image

Thunder issuing from the earth with a crashing noise. The ancient kings composed their music and did honour to virtue, presenting it especially and most grandly to God, when they associated with Him at the service, their highest ancestor and their father.

Dwelling on the power and mystery of the spiritual brings harmony and happiness.

Line readings

Line 1: *One proclaims one's pleasure and satisfaction. There will be misfortune.*

If you are boastful or overbearing then people will distance themselves from you.

Line 2: *One is as firm as a rock. One sees a thing without waiting till it has come to pass. With firm correctness there will be good fortune.*

Make sure your enthusiasm doesn't carry you or others away; temper it with common sense and your sense of responsibility to yourself and others.

Line 3: *One looks upwards for favours while indulging the feeling of pleasure and satisfaction. If one does change there will be occasion for repentance.*

Act out of your own sense of judgement and your enthusiastic desire for getting something done now. Don't allow yourself to be swayed or led astray by those above you who you find glamorous or exciting. Have faith in yourself and your own judgement.

Line 4: *He who brings harmony and satisfaction. Great is the success which he obtains. Let him not allow suspicions to enter his mind, and thus friends will gather around him.*

Others admire and respect your honesty and sincerity of commitment. Your support of them will be reciprocated.

Line 5: *He has a chronic complaint, but lives on without dying.*

Feeling under pressure, although onerous and disliked, is sometimes the impetus you need to take appropriate and effective action.

Line 6: *One with darkened mind is devoted to the pleasure and satisfaction of the time; but if he change his course even when it may be considered as completed, there will be no error.*

You have been carried away by your enthusiasm and your delight in yourself. It is necessary to come back down to earth and view yourself and your circumstances objectively. This clarity of perception can only be of benefit to you in the future.

Hexagram 17
Sui—Following

Component Trigrams
Primary: Tui—Marsh (upper), Chen—Thunder (lower). Nuclear: Sun—Wind (above), Ken—The Mountain (below).

Keywords
Marsh, thunder, listening, following, cooperation, opportunity, counsel.

Commentary
Let others take the initiative just now. Follow their guidance and advice about the direction you should take and the goal you should aim for and your undertaking will be a success, with great benefits for you. If you rashly go your own way and ignore good advice then you put yourself at risk of failure and subsequent remorse. Those who you assume to be in opposition to you could in fact be willing and ready to help you. If you successfully obtain the help of others then you will be closer to obtaining a great reward.

Judgement
There will be great progress and success. But it will be advantageous to be firm and correct. There will then be no error.

Those who lead must be worthy of the faith and trust that others put in them. If they are not, the result will be failure for all.

Interpretation

In the hexagram's structure the arousing (thunder) humbles itself beneath delight (the lowly marsh). The upper trigram also signifies the eldest son and the lower signifies the youngest daughter. These suggestions combine to yield the ideas of following and follower. Knowing when to follow rather than lead is a wise attribute. Happiness creates harmony. If you are happy and content and have faith and trust in those around you then no harm can come from following them. Also, the one who is being followed must show in his character and actions that he is worthy of the support that he receives.

Image

Thunder hidden in the midst of the marsh. The wise man, when it is getting towards dark, enters his house and rests.

As situations change, so should you; but stay true to yourself. Being flexible and adaptable is more realistic and sensible than stubbornly trying to resist change.

Line readings

Line 1: *One changes the object of one's pursuit; but if one is firm and correct, there will be good fortune. Going beyond one's own gate to find associates, one will achieve merit.*

Open your self and your mind up to the views and attitudes of others. Be prepared to abandon your ideas for new ones suggested by others. Widen the circle of people that you listen and relate to, even at the risk of possible conflict.

Line 2: *One cleaves to the little boy, and lets go the man of age and experience.*

You must be wary of becoming involved with those who are not honest and sincere. They will ensnare you in their weakness. Distance yourself from them.

Line 3: *One cleaves to the man of age and experience, and lets go the little boy. Such following will get what it seeks; but it will be advantageous to adhere to what is firm and correct.*

You must decide for yourself the direction that will also allow you to keep faith with yourself. Then bond yourself with those who share common cause with you.

Line 4: *One is followed and obtains adherence. Though one is firm and correct, there will be misfortune. If one is sincere however in one's course, and makes that evident, into what error will one fall?*

When you are in a position of authority don't be swayed or misled by the insincere praise of those who wish to gain influence with you. Make your decisions from your own honest judgement, remembering your responsibility to yourself and others, and then make them clear to those around you.

Line 5: *The ruler is sincere in fostering all that is excellent. There will be good fortune.*

Be guided by the powers of virtue and truth in the path you chose. Stay true to yourself and you will succeed.

Line 6: *Sincerity firmly held and clung to, and bound fast. With it, the king presents his offerings on the western mountain.*

Ask a more experienced and wiser person than yourself to give you help and advice in your undertaking. It will be of benefit to you both.

Hexagram 18
Ku—Work on disruption

Component Trigrams
Primary: Ken—The Mountain (upper), Sun—Wind (lower). Nuclear: Chen—Thunder (above), Tui—Marsh (below).

Keywords
The mountain, wind, corruption, disorder, illicitness, sickness, past errors, reconciliation.

Commentary
You find yourself in an unusually difficult and confused situation, but one which also presents you with a great opportunity. There is a deep-rooted disorder in your circumstances, perhaps in your self and your relationships. The possibility is there, though, of restoring this situation to one of health and harmony. It will require much of you: in terms of strength of mind and character, your sincerity and good faith, and prolonged effort. You will have to discover the root causes of the problem and remedy them accordingly. When things are restored to wholeness, you will receive great benefits.

Judgement
There will be great progress and success. There will be advantage in crossing the great stream. One should weigh well the events of three days before the turning point, and those to be done three days after it.

You must apply yourself with strength and energy to finding the origins of the present decay and disorder, in order to bring it to and end and restore the situation to well-being.

Interpretation

This hexagram expresses a state of decay. The mountain blocks the wind. Stagnant air is redolent with corruption. But the hexagram also presents a reversal of this. A restoration of wholeness that will be the precursor to eventual success. This will only be achieved by great effort though. There is festering corruption around you which has been bred by dishonesty and deceit. You must counter this by bringing the qualities of clear-sightedness, honesty and sincerity to bear on it.

Image

The wind blows low on the mountain. The wise man addresses himself to help the people and nourish his own virtue.

This image embodies the message of the hexagram's component trigrams. It emphasizes how others can help if given the right lead: making clear what is required and being honest and sincere.

Line readings

Line 1: *A son deals with the troubles caused by his father. If he be an able son, the father will escape the blame of having erred. The position is perilous, but there will be good fortune in the end.*

To get to the bottom of this situation and change it, it will be necessary for you to re-examine the basis on which you act and form relationships, your guiding principles, and reform them if necessary. But be very cautious as this will have lasting and far-reaching consequences.

Line 2: *A son deals with the troubles caused by his mother. He should not carry his firm correctness to the utmost.*

Patience and sensitivity to others, the use of tact and diplomacy: these must be the means to making the changes that are required.

Line 3: *A son deals with the troubles caused by his father. There may be small occasion for repentance, but there will not be any great error.*

You must commit yourself to making the necessary changes with wholehearted effort and energy. This will bring about resentment from others but you must persist, all the same.

Line 4: *A son views indulgently the troubles caused by his father. If he go forward, he will find cause to regret it.*

There is no time to waste, you must act now to transform the corrupt situation and you must keep up your efforts no matter what setbacks you face along the way. Be vigilant over any tendency in yourself to turn away or slacken off.

Line 5: *A son deals with the troubles caused by his father. He obtains the praise of using the fit instrument for his work.*

Others will applaud your honesty and courage in acknowledging your responsibility for things being as bad as they are and your determined efforts to change yourself and transform the situation. They may be inspired to join you and work with you.

Line 6: *One does not serve either king or prince, but in a lofty spirit prefers to attend to one's own affairs.*

Your responsibility is to the future, to the effort and selfless concern needed to create a fresh, new beginning. Don't concern yourself with what is past and troublesome. Dwell instead on happy things with their invigorating and restorative value. In this spirit focus on yourself and your motivating principles. Work toward change for yourself and others.

Hexagram 19
Lin—Advance

Component Trigrams

Primary: K'un—Earth (upper), Tui—Marsh (lower). Nuclear: K'un— Earth (above), Chen—Thunder (below).

Keywords

Earth, marsh, ascent, increasing power, moral strength, generosity, benevolence.

Commentary

You are in a very auspicious situation. What you are about to undertake will be highly effective and successful. There will be no need for force. What will be required is proper conduct and a sense of caution. You are in an impressively favourable situation but remember that it won't last. Beware of letting your good fortune go to your head. Keep in mind that things change; maintain honesty and sincerity. Share your good fortune with others. While your star remains in the ascendancy, and you continue to act properly, you can enjoy your success.

Judgement

There will be great progress and success, while it will be advantageous to be firmly correct. In the eighth month there will be evil.

Spring brings new growth and gladness. But as the seasons change, so do all situations. Therefore, all you should do now is continue to ensure the worth of your principles and conduct.

Interpretation

The hexagram has two strong yang lines advancing on four yielding yin lines, which gives an image of the advent of expanding power and authority. This is a hexagram of growth and strength. You are required to remain steadfast to true aims and motives in the midst of favourable, but ephemeral, time. The undertaking you are about to begin will have great power and impact and will be a success. Don't be impetuous and forceful. All you need do is proceed with due care, and with regard for good conduct and respect toward others, and success is inevitable.

Image

The waters of a marsh and the earth above it. The wise man has his purposes of instruction that are inexhaustible, and nourishes and supports the people without limit.

Change is infinite and eternal. So is learning and knowledge. The wise man knows this and will seek to teach others.

Line readings

Line 1: *One advances in company. Through firm correctness there will be good fortune.*

You are being effortlessly carried forward by favourable circumstances. Don't lose your head.

Line 2: *One advances in company. There will be good fortune; advancing will be in every way advantageous.*

You cannot neglect your spiritual nature while you are enjoying worldly success, as nothing on earth endures.

Line 3: *One is well-pleased to advance, but one's action will be in no way advantageous. If one becomes anxious about it however, there will be no error.*

Don't get arrogant or complacent. Think of others and be generous to them. Correct any faults in yourself and your conduct.

Line 4: *One advances in the highest mode. There will be no error.*

New people may now come into your life; you should welcome them and be open and supportive.

Line 5: *The advance of wisdom, such as befits the great ruler. There will be good fortune.*

Choose carefully who will help you and the tasks that you give them. Trust them to fulfil their allotted tasks successfully, as they trust you to fulfil yours.

Line 6: *The advance of honesty and generosity. There will be good fortune and no error.*

From the solitary, spiritual region of your joy and success, it is now time to return to the world and share with others what you have learned.

Hexagram 20
Kuan—Contemplating

Component Trigrams

Primary: Sun—Wind (upper), K'un—Earth (lower). Nuclear: Ken—
The Mountain (above), K'un—Earth (below).

Keywords

Wind, earth, manifestation, showing, watching, perception, observance.

Commentary

Look, listen and learn: these are the keywords. It would be better, more
prudent, to stay in your present situation and scrutinize it carefully than
attempt to move forward into new and unknown territory. There may
soon be a change for the worse in your circumstances. Study closely the
direction and aims, the motives and conduct of yourself and those you
are closely associated with. Be prepared to accept just criticism and
advice. Only when you have thoroughly assessed, in a clear and objective light, your present situation will you then be able to consider moving forward. Through this process of review you may discover an important matter, with close relevance to you and your situation. Deal
with it carefully and thoughtfully and you will then be better equipped
to continue on your course.

Judgement

*The worshipper has washed his hands but has not yet presented his offerings. His
sincerity and dignity commands a reverent regard.*

Everything is able to be seen: past, present and future.

Interpretation

In the hexagram the four weak yin lines look up reverently to the two
strong yang lines. This symbolizes the strength and authority of the
wise man manifesting itself to others he can show and teach. A great
wind (the upper trigram) blows across the earth (the lower trigram). It
would be better to survey the landscape before venturing forward into
such a wind. This refers to the idea of contemplating the present situation. Cultivate clear-sightedness and the proper way. Be an example
that others can recognize and follow.

Image

The wind moves across the earth. The ancient kings examined the different regions of the kingdom, to see the ways of the people, and set
forth their instructions.

The ruler comes among the people to observe and teach. His gratified people show their respect and loyalty.

Line readings

Line 1: *A thoughtless boy; not blameable in men of inferior rank, but matter for regret in wise man.*

Don't just look at the superficial, the fanciful and sensational. To grow in wisdom you must grow in your understanding of others. Look more deeply at others in order to understand their action's and their motives.

Line 2: *One peeps out from a door. It would be advantageous if it were merely the firm correctness of a female.*

Only if you take a wider view of things will you be able to see them clearly and put them into a proper perspective.

Line 3: *One looks at the course of one's life, to advance or recede accordingly.*

You must try to see yourself as other people see you. Examine yourself thoroughly before you decide on the direction which you should take.

Line 4: *One contemplating the glory of the kingdom. It will be advantageous for him, being such as he is, to seek to be guest of the king.*

Having learned from the past you should seek positions of responsibility and authority.

Line 5: *One contemplates one's own life-course. A wise man will thus fall into no error.*

To be worthy of others' respect you should conscientiously survey all aspects of yourself. But remember that the point of this introspection is to make self-judgements and then act on those judgements.

Line 6: *One contemplates one's character to see if it be indeed that of a wise man. One will not fall into error.*

At this stage you have completed you period of inner contemplation. Although you are moving on, purged of your past faults and weakness, don't forget the past: otherwise you will repeat the mistakes of the past in the future.

Hexagram 21
Shih Ho—Biting through

Component Trigrams

Primary: Li—Fire (upper), Chen—Thunder (lower). Nuclear: K'an—Water (above), Ken—The Mountain (below).

Keywords

Thunder, lightning, clarity, shining brilliance, justice, attachment, clinging, union.

Commentary

You must not flinch from your purpose despite the obstacles you face. Rely on the rightness of your cause and maintain your commitment and you will win through. Remain in harmony with those above and below you. Working in tandem with others to achieve your goal will allow you to robustly defend your worthy course. Don't forsake your basic principles and your forceful action will be successful. Prepare, though, to cope with conflict on the way.

Judgement

There will be successful progress. It will be advantageous to use legal restraints.

You have to act now to remove obstacles from your path, but you must not do this by unworthy conduct.

Interpretation

The name of the hexagram derives from its shape: the top and bottom yang lines are the lips, the yin lines are teeth and the fourth yang line is something being bitten through. High and low must unite: what separates the two jaws must be bitten through. The trigram images of thunder and fire symbolize the rule of law. You may need to employ some kind of force to reach your goal. The hexagram is to do with biting past obstacles, eliminating problems and disunion, curbing spiteful threats and sorting out legal difficulties.

Image

Thunder and lightning. The ancient kings framed their penalties with intelligence, and promulgated their laws.

A just, open and clear set of rules, with clearly identified penalties for transgressions, is necessary to deal with those who don't follow the right conduct.

Line readings

Line 1: *One with his feet in the stocks and deprived of his toes. There will be no error.*

First offences should be treated less severely than further transgressions. Having erred, though, there is still scope for remorse and atonement. Return to the right path and there will be no lasting harm.

Line 2: *Biting through the soft flesh, and going on to bite off the nose. There will be no error.*

In response to provocation you are meting out penalties which are too severe. Perhaps you are justified.

Line 3: *One gnaws dried flesh, and meets with what is disagreeable. There will be occasion for some small regret, but no great error.*

Don't concern yourself with issues that are dead and buried.

Line 4: *One gnaws the flesh dried on the bone, and gets pledges of money and arrows. It will be advantageous to him to realize the difficulty of the his task and be firm, in which case there will be good fortune.*

Your obstacles and enemies are strong; you must be stronger and harder. Be firm and unwavering and you will win through.

Line 5: *One gnaws at dried flesh, and finds the yellow gold. Let him be firm and correct, realizing the peril of his position. There will be no error.*

What you have to do may be clear and simple but don't relax your attitude of rigorous purpose. Be steadfast and don't retreat before vigorous opposition.

Line 6: *One is wearing the wooden yoke and is deprived of his ears. There will be misfortune.*

The transgressor, and that may be yourself, is arrogant, stubborn and shameless. These faults and weaknesses must be tackled and remedied.

Hexagram 22
Pi—Adornment

Component Trigrams
Primary: Ken—The Mountain (upper), Li—Fire (lower). Nuclear: Chen—Thunder (above), K'an—Water (lower).

Keywords
Mountain, fire, grace, beauty, sunsets, coherence, the arts.

Commentary
Your present situation is settled but as you go forward you will encounter surprises. It is wiser to not to be too ambitious and to restrict yourself to what you can cope with. Put your efforts and energy into maintaining proper conduct and a harmonious balance between yourself and your environment, and between yourself and others.

Judgement
There should be free course. There will be little advance, however, if it be allowed to advance and take the lead.

Concern with adornment must not become excessive or obsessive;

there are other matters to attend to. The quality of just and elegant rules depends on the merit of those who administer them.

Interpretation

The hexagram combines clarity (lower trigram) with the unmoving (upper). At night the fire illuminates the mountain. This introduces the symbol of adornment and beauty. The hexagram is about elegance and brightness. Its concern is with artistic and theoretical activities rather than prosaic, everyday ones. It intimates that one should simply occupy oneself with artistic adornment while remaining true and humble. But if required one should relinquish this in the face of trouble. Grace and elegance, nevertheless, are worthy of attainment. This hexagram is about the value of beauty and harmony and those who create and admire these qualities. It also refers to the impression we make on others and how this accords with our view of ourselves.

Image

Fire illuminates the mountain. The wise man throws a brilliancy around his various processes of government, but does not dare in a similar way to decide cases of criminal litigation.

Meditation brings peace but it does not remove the necessity for choice and action.

Line readings

Line 1: *One adorns the way of his feet. One can discard a carriage and walk on foot.*

Don't always take the easy option. People will respect you for taking on what is difficult.

Line 2: *One adorns one's beard.*

Trying simply to please other people has an adverse effect on your character.

Line 3: *One is adorned and bedewed with rich favours. But maintain firm correctness, and there will be good fortune.*

Don't let yourself be corrupted by love of the good things in life.

Line 4: *One is adorned, but only in white. As if mounted on a white horse, and furnished with wings, he seeks union, while another pursues, not as a robber, but intent on a matrimonial alliance.*

Don't neglect your true path and friends in order to impress the wider world.

Line 5: *One is adorned by the occupants of the heights and gardens. He bears his roll of silk, small and slight. He may appear stingy; but there will be good fortune in the end.*

Bonding with a soul mate after the glitter of the superficial world will at first make you feel humble and unworthy. But this sincere friendship will be valuable.

Line 6: *One's only ornament is white. There will be no error.*

Some happy people have simple grace from within and have no need of the external trappings of beauty.

Hexagram 23
Po—Splitting apart

Component Trigrams
Primary: Ken—The Mountain (upper), K'un—Earth (lower). Nuclear: K'un—Earth (above), K'un—Earth (below).

Keywords
Mountain, earth, division, disintegration, challenge, contemplation, endurance.

Commentary
This inauspicious situation should be viewed as a salutary reminder of the fickleness of fortune and of the need to be adaptable to changing circumstances. You are threatened by subversive forces but if you maintain strength of character and use your faculties of wise discernment and judgement, then you will be able to decide on the best courses of action. You must unflinchingly commit yourself to a preparatory period of self-examination. Although you may suffer a setback you will come back from it stronger for the experience.

Judgement
It will not be advantageous to make a movement in any direction whatever.

It is better to stay in the background when the worst 'are full of a passionate conviction' and making all the running.

Interpretation
The solid top yang line seems about to give way to the division below it. The mountain sits uneasily on the unreliable earth. The hexagram deals with how one survives in threatening and destructive circumstances. It reminds of the fickleness of fate and the necessity of having the correct resources to deal with adversity. The situation is unbalanced and lacks harmony. You should refrain from action until the position improves.

Image
The mountain adheres to the earth. Superiors seek to strengthen those

below them, to secure the peace and the stability of their own position.

Authority and respect, love and loyalty can only be attained and survive by generosity towards others.

Line readings

Line 1: *One overturns the couch by injuring its legs. The injury will go on to the destruction of all firm correctness, and there will be misfortune.*

Others are trying to subvert your position but if you act now you will fail. Wait.

Line 2: *One overthrows the couch by injuring its frame. The injury will go on to the destruction of all firm correctness, and there will be misfortune.*

You feel isolated and helpless and are responding prematurely to the subverting challenge. Be careful, as this will result in failure.

Line 3: *One is among the overthrowers; but there will be no error.*

Because of your isolation you decide to make an accommodation with those who threaten you and call a truce. This is forgivable.

Line 4: *One has overthrown the couch, and is going to injure he who lies on it. There will be misfortune.*

A line of abject failure and total defeat. It is your fate and you must endure it.

Line 5: *One leads on the others like a string of fishes, and obtains for them the favour that lights on the inmates of the palace. There will be advantage in every way.*

You recover and take action, which improves your situation financially and in other ways. You may be helped by someone.

Line 6: *A great fruit has not been eaten. The wise man finds the people again as a chariot carrying him. The small men by their course overthrow their own dwellings.*

You have suffered and endured but things are not the same nor as good as they were before. All you can do is accept it and start anew from where you are. It is pointless and useless to dwell on the past and what has been lost. Be optimistic and look to the future. Others will come to your aid at this time of need.

Hexagram 24
Fu—Returning

Component Trigrams

Primary: K'un—Earth (upper), Chen—Thunder (lower). Nuclear: K'un—Earth (above), K'un—Earth (below).

Keywords

Thunder, earth, turning point, approaching spring, ascent, gradual, improvement, reinforcement.

Commentary

This is a time of growing good fortune and especially favourable for any new undertaking. Be cautious though, don't get too far ahead of the awakening forces that will support you. Conserve your energies and concentrate on keeping to your true path and character. Your time is arriving and you will undoubtedly benefit.

Judgement

There will be free course and progress. One finds no-one to distress one in one's exits and entrances; friends come to one and no error is committed. One will return and repeat one's proper course; in seven days comes return. There will be advantage in whatever direction movement is made.

As you wait for the full effects of this time of beneficial change to emerge, you should think carefully and plan for the future.

Interpretation

The trigram positions show thunder within the earth, representing the first tremors of great force. The hexagram describes the unending, cyclic movements of decay and renewal. This is an auspicious hexagram, marking the beginning of a period of recovery after reaching the nadir of decline. As the seasons change and winter begins the long preparation for spring, so your fortunes will change for the better.

Image

Thunder silent in the midst of the earth. The ancient kings on the day of the winter solstice, shut the gates of the passes from one state to another, so that the travelling merchants could not then pursue their journeys, nor the princes go on with the inspection of their states.

Winter was a time of rest and recuperation, a withdrawing inwards to aid the renewal of energy.

Line readings

Line 1: *One returns from an error of no great extent, which will not proceed to anything requiring repentance. There will be great good fortune.*

Don't stray off your own true path or you may end up doing something you will later regret.

Line 2: *An admired return. There will be good fortune.*

Encouraged by being surrounded by influential people, you sense a new beginning. You are considering an offer of help you have received.

Line 3: *One has made repeated returns. The position is perilous, but there will be no error.*

Remember: 'The only thing we have to fear, is fear itself.' Don't be afraid to grasp your new opportunities. Change is inevitable and you should eagerly welcome it when it brings you good fortune. Your stop-go attitude is wasteful and self-defeating. You must go forward optimistically without stopping or turning back.

Line 4: *One moves in the centre among others, and yet returns alone to one's proper path.*

You have to go your own way even at the risk of offending others. Don't feel bad about that. A respected person will give you help.

Line 5: *One makes a noble return. There will be no ground for repentance.*

You have to accept and go along with change and others around you will eventually realize this. Your exemplary attitude and behaviour may encourage them to follow you.

Line 6: *One is all astray on the subject of returning. There will be misfortune. There will be calamities and errors. If with his views he puts the troops in motion, the end will be a great defeat, whose issues will extend to the ruler of the state. Even in ten years he will not be able to repair the disaster.*

Afraid of forsaking the old and familiar you have let the opportunity of change for the better pass you by. This is a profound error which may have lasting detrimental consequences for you. This was your decisive moment; you may never have another. You have rejected a rare opportunity and all you can do now is wait for a lesser opportunity to come round.

Hexagram 25
Wu Wang—Correctness

Component Trigrams

Primary: Ch'ien—Heaven (upper), Chen—Thunder (lower). Nuclear: Sun—Wind (above), Ken—The Mountain (below).

Keywords

Heaven, thunder, beginnings, passivity, naturalness, innocence, guilelessness, sincerity.

Commentary

If you act rashly or selfishly in your present situation you will be afflicted with unusually severe ill-luck. Be modest, sincere and honest with others. Don't try to force your own way just now. Be content to go along with things as they unfold naturally and you will be fine. Take great care not to act impetuously or in a domineering way for purely selfish ends. If your motives and acts are impure you will face great misfortune.

Judgement

There will be great progress and success. It will be advantageous to be firm and correct. If one is not correct, one will fall into errors, and it will not be advantageous to move in any direction.

By following the way of heaven in all innocence one is as one should be. Failure awaits lack of innocence.

Interpretation

Beneath heaven, thunder sounds; elemental energy which is innocent. Those who act out of innocent selflessness: good fortune. For those who conspire for their own selfish gain: evil fortune. The hexagram signifies being in tune with one's true nature and the way of heaven. This is the state of harmony and innocence.

Image

The thunder rolls under heaven, and to everything there is given its nature, free from all insincerity. The ancient kings made their regulations in complete accordance with the seasons, thereby nourishing all things.

Thunder brings rain which nourishes the germination and growth of plants. It is wise to act in harmony with natural forces.

Line readings

Line 1: *One is free from all insincerity. One's advance will be accompanied with good fortune.*

Trust your intuition and you will have good fortune.

Line 2: *One reaps without having ploughed, and gathers the produce of his third year's fields without having cultivated them the first year for that end. To such a one there will be advantage in whatever direction he may move.*

Don't try to achieve everything by one action now; you will fail. But if your action is for short-term aims then it is fine.

Line 3: *Calamity happens to one who is free from insincerity, as in the case of an ox that has been tied up. A passerby finds it and carries it off, while the people in the neighbourhood have the calamity of being accused and apprehended.*

Be stoic and fatalistic about the ill-fortune that surrounds you. Your loss is another's gain.

Line 4: *If one remains firm and correct, there will be no error.*

Keep to the path you know is yours and don't be influenced by others.

Line 5: *One is free from insincerity, and yet has fallen ill. Not using medicine, one will have occasion for joy in one's recovery.*

The ill-fortune that dogs you will end and, in time, you will recover. Being anxious will only make your position worse.

Line 6: *One is free from insincerity, yet sure to fall into error, if one take action. One's action will not be advantageous in any way.*

Refrain from all action, even that prompted by intuition, and wait patiently.

Hexagram 26
Tach'u—Taming force

Component Trigrams
Primary: Ken—The Mountain (upper), Ch'ien—Heaven (lower). Nuclear: Chen—Thunder (above), Tui—Marsh (below).

Keywords
The mountain, heaven, stillness, creativity, restraint, accumulation, virtue.

Commentary
Cultivate your talents and strive to be of good character and conduct. You will be able to tackle even formidably difficult undertakings and be sure of help from influential others and success. You show your worthiness by accumulating these heavenly creative energies within. To use them for some common good would be an even worthier act, and you should consider this. Use what you glean from the experience and example of others and you will overcome immediate obstacles and find lasting success.

Judgement
It will be advantageous to be firm and correct. If one does not seek to enjoy one's revenues in one's own family, without taking service at court, there will be good fortune. It will be advantageous to cross the great stream.

The wise man partakes of periods of stillness each day to strengthen his character. Any activity to do with the public good is favourable.

Interpretation
Heaven resides within the mountain; great potential is stored up. The hexagram conveys the idea of containment and restraint, and this causing great forces to build up. There is great potential within you which you should use wisely. This hexagram signifies the balance of inner strength with outward calmness. It is about containment and restraint, steadfastness and strength of purpose.

Image
Heaven within the mountain. The wise man stores largely in his memory

the words and deeds of former men, to subserve the accumulation of his virtue.

Learning from past errors and past successes ensure future success.

Line readings

Line 1: *One is in a position of peril. It will be advantageous to stop advancing.*

Forging forward at this time will only produce error and failure. Wait patiently.

Line 2: *A carriage has its braking strap removed from underneath.*

If you find yourself in a weak position the pragmatic and sensible thing is to do nothing and wait.

Line 3: *One urges his way with good horses. It will be advantageous for him to realize the difficulty of his course, and to be firm and correct, exercising himself daily in his charioteering and methods of defence; then there will be advantage in whatever direction he may advance.*

Well-prepared for the problems you will face ahead, you can go forward towards your goal with confidence.

Line 4: *A young bull has a piece of wood over his horns. There will be great good fortune.*

Immediate action will neutralize any potential harm.

Line 5: *The tusk of a gelded hog. There will be good fortune.*

Action now to affect the nature of your potential enemies will diminish the threat they pose to you.

Line 6: *One is in command of the firmament of heaven. There will be progress.*

Everything has been favourable and you have achieved your goals.

Hexagram 27
I—Nourishment

Component Trigrams
Primary: Ken—The Mountain (upper), Chen—Thunder (lower). Nuclear: K'un—Earth (above), K'un—Earth (lower).

Keywords
The mountain, thunder, temperance, self-discipline, discretion, opportunity.

Commentary
This is an auspicious time. You have to chose what is to be nourished —in yourself or in another—after proper and worthy deliberation. The path to this choice being true you will achieve particular success. This

is a remarkable opportunity and if you chose that aspect of your own nature or another's that most deserves this enrichment then you will benefit from good fortune. However, if you merely satisfy the cruder appetites you will come to regret it.

Judgement

With firm correctness there will be good fortune. We must look at what we are seeking to nourish, and by the exercise of out thoughts seek for the proper sustenance.

Be sensible and careful about your material and other nourishment. Look after yourself and others who require it.

Interpretation

Thunder at the base of the mountain; movement below stillness: the first stirrings of life activity. Taken together with the visual symbolism of a mouth in the hexagram, this suggest the idea of nourishment: physical, mental and spiritual. Be careful what you consume in terms of food and drink as it may not be nourishing, just as you may be wrong about your own nature. Think of your spiritual needs.

Image

Thunder within the mountain. The wise man enjoins watchfulness over our words, and the temperate regulation of our eating and drinking.

Being temperate and thoughtful in what you say and in the nourishment you take, and your consideration for yourself and others, will bring you to wisdom.

Line readings

Line 1: *One leaves his efficacious tortoise, and looks at the other till his jaw hangs down.*

You render yourself unworthy and obnoxious with envy and greed

Line 2: *One looks downward for nourishment, which is contrary to what is proper; or seeking it from the height above, advance towards which will lead to misfortune.*

You must look first of all to yourself for nourishment and succour. To lazily seek others to provide it is bad.

Line 3: *One acts contrary to the method of nourishing. However firm he may be, there will be misfortune. For ten years let him not take any action, for it will not be in any way advantageous.*

You are lost in the worthless pursuit of sensational pleasure.

Line 4: *One looks downwards for the power to nourish. There will be good fortune. Looking with a tiger's downward unwavering glare, and with his desire that impels him to spring after spring, one will fall into no error.*

You know that you need and must enlist the support of others to enable you achieve your aims. Seize any opportunity that comes your way.

Line 5: *One acts contrary to what is regular and proper; but if one abides in firmness, there will be good fortune. One should not, however, try to cross the great stream.*

Don't take on too much. Know your limitations and seek the right help.

Line 6: *He who brings the nourishing. His position is perilous, but there will be good fortune. It will be advantageous to cross the great stream.*

You are fortunate. Your nourishing spiritual nature can be used for the good of others What you undertake for the benefit of others will be successful.

Hexagram 28
Ta Kuo—Exceeding greatness

Component Trigrams
Primary: Tui—Marsh (upper), Sun—Wind (lower). Nuclear: Ch'ien—Heaven (above), Ch'ien—Heaven (below).

Keywords
Marsh, tree, heaviness, flexibility, caution, great developments, renunciation, solitude, continuation.

Commentary
You are in a particularly critical situation but if you have the right and proper attitude you can expect things to favour your winning through. Act boldly and confidently and this unusually threatening situation may be completely defused. Assessing how you should go about this undertaking is an important prior step, taking your own nature and all other circumstances into consideration. Then take the action you consider the most appropriate and you will be successful. The needs of the situation should decide your actions, not your inflexible inclinations.

Judgement
The beam is weak. There will be advantage in moving in any direction whatever; there will be success.

It is necessary to find some means to redress the imbalance, as there is not enough strength.

Interpretation
The Sun trigram here represents a solitary tree with the water risen above it, symbolizing solitude and renunciation. This is the recommended course during times of severe trouble and conflict. The hexagram has two weak outer lines and four strong inner lines, and resem-

bles a roof with a strong centre but weak edges. The centre is in danger of falling. The hexagram signifies caution and the need for change.

Image

Trees hidden beneath the waters of the marsh. The wise man stands alone, has no fear, and keeps retired from the world without regret.

Isolation may be necessary to survive this testing time.

Line readings

Line 1: *One spreads rush-mats under things set on the ground. There will be no error.*

Be cautious and take precautions, and ignore others' comments. Provide a firm basis for any new venture.

Line 2: *A decayed willow produces shoots, an old husband with a young wife. There will be advantage in every way.*

The outlook is providential for a new undertaking, new love, new spirituality.

Line 3: *A beam is weak. There will be misfortune.*

You have ignored warning-signs and taken no precautions. It would be too dangerous to do anything for the time being.

Line 4: *A beam curves upwards. There will be good fortune. If one looks for other help there will be cause for regret.*

Welcome help has come from another but don't exploit this person for your own ends otherwise you will regret it.

Line 5: *A decayed willow produces flowers, an old wife with a young husband. There will be occasion neither for blame nor for praise.*

Don't arrogantly forsake old friendships when you are successful. They are still part of your destiny, you have not changed as much as you think.

Line 6: *One wades with extraordinary boldness through a stream, till the water hides the crown of his head. There will be misfortune, but no ground for blame.*

Through lack of caution and foresight, your own enthusiasm and commitment has brought you into hard times. But you can learn from what is only a temporary setback.

Hexagram 29
K'an—The deep

Component Trigrams

Primary: K'an—Water (upper), K'an—Water (lower). Nuclear: Ken—The Mountain (above), Chen—Thunder (below).

Keywords
Water, danger, decline, lack of bearings, caution.

Commentary
You are in a position of danger. The best way to overcome this is to move boldly and remain true to yourself. You must assess your situation carefully and though the choices open to you at the moment are unappealing, with patience and clearsightedness you should arrive at a better situation. You may be faced with great challenges and fearful situations, but if you maintain strength of heart and remain true you will survive, having learned valuable things.

Judgement
When one is sincere, the mind is penetrating. Actions will be of high value. Remain steadfast in the face of danger, and true to yourself. Keep going forward, as any hesitation could be disastrous.

Interpretation
This hexagram concerns danger. The trigrams are water upon water, and suggest not only dangerous waters but also perilous pits, hazardous caves and other similar situations. The hexagram is about how to meet danger, what effects it can have on you, and how to escape and survive it.

Image
Water flowing continuously on. The wise man maintains constantly the virtue of his heart and the integrity of his conduct, and practices the business of instruction.

If you remain virtuous then you will not be swamped by danger.

Line readings
Line 1: *One is in the double defile, and yet enters a cavern within it. There will be misfortune.*

Do not make the mistake of becoming casual about danger if it is always around you. Remain vigilant.

Line 2: *One is in all the peril of the defile. One will, however, get a little of the deliverance that one seeks.*

Focus on achieving limited aims rather than going all out.

Line 3: *One is confronted by a defile, whether one comes or goes. All is peril and unrest. One's endeavours will lead into the cavern of the pit. There should be no action in such a case.*

When you seem to be in a 'no-win' situation it is time to halt temporarily to think your way out. Continuing to act is foolish.

Line 4: *One is at a feast with a simple bottle of spirits and a basket of rice, while the cups and bowls are only of earthenware. One introduces important lessons as the ruler's intelligence admits. There will in the end be no error.*

You must cut you losses and settle for less and accept help from areas you would have previously scorned. Be grateful to those who help and accept the help in the sincere and honest spirit in which it is given.

Line 5: *The defile is almost full of water; but order will soon be brought about. There will be no error.*

There is still danger around so don't embark on anything new. Keep everything simple.

Line 6: *One is bound with cords and placed in the thicket of thorns. But in three years he does not learn the course for him to pursue. There will be misfortune.*

Everything has come down upon your head at once. You have brought this upon yourself. You have to carefully trace the relation between your motives and this calamitous outcome. Examine your character and remedy whatever is at fault.

Hexagram 30
Li—Fire

Component Trigrams
Primary: Li—Fire (upper), Li—Fire (lower). Nuclear: Tui—Marsh (above), Sun—Wind (below).

Keywords
Beauty, sunlight, shining brilliance, intelligence, clinging.

Commentary
You have an opportunity to be creative. Stay on a true path, be humble and listen to advice from experienced others. Give careful though to the advice before accepting or rejecting it. Your collaboration with others will be successful if you follow these precepts. Think of the long term and don't act impulsively for any perceived short-term advantage or out of provocation. By keeping faith with what is true and remaining honest, as you proceed towards your goal, you are guaranteed to be successful. If you go against your intuition or your conscience, you will fail.

Judgement
It will be advantageous to be firm and correct. There will be free course and success. Let one also nourish a docility like that of a cow, and there will be good fortune.

Be calm and humble and remain committed to what you believe to be right and true.

Interpretation

Both primary trigrams represent fire and light, the sun represents the source of all light, and its illuminating radiance. It is the symbol for intelligence.

Image

Brightness everywhere. The wise man cultivates more and more his brilliant virtue, and diffuses its brightness over the four quarters of the land.

Don't hoard your wisdom, but use it for the benefit of all.

Line readings

Line 1: *One is ready to move with confused steps. But if one treads reverently at the same time, there will be no mistake.*

Keep calmly and consistently to the path of truth and rightness, and resist any attempts to make you deviate from this.

Line 2: *One is in one's place in yellow. There will be great good fortune.*

Everything is favourable and going well.

Line 3: *One is in a position like that of the declining sun. Instead of playing on his instrument of earthenware, and singing to it, he utters the groans of an old man of eighty. There will be misfortune.*

'What will be, will be': don't worry or grieve over the future or your own mortality.

Line 4: *How abrupt it is, as with fire, with death, to be rejected by all!*

Don't waste your energies on short-lived ventures.

Line 5: *One flows with torrents of tears, and groans in sorrow. There will be good fortune.*

Don't succumb to downheartedness. Keep looking clearly towards your goal and remain humble and persevering. Be heartened by the concern of others and spare some of your thoughts and concern for them.

Line 6: *The king employs one in his punitive expeditions. Achieving admirable merit, one breaks only the chiefs of the rebels. Where his prisoners were not their associates, he does not punish. There will be no error.*

Although you still have faults despite all your laudable attempts to remove all your faults, it is praiseworthy that you own to them, though they are not great. Retain your strength and generosity, particularly to those you are competing with.

Hexagram 31
Hsein—Courtship

Component Trigrams
Primary: Tui—Marsh (upper), Ken—The Mountain (lower). Nuclear: Ch'ien—Heaven (above), Sun—The Wind (lower).

Keywords
Lake, mountain, reciprocity, objectivity, emptiness, correct mutual assistance.

Commentary
In the situation in which you find yourself, being sensitive and bringing to bear a proper influence which will result in a worthy end will successfully resolve the situation. Your influence should not be purposive or self-seeking, but selfless, passive and benign. Nevertheless, this position will lead to reward and mutual benefit for you and others. You must cultivate keeping an open mind and a responsiveness which will immediately instigate the right and appropriate action for any circumstance.

Judgement
There will be free course and success. It will be advantageous to be firm and correct. In marrying a young lady, there will be good fortune.

Responsiveness and influence are reciprocated by another. Be sensitive to the needs of the other and remain inwardly calm even when you are outwardly excited and happy.

Interpretation
On a mountain there is a lake; it conforms to the mountain and the mountain obtains rain from the clouds for the lake. The hexagram is about reciprocal relationships and self-less mutual influence. The primary trigrams also signify young women and men in courtship, with their selfless concern for each other and their harmonious relations.

Image
A lake on top of a mountain. The wise man keeps his mind free from preoccupation, and open to receive the influences of others.

The wise man knows that he still has everything to learn, and is always open to new ideas and fresh perspectives. You should remember that you still have much to learn from others and should humbly strive to emulate the example of the wise man.

Line readings

Line 1: *One moves only one's great toes.*

You need to consider the changes you must make to yourself in order to proceed in your direction, from minor changes to more radical. For the time being others will be unaware of your intention to change.

Line 2: *One moves the calves of one's legs. There will be misfortune. If one abides quiet in one's place, there will be good fortune.*

This is not the time for making changes or for action. You must wait otherwise you will fail.

Line 3: *One moves one's thighs, and keeps close hold of those whom one follows. Going forward in this way will cause regret.*

Seeking to use your influence for selfish ends is wrong. You must reeducate your thinking, and clarify your thoughts.

Line 4: *Firm correctness will lead to good fortune, and prevent all occasion for repentance. If one be unsettled in one's movements, only one's friends will follow one's purpose.*

Keep a clear mind and course and follow the promptings of your intuition and your conscience. Don't try to manipulate situations and others for your own advantage.

Line 5: *One moves the flesh along the spine above the heart. There will be no occasion for repentance.*

You must be more flexible and less rigid in your approach and ideas. You will gain approval and respect from others.

Line 6: *One moves one's jaws and tongue.*

'All talk and no action': you must avoid gaining this unenviable reputation. It is better to let your correct and worthy actions speak for you.

Hexagram 32
Heng—Persistence

Component Trigrams

Primary: Chen—Thunder (upper), Sun—Wind (lower). Nuclear: Tui—Marsh (above), Ch'ien—Heaven (below).

Keywords

Thunder, wind, perseverance, persistence, commitment, endurance, constancy.

Commentary

You should persevere on your chosen path, confident in its rightness. Maintain your responsibilities and everything will be fine. You must be sure what your function is and act accordingly, whether it is to be a faithful follower or a conscientious leader. At the end of your chosen path is success and a new beginning.

Judgement

There will be successful progress and no error. Advantage will come from being firm and correct. Movement in any direction whatever will advantageous.

Change is a fact in our lives and we must be responsive to it and change accordingly. But there should always remain at the heart of all our changes an unchanging core of meaning.

Interpretation

The images of thunder and wind convey the ideas of moving, involving and enduring. The primary trigrams signify eldest son and eldest daughter, and symbolize a long and harmonious marriage. Using the wisdom gained from the lessons of the past to live more successfully in the present is the message of the hexagram.

Image

Thunder and wind. The wise man stands firm, and does not change his method of operation.

Be flexible in the face of change but be steadfast in your commitment to your direction.

Line readings

Line 1: *One is deeply desirous of long continuance. Even with firm correction there will be misfortune; there will be no advantage in any way.*

An impetuous act has altered your course and you have lost touch with your past and a sense of direction towards your future. Taking on too much too soon leads to failure.

Line 2: *All occasion for repentance disappears.*

Learn to be guided by your intuition and know your limitations.

Line 3: *One does not continuously maintain one's virtue. There are those who will impute this to one as a disgrace. However firm one may be, there will be grounds for regret.*

Your actions have led you into situations where you have felt publicly embarrassed. You must learn to be more robust in such situations and not let them get to you. Use any such occasion as an opportunity to learn something valuable for yourself.

Line 4: *A field where there is no game.*

You must be clearheaded and clearsighted in order to deal with difficulties: only then can you make valid and worthwhile decisions.

Line 5: *One continuously maintains the indicated virtue. In a wife this will be fortunate; in a husband, unfortunate.*

In any union or partnership you should be flexible and be prepared, if necessary, to depart from custom and convention as a response to changing situations. But never adapt to the point of losing touch with your true self.

Line 6: *One excites oneself to long continuance. There will be misfortune.*

'More haste, less speed': hurry and constant activity are wasteful and harmful. Measured and thoughtful progress towards your goal is more efficient and more likely to succeed.

Hexagram 33
Tun—Withdrawal

Component Trigrams
Primary: Ch'ien—Heaven (upper), Ken—The Mountain (lower). Nuclear: Ch'ien—Heaven (above), Sun—Wind (below).

Keywords
Heaven, the mountain, poise, strategic retreat, persistence, endurance, unfavourable forces.

Commentary
Heaven moves upwards in response to increasing power; it is time for strategic retreat. With threatening forces ranged against you, your success in mitigating their harmful effects depends on the timing and the direction of your withdrawal. You have to proceed carefully, remaining modest and virtuous in the small steps you take; this will allow you to make the best out of the situation. Be realistic and accept that you cannot defeat the forces that you face; all you can do is find the best way of accommodating them, with the least harm to yourself. You are not forsaking your path but seeking better ways of continuing on it. Avoid false and dubious characters if you can, but keep them at a safe distance if you can't. Stay away from conflict with such disruptive types. Maintain your own balance and strength and protect yourself as needs be from their adverse influence.

Judgement
There will be successful progress. To a small extent it will still be advantageous to be firm and correct.

Act economically and timeously. Fail to do this and you will lose respect and authority and encounter further conflict.

Interpretation

Heaven above, the mountain below. The hexagram signifies the superior person moving away from the inferior. When faced with overwhelming odds from a host of malicious adversaries, the virtuous person makes a strategic withdrawal.

Image

Heaven is above the mountain. The wise man keeps small men at a distance, not by showing that he hates them, but by his own dignified gravity.

One retains one's dignity and balance by withdrawing into inner contemplation.

Line readings

Line 1: *A retiring rearguard. The position is perilous. No movement in any direction should be made.*

Your retreat has been mis-timed and you are open to attack. Pause and do nothing which will provoke others.

Line 2: *One holds one's purpose fast as if by a thong made from the hide of a yellow ox, which cannot be broken.*

You must maintain strength of purpose and conviction, and show exemplary conduct, in order to endure. Be prepared to accept help from someone stronger.

Line 3: *One is retiring but bound, to one's distress and peril. To deal with one's binders as in nourishing a servant or concubine would be fortunate for one.*

Your priority is withdrawal from a dangerous situation. Those who are holding you back are compounding the danger. If they can't be enlisted to help you then you must escape from them.

Line 4: *One retires, irrespective of one's personal inclinations. In a wise man this will lead to good fortune; a small man cannot attain to this.*

Retreat is not the same as surrender. You are taking the wise course by withdrawing, and there is no need to feel guilty.

Line 5: *One retires in an admirable way. With firm correctness there will be good fortune.*

Remain committed to the course you have chosen, rem,main determined and don't allow yourself to be diverted. Others will now see what you are doing.

Line 6: *One retires in a noble way. It will be advantageous in every respect.*

Sometimes the correct response to setbacks and disappointments is simply to move away with humility, as you are doing now. Remain positive and optimistic in the face of unavoidable fate.

Hexagram 34
Tachuang—The power of the great

Component Trigrams

Primary: Chen—Thunder (upper), Ch'ien—Heaven (lower). Nuclear: Tui—Marsh (above), Ch'ien—Heaven (below).

Keywords

Thunder, the heavens, strength, power, influence, authority, self-restraint, propriety.

Commentary

You are in the fortunate position of being able to exercise considerable power. Use this power wisely, for the benefit of all and not just yourself. Don't get obsessed with power for its own sake, and smugly preen your own ego. Use it selflessly for good ends and make sure that you stay in harmony with yourself and those around you. Be strong of character when wielding this power, and use it correctly, and anything will be possible. If you misuse the power you have then unhappiness and failure will be the result.

Judgement

It will be advantageous to be firm and correct.

Act cautiously and prudently. Sometimes the best way forward is to pause and wait for a while.

Interpretation

An auspicious situation. Thunder resounds in the heavens: great forces are readying their strength. But this power will have to be employed with a firm sense of moral propriety if it is to be effective in achieving successful aims.

Image

Thunder in its place in heaven. The wise man does not take a step which is not according to propriety.

You must be a moral exemplar at this time, so avoid dubious company and don't deviate from the worthy course you have chosen.

Line readings

Line 1: *One manifests one's strength. But advance will lead to misfortune, most certainly.*

Don't rush into action as this will result in failure.

Line 2: *With firm correctness there will be good fortune.*

Things are beginning to go well so continue with the same commitment, without slacking off.

Line 3: *The small man uses all his strength; the wise man's rule is not to do so. Even with firm correctness the position would be perilous. A ram butts against a fence and gets his horns entangled.*

Things may going well but exercise restraint. Don't charge ahead regardless.

Line 4: *Firm correctness leads to good fortune, and occasion for repentance disappears. The fence opens without the horns being entangled. Strength like the wheel-spokes of a large waggon.*

Follow through with your intentions. The effectiveness of your power depends on your motives. Take time to sort them out.

Line 5: *One loses one's ram-like strength in the ease of one's position. But there will be no occasion for repentance.*

Doing something about the negative aspects of your character is a good thing. Exercise tolerance.

Line 6: *A ram butts against the fence and is unable either to retreat, or to advance as he would fain do. There will not be advantage in any respect; but if one realizes the difficulty of one's position, there will be good fortune.*

Avoid overreaching yourself; you risk coming up against something that will halt your progress. If you are already in a deadlock situation, then back away.

Hexagram 35
Chin—Advancement

Component Trigrams
Primary: Li—Fire (upper), K'un—Earth (lower). Nuclear: K'an—Water (above), Ken—The Mountain (below).

Keywords
Sunrise, earth, shining brilliance, clarity, accumulating virtue.

Commentary
You luckily find yourself in the right place at the right time and have the opportunity, perhaps with the help of influential people, of furthering your plans and taking action which will achieve great success. It is a favourable time for partnerships and you should seek one with a sympathetic authoritative person. Your joint venture has considerable potential for substantial benefits for you. You should go all out and aim for the heights during this highly auspicious period of change and

growth. Keep your integrity, and the full potential of your talents and character will almost effortlessly be realized during this time.

Judgement

A prince secures tranquillity for his people. The king presents him with numerous horses. Three times in one day he is received at interviews.

A good leader only takes others with him if he has their respect and loyalty. He earns this by his desire to act for their welfare.

Image

The bright sun rising above the earth. The wise man gives himself to make more brilliant his bright virtue.

The wise man remains committed always to the path of light and truth, disdaining the shallow and futile temptations of the material world.

Line readings

Line 1: *One wishes to advance but is kept back. Let one be firm and correct, and there will be good fortune. If trust be not reposed in one, let one maintain a large and generous mind, and there will be no error.*

Don't let yourself be upset by minor setbacks. If you remain calm and committed you may also inspire others to your cause.

Line 2: *One advances and yet one is sorrowful. If one be firm and correct, there will be good fortune. One will receive this great blessing from a kind and generous ruler.*

You feel that barriers are being put between you and the person who can help you. Maintain your strength of purpose and consider other tactics.

Line 3: *One is trusted by all around one. All occasion for repentance will disappear.*

Entering into a partnership is a good idea at this time.

Line 4: *One advances like a marmot. However firm and correct one may be, the position is one of peril.*

Trying to be as inconspicuous and innocuous as you can is not the way to proceed.

Line 5: *All occasion for repentance disappears. But let one not concern oneself about failing or succeeding. To advance will be fortunate, and in every way advantageous.*

Don't be so concerned with achievement. The most important thing is the worth of your character. Stay loyal to those who may be helping you at the moment, even if you are not progressing towards your goal.

Line 6: *One advances with strength. But one only uses it to punish the rebellious people of one's own city. The position is perilous, but there will be good fortune. Yet however firm and correct one may be, there will be occasion for regret.*

Don't move forward too quickly, but keep moving forward. Concentrate on husbanding your resources and energies and sticking to the path.

Hexagram 36
Ming I—Darkening of the light

Component Trigrams

Primary: K'un—Earth (upper), Li—Fire (lower). Nuclear: Chen—Thunder (above), K'an—Water (below).

Keywords

Earth, light, repression, obstruction, misfortune, honour, resolve.

Commentary

This is an inauspicious occasion. Perhaps there has been a lack of loyalty from those around you. Be wary of the malicious intent of authority figures or their lack of competence. You will only overcome any difficulties posed by an authority figure, with great effort and strength of purpose. Begin by accepting the fact of the obstacles that have been placed in your way; and then pursue a course of strengthening the virtuous aspects of your character. Show steadfastness in the face of this adversity, and bring into play a strategic cunning in order to find the best way through. In times of such crisis you are entitled to use your wit in ways you would disdain at other times. Crafty ploys are acceptable survival tactics.

Judgement

It will be advantageous to realize the difficulty of the position and maintain firm correctness.

The wise thing to do in the midst of trouble and confusion is to stay calm and think clearly, bringing your own light to bear on the situation. Then with perseverance you can overcome any difficulties.

Interpretation

The light falls into the depths of the earth; the brilliance of virtue is obscure, but not blotted out. The hexagram is about the proper and effective response to situations where the light of reason and virtue is obscured.

Image

The sun sinks into the earth. The wise man conducts his management of men; he shows his intelligence by keeping it obscured.

Act cautiously and conduct yourself properly with others. Don't brag or be arrogant towards others.

Line readings

Line 1: *One flies with drooping wings. When the wise man is resolving his going away, he may be for three days without eating. Wherever he goes, the people there may speak derisively of him.*

You must face up to the problem at hand. Not doing so will bring unwanted attention from others.

Line 2: *One is wounded in the left thigh. One saves oneself by the strength of a swift horse; and is fortunate.*

Although things are bad they can still be remedied. Accept help from others and be prepared to give them help in turn.

Line 3: *One hunts in the south and captures the great chief of the darkness. One should not be eager to make all correct at once.*

Expect those you have offended to be angry. Take any opportunity to right any wrongs you have committed.

Line 4: *One enters the left side of the belly of the dark land. But one is able to quit the gate and the courtyard of the lord of darkness.*

You are in a tense and difficult situation. Stay calm and move cautiously away from it.

Line 5: *One does one's duty. It will be advantageous to be firm and correct.*

Sometimes the only way to protect yourself is to conceal your true self; but remain inwardly and steadfastly committed to that true self and its direction.

Line 6: *There is no light, but only obscurity. It had at first ascended to the top of the sky; its future shall be to go into the earth.*

Your strength, patience and faith are now rewarded as the bad times recede and the darkness is replaced by the light.

Hexagram 37
Chia Jen—Family

Component Trigrams
Primary: Sun—Wind (upper), Li—Fire (lower). Nuclear: Li—Fire (above), K'an—Water (below).

Keywords
Wind, fire, family, harmony, balance, propriety, adherence to structure.

Commentary
You are in a fortunate situation and with harmony and a due attendance to your responsibilities you can attain your desired goal. Apply yourself and avoid distractions. Work together with others and if everyone performs their allotted tasks to the best of their ability then everything will prosper. Whatever your position in this joint enterprise you

should ensure that the spirit—and the letter—of harmony and coordination, especially with the course of the leader, prevails. Mutual respect and proper consultation within the group are required. If you then work to the best of your ability then things will go well.

Judgement

For the regulation of the family, what is most advantageous is that the wife be firm and correct.

Even if you are in a supporting role in a group you have responsibilities towards all the others, including the leader of the group.

Interpretation

This hexagram uses the symbol of the family. The order and harmony of the family group, with everyone performing their allotted tasks to the best of their ability, is the model for society at large. Their are moral aspects to this family coherence, in attitudes and conduct, and also the virtues of love, respect and loyalty.

Image

Wind coming forth from fire. The wise man orders his words according to the truth of things, and his conduct so that it is uniformly consistent.

Make sure there is a correspondence between what you say and what you do. Don't be a hypocrite.

Line readings

Line 1: *One establishes restrictive regulations in one's household. Occasion for repentance will disappear.*

Setting or knowing ground rules and keeping to them are the prerequisites for the growth of any joint endeavour or any relationship.

Line 2: *The wife takes nothing on herself, but in her central place attends to the preparation of the food. Through her firm correctness there will be good fortune.*

Don't be tempted to start anything new.

Line 3: *One treats the members of the household with stern severity. There will be occasion for repentance; there will be peril, but there will also be good fortune. If the wife and the children were to spend their time smirking and chattering, in the end there would be occasion for regret.*

Working towards maintaining an effective balance between the individual wishes of the group and the responsibilities they owe to the group is the best thing to do just now.

Line 4: *The wife enriches the family.*

Things are in proper harmony as you have the love and respect of others for your selflessness and fairness.

Line 5: *The influence of the king extends to one's family. There need be no anxiety; there will be good fortune.*

You are confident in your own ability, and your sense of well-being and happiness expresses itself with love and respect for others.

Line 6: *One is possessed of sincerity and arrayed in majesty. In the end there will be good fortune.*

With your growing status and influence, you should aspire to be a consistent source of stability and strength to those you are responsible to, allowing them to rely on your sense of Judgement and strength of character. Always, though, remain true to yourself, as you cannot grow without inner consistency, and the continuing harmony of the group depends on this.

Hexagram 38
K'uei—Opposition

Component Trigrams
Primary: Li—Fire (upper), Tui—Marsh (lower). Nuclear: K'an—Water (above), Li—Fire (below).

Keywords
Fire, marsh, disunity, alienation, neutrality, division, disagreement.

Commentary
There is disunity which will make it very difficult to achieve anything worthwhile. The conflict and division that you will face is only temporary, though, and harmony will eventually be restored. In the meantime keep your sights set low, attempting only small undertakings, and try to find common ground wherever you can. Respond calmly and resolutely to difficulties that arise. Act honestly and sincerely at all times and do things properly. Don't take advantage of others and make sure that no-one takes advantage of you. Remain optimistic in the face of challenges ahead, remembering that opposition will eventually be superseded by harmony.

Judgement
In small matters there will still be good success.

Don't try to sort everything out at once when things are going badly. You will get back to a harmonious situation by taking things one step at a time.

Interpretation
Fire flames upwards, water flows downwards; the opposing directions

cause a state of disharmony. The hexagram is about a social state in which discord and mutual rejection are the rule. There is dissent, conflict and stalemate. It also conveys the idea of being tugged in two opposing directions. The hexagram suggests what modest steps can be taken to heal breaches.

Image

Fire above the waters of the marsh. The wise man, where there is general agreement, still admits diversity.

Retaining your integrity and freedom of thought and will are the most important things in life.

Line readings

Line 1: *Occasion for repentance will disappear. One has lost one's horses, but let one not seek for them; they will return of themselves. Should one meet with bad men, one will not err in communicating with them.*

You feel you have lost something from your life, but you should not dwell on this as it is an inevitable part of changing and growing. Look to what is new; be responsive to things that you gain as a result of change in your life. If you pursue what you feel you have lost, you will find that it just moves further away. The same applies to people who are no longer a part of your life. Avoid those who have lost their principles as you cannot change this fact.

Line 2: *One meets one's lord in a side-street. There will be no error.*

An accidental and unavoidable meeting with someone will turn out well for you. Things will change for the better as a result of this meeting with a person you may have been trying avoid.

Line 3: *One's carriage is dragged back, while the oxen in it are pushed back, and one is subjected to the shaving of one's head and the cutting off of one's nose. There is no good beginning but there will be a good end.*

You are in a stagnant situation, with no progress possible and this frustrates you. Things will improve in time. For the time being it is best to simply accept what you have and where you are.

Line 4: *One is solitary amidst the prevailing disunion. But one meets with the good man and they blend their sincere desires together. The position is one of peril, but there will be no mistake.*

You will feel less solitary and better able to manage your problems when you meet someone in a similar situation to yourself, with whom you are in tune.

Line 5: *Occasion for repentance will disappear. With one's relative and one's helper, one unites closely and readily as if one were biting through a piece of skin. When one goes forward with this help, what error can there be?*

You are fortunate as you have a sympathetic and happy relationship with an honest and sincere friend, which has ameliorated your feeling of isolation.

Line 6: *One is solitary amidst the prevailing disunion. One seems to see a pig bearing on its back a load of mud, or fancies there is a carriage full of ghosts. One first bends one's bow against him, and afterwards unbends it, for one discovers that he is not an assailant to injure, but a near relative. Going forward, one shall meet with genial rain, and there will be good fortune.*

Don't misjudge your companions as this creates unnecessary and avoidable friction and conflict. Reciprocate their honesty and sincerity and you will be able to relate to one another again.

Hexagram 39
Chien—Barriers

Component Trigrams
Primary: K'an—Water (upper), Ken—The Mountain (lower). Nuclear: Li—Fire (above), K'an—Water (below).

Keywords
Water, mountain, blockage, danger, dilemmas, caution, dangerous pathways.

Commentary
During times of danger and stalemate you must focus on the development of your true self. Fulfilling the potential of your character will give you the strength to overcome the formidable obstacles in front of you. Knowing when and when not to act is a wise capacity and you may need to develop this ability in order to deal with the present situation. Exercise caution before moving forward and seek the advice of experienced elders.

Judgement
Advantage will be found in the south-west and the contrary in the north-east. It will be advantageous also to meet with the great man. In these circumstances, with firmness and correctness, there will be good fortune.

To prepare for the proper action to deal with the difficult situation that faces you, it would be advisable to seek the necessary wisdom through meditation and the consulting of wise and experienced people.

Interpretation
Water is trapped at the top of the mountain, it cannot follow its natural

course. The hexagram is about how to deal with obstructions or impediments, or possible debilitating injury. A wise equanimity is required.

Image
Water atop a mountain. The wise man turns round and examines himself, and cultivates his virtue.

Developing your insight and heightening your awareness is necessary, in order to see a way through severe difficulties and obstacles.

Line readings
Line 1: *Advance will lead to greater difficulties, while remaining stationary will afford ground for praise.*

It is better to pause and wait rather than rashly proceed, creating further problems.

Line 2: *The servant of the king struggles with difficulty on difficulty, and not with a view to his own advantage.*

You must face up to inescapable problems.

Line 3: *One advances but only to greater difficulties. One remains stationary, and returns to one's former associates.*

You are responsible to others so it would be irresponsible to act just now when that action will have consequences for others. Take time to think about the situation to find the best way of proceeding. You will then be able to move forward with renewed energy.

Line 4: *One advances but only to greater difficulties. One remains stationary, and unites with others.*

You need help from others, despite what you may think. Others are ready to help but you must ask them as they believe their help would not be welcomed by you.

Line 5: *One struggles with the greatest difficulties, while friends come to help one.*

In an attempt to help another you have become entangled in difficulties. But you can expect others to come to your aid as they saw the honesty of your motives. You will overcome the obstacles which have halted you.

Line 6: *One goes forward, only to increase the difficulties, while remaining stationary will be productive of great merit. There will be good fortune, and it will be advantageous to meet with the great man.*

Your period of withdrawal in order to meditate on your difficult situation cannot be extended indefinitely. You are not a wise man who can renounce the world and live in solitude. You should now be able to see more clearly how to proceed; so it is time to return to your difficulties and face them, unpalatable as that may be.

Hexagram 40
Chien—Removing obstacles

Component Trigrams
Primary: Chen—Thunder (upper), K'an—Water (lower). Nuclear: K'an—Water (above), Li—Fire (below)

Keywords
Thunder, rain, spring, release, growth, joy, vitality, dispersal.

Commentary
This is a propitious time. After a prolonged period of trial and obstruction a great new direction is open to you. You have a great opportunity. As all the troubles that have beset you fade away, and you approach an unprecedented time of growth and development, you are in a position to forgive and forget. The only thing you have to guard against now is failing to act boldly and timeously in progressing towards a worthy aim. Take full advantage of your fortunate circumstances.

Judgement
Advantage will be found in the south-west. If no further operations be called for, there will be good fortune in coming back to the old conditions. If some operations be called for, there will be good fortune in the early conducting of them.

You must move forward quickly on your chosen path in order to alleviate the stresses that threaten to derail you; but don't overreach yourself.

Interpretation
The hexagram suggests the tension-releasing, cleansing effect of a massive thunderstorm. The ideas of releasing pent-up power and of deliverance from constraint are suggested. It is time to move into a better future and forget the troubles of the past. But don't get carried away as your good fortune has still to arrive.

Image
Thunder and rain acting together. The wise man forgives errors and deals gently with crimes.

'Clearing the air' is necessary to resolve disputes and tensions, and come to better terms with things and people so that you can move forward. You will also be able to see more clearly the best direction for you.

Line readings
Line 1: *One will commit no error.*

You can take time out from your problems and recharge your depleted batteries in peace and quiet.

Line 2: *One catches, in hunting, three foxes, and obtains the golden arrows. With firm correctness there will be good fortune.*

Be wary of those who may seek to exploit you because they see your good fortune coming. Preserve your energies and be careful.

Line 3: *A porter rides in a carriage with his burden. He will only tempt robbers to attack him. However firm and correct he may try to be, there will be cause for regret.*

Don't advertise your good fortune as there are potential dangers lurking in the circle that surrounds you. Some of your friends are deceiving you. Be careful.

Line 4: *One is instructed to remove his toes. Friends will then come, between him and them there will be mutual confidence.*

You must be realistic and sensible and confront those who are not genuine friends with the fact of your knowledge of their duplicity. Remove them from your circle, otherwise you could be faced with your genuine friends leaving.

Line 5: *The wise man executes his function of removing what is harmful, in which case there will be good fortune, and confidence in him will be shown even to the small men.*

As you move those who are undesirable from your circle of friends, so you must discard those regressive aspects of your character and achieve greater clarity of mind and grow in wisdom.

Line 6: *A prince with his bow shoots at a falcon on the top of a high wall, and hits it. The effect of his action will be in every way advantageous.*

It is best to ponder a situation and then act in due time and appropriately. But to resolve a situation it is sometimes necessary to use force.

Hexagram 41
Sun—Reduction

Component Trigrams

Primary: Ken—The Mountain (upper), Tui—Marsh (lower). Nuclear: K'un—Earth (above), Chen—Thunder (below).

Keywords

The mountain, marsh, sacrifice, restraint, self-control, discipline, attendance to excess.

Commentary

This is a time of loss, which will in turn bring gain and a new beginning. You are in a situation where it is paramount that you curb your own excesses. You will have to do whatever it takes to return your self to balance and health, in order to act correctly again. If you are sincere and unremitting in your efforts at self-improvement then you will reap the rewards. Even if the necessary improvement only needs to be small, it will be enough if it is done with genuine wholeheartedness. There must be a persistent effort to improve your character and you must avoid loss of self-control leading you into mistakes.

Judgement

If there is sincerity there will be great good fortune: freedom from error; firmness and correctness that can be maintained; and advantage in every movement that shall be made. In what shall this sincerity be employed? In sacrifice two baskets of grain may be presented, though there be nothing else.

The experience of loss can be valuable and profitable. Respond to it with sincerity and optimism.

Interpretation

The trigrams' symbolism: the marsh water below the mountain evaporates and nourishes the vegetation above. The hexagram's form suggests the image of the lower trigram of strong yang lines generously yielding its top line to the upper trigram of weak yin lines. The idea is of voluntary loss or relinquishing, curbing excess for a greater purpose, which will deliver reward.

Image

The lake below the mountain. The wise man restrains his wrath and represses his desires.

Unrestrained passions and indulgence in excess lead you into difficulties. It is time to exercise self-control and restraint.

Line readings

Line 1: *One suspends one's own affairs, and hurries away to help another. One will commit no error, but let one consider how far one should contribute what is one's own to the other.*

Use this time of restraint and lack of movement to help, modestly and humbly, those others who need it. If it is you who is seeking help, don't become a burden to others.

Line 2: *It will be advantageous to maintain a firm correctness, and action will bring no misfortune. One can give increase to another without taking from oneself.*

Don't do anything which goes against your principles. Retain your honour and dignity.

Line 3: *Three men walk together, then the number is diminished by one; and one, walking, finds his friend.*

There is conflict in your group, animosities and jealousies, resulting from there being one person in the group who should no longer be a member. This person must leave. If it is you who has to leave then it is best that you take a companion with you.

Line 4: *One diminishes the ailment under which one labours by making another hasten to one's help and make one glad. There will be no error.*

Welcome help in your efforts when it is offered. It comes from a genuine desire to contribute.

Line 5: *The ruler's subjects add to his stores ten pairs of tortoise shells, and accept no refusal. There will be great good fortune.*

This is a time of great good fortune, when you have success in everything.

Line 6: *One gives increase to others without taking from oneself. There will be no error. With firm correctness there will be good fortune. There will be advantage in every movement that shall be made. One will find ministers more than can be counted by their clans.*

You will achieve your goals if you persist in your course with sincerity and honesty. Your genuineness will encourage others to come to your help in the spirit of friendship.

Hexagram 42
I—Increase

Component Trigrams
Primary: Sun—Wind (upper), Chen—Thunder (lower). Nuclear: Ken—The Mountain (above), K'un —Earth (below)

Keywords
Wind, thunder, reinforcement, addition, augmentation, abundance, gain.

Commentary
A highly auspicious time. You will overcome all obstacles and achieve success in your undertakings. But during your time of prosperity and success it is your responsibility and honour to share your good fortune with others. All you achieve and are granted by fortune is only to give you the opportunity to be selfless and show generosity to others by helping to improve their situations.

Judgement
There will be advantage in every movement which shall be undertaken. It will even be advantageous to cross the great stream.

You should savour your time of success and good fortune while it lasts and use it to enable you to give as much help to others as possible. In this will be true reward.

Interpretation
In the hexagram we have wind above and thunder below; each strengthens the other. Thus we derive the ideas of growth and increase. Increase is also conveyed by the donation of the yang line from the upper trigram to the lower, to strengthen it. The upper trigram also signifies the wood from which a boat is constructed. A journey over water may feature in the good fortune which will be heaped upon you.

Image
Thunder and wind together. When the wise man sees what is good, he moves towards it; and when he sees his errors, turns from them.

Follow the moral example of the wise man and cultivate the self-awareness which will allow you to identify and eradicate the weaknesses and faults in your nature. Compare yourself objectively with the good character of others.

Line readings
Line 1: *It will be advantageous for one to make a great movement. If it be greatly fortunate, no blame will be imputed to one.*

Your position of great good fortune should encourage you to achieve great aims. Your selflessness and the selfless help of others will bring about success.

Line 2: *The people add to the rulers stores ten pairs of tortoise shells whose oracles cannot be gainsaid. Let one persevere in being firm and correct, and there will be good fortune. Let the king employ the people in presenting his offerings to God, and there will be good fortune.*

Everything in your life is in harmony and everything you do achieves success. Remember to keep to your true path in the midst of your good fortune.

Line 3: *One receives increase by misfortune, so that one shall be led to good, and be without blame. Let one be sincere and pursue the path of the Mean, so shall one secure the recognition of the ruler, like an officer who announces himself to his prince by the symbol of his rank.*

Someone is in need and you should take the opportunity to unselfishly give them help. This will bring its own rewards.

Line 4: *One pursues the due course. One's advice to one's prince is followed. One can with advantage be relied on in such a movement as that of removing the capital.*

You should take the opportunity that presents itself of being a mediator. It is good that you are respected and trusted enough to be offered this role. Accept the responsibility with a good heart.

Line 5: *One seeks with sincere heart to benefit all below. There need be no question about it; the result will be great good fortune. All below will with sincere heart acknowledge one's goodness.*

Generosity and benevolence are exercised for their own sake and with no other motives. You will be respected for such acts.

Line 6: *None will contribute to one's increase, while many will seek to assail one. One observes no regular rule in the order of one's heart. There will be misfortune.*

It is not enough to exercise an impersonal kind of kindness and benevolence. You must open yourself genuinely to others in order to have friendships and companionship. You must give of yourself and your time to others, and not just rely on your actions.

Hexagram 43
Kuai—Displacing

Component Trigrams

Primary: Tui—Marsh (upper), Ch'ien—Heaven (lower). Nuclear: Ch'ien—Heaven (above), Ch'ien—Heaven (below).

Keywords

Marsh, heaven, threatening skies, corruption, virtue, resolve.

Commentary

You will have to do something regarding influential and powerful people who are unworthy of their positions and authority. You cannot ignore their abuses of power nor can you directly challenge them. You will have to use your own strength of character and sense of moral purpose, along with help from those who are inspired by your example, to change things for the better. Making the offences known to someone in authority who can be trusted is a worthwhile tactic, as is enlisting the public on your side. The main thing, though, is to remain convinced of the rightness of your cause and to maintain good relations with others. You should not set out to act because you have a personal axe to grind with someone.

Judgement

The culprit's guilt should be made known in the royal court, with a sincere and earnest appeal for sympathy and support. There will be peril. One should also make announcement in one's own city, and show that it will not be well to have recourse at once to arms. In this way there will be advantage in whatever one goes forward to.

Don't use force to achieve your aim, but rely on your own virtuous character. You have to show steadfastness, honesty and strength in pursuing this worthwhile course.

Interpretation

The marsh waters have evaporated and changed into clouds which have ascended up to the heavens. A cloudburst is imminent. The hexagram is about how you can avoid social and political storms and the disorder they create. The form of the hexagram symbolizes the inferior person in a position of influence (the top yin line) who confronts and opposes those who are true and honest. It suggests that those of virtue will successfully resist and overwhelm the threat to them.

Image

The waters rise to heaven. The wise man bestows reward on those below him, and dislikes allowing his gifts to accumulate undispensed.

Be flexible and cultivate self-awareness in order to remedy your faults.

Line readings

Line 1: *One advances in the pride of one's strength. One goes forward, but will not succeed. There will be ground for blame.*

Know your limitations and be cautious with any new undertaking.

Line 2: *One is full of apprehension and appeals for sympathy and help. Late at night hostile measures may be taken against one, but one need not be anxious about them.*

If you remain wary and anticipate problems before they appear then you will be able to deal confidently with them.

Line 3: *One is about to advance with strong and determined looks. There will be misfortune. But the wise man, bent on cutting off the criminal, will walk alone, and encounter the rain, till he be hated by his proper associates as if he were contaminated by the others. In the end there will be no blame against him.*

Keeping to your own true path and remaining calm and in control is the best way to conduct yourself, when you are isolated and surrounded by the animosity of others.

Line 4: *One has been punished by whipping, and one walks slowly and with difficulty. If one could act like a sheep led after its companions, occasion for repentance would disappear. But though one hear these words, one will not believe them.*

This is an inauspicious time to try and move forward. Remain where you are and don't stubbornly reject advice.

Line 5: *The small men are like a bed of weeds, which ought to be uprooted with the utmost determination. Having such determination, one's action, in harmony with one's central position, will lead to no error or blame.*

You cannot eradicate all evil in the world. You must live with this realization. What you can do successfully and continually is promote the power of good.

Line 6: *One has no helpers on whom to call. One will end with misfortune.*

Be extra-vigilant with yourself when it seems that you have achieved your purpose and the bad times are finally over. Don't become blase. What to do with victory can be a great responsibility and the situation demands the right thought and action.

Hexagram 44
Kou—Encountering

Component Trigrams
Primary: Ch'ien—Heaven (upper), Sun—Wind (lower). Nuclear: Ch'ien—Heaven (above), Ch'ien—Heaven (below).

Keywords
Wind, heaven, pernicious influences, temptation, corruption, encroachment.

Commentary
There are strong influences for the good at work in your life but you should still be careful in your choice of those who work with you and for you; be alert for negative influences at work among them that are likely to stir up trouble. There is a weak negative force attempting unsuccessfully at the moment to affect your life, but if you ignore it, it could become more effective. Try to prevent anyone of doubtful or bad character getting the chance to exert any influence. If they do they will draw others into their fold and cause your fortunes to gradually diminish. If you act swiftly and boldly you will be able to prevent such a decline. But if you hesitate or try to elaborate a plan, then the negative forces will entrench themselves and prosper to your disadvantage.

Judgement
A female who is bold and strong. It will not be good to marry such a female.

Those of poor character attain positions of influence because those of good character allow themselves to be duped. They support bad characters who present themselves as innocent and reliable.

Interpretation
The upper trigram, representing royalty, uses the penetrating power of the wind. The image is of a prince's will being taken to all corners of

the land. The single yin line at the bottom signifies a harmful force in a futile attempt to get into the situation.

Image

Wind below heaven. The ruler delivers his charges, and promulgates his announcements throughout the four corners of the kingdom.

It is better and wiser to delegate responsibilities to others, thus gaining respect for the soundness of your leadership.

Line readings

Line 1: *One should be like a carriage tied and fastened to a metal drag, in which case with firm correctness there will be good fortune. But if one move in any direction, misfortune will appear. One will be like a lean pig, which is sure to keep jumping about.*

Irrespective of the forces or obstacles there may be against you, you should keep resolutely going forward on your chosen path.

Line 2: *One has a wallet of fish. There will be no error. But it will not be well to go forward to the guests.*

Your lack of progress and your feelings of frustration are the result of your own actions. You must suppress your frustrated feelings as expressing them at this time will cause you problems.

Line 3: *One has been punished by whipping and walks with difficulty. The position is perilous, but there will be no great error.*

By shrewdly anticipating likely difficulties you are better able to deal with them when they arrive. Retain your self-control and equanimity and don't give way to anything you disagree with.

Line 4: *One has one's wallet, but no fish in it. This will give rise to misfortune.*

Don't make the mistake of cutting yourself off from people because you have attained a position of power. You still need these people. Alienate them now and you would have no-one if you were deposed from your present position.

Line 5: *A medlar tree overspreads the gourd beneath it. If one keeps one's brilliant qualities concealed, a good issue will descend as from heaven.*

If you remain virtuous in your character and path, then you will have good fortune. Be content in yourself. All you have to impress on others is your genuine concern for them.

Line 6: *One receives others on one's horns. There will be occasion for regret, but there will be no error.*

You have removed yourself from the situation, having done what you set out to do. Others may express antipathy and hostility to you for withdrawing. You should pay no heed as you have remained true to yourself. They will have to deal for themselves with the consequences of harbouring these negative feelings.

Hexagram 45
Ts'ui—Gathering

Component Trigrams

Primary: Tui—Marsh (upper), K'un—Earth (lower). Nuclear: Sun—Wind (above), Ken—The Mountain.

Keywords

Marsh, earth, unity, prosperity, boundaries, order, happiness, obedience.

Commentary

This is a time of unity, and efforts should be made to maintain such a state. You should enjoy and take full advantage of this favourable period. Be wary, though, of those within and without your circle who may seek from jealousy or spite to destroy your harmonious situation. You will be able at this time to draw on substantial personal and material resources. You should be willing to listen to and act on good advice from trusted and respected figures. They can help you get the most out of this time of success. Remain cautious regarding threats to your situation. But with the cooperation of others you will be able to look forward to great rewards.

Judgement

The king will repair to his ancestral temple. It will be advantageous also to meet with the great man; and then there will be progress and success, though the advantage must come through firm correctness. The use of great victims will conduce to good fortune; and in whatever direction movement is made, it will be advantageous.

By maintaining strength and a calm purpose you will enlist others in your propitious undertakings.

Interpretation

The upper trigram signifies happiness and the lower, obedience. The hexagram as a whole indicates an auspicious time when you gather together with others and form a harmonious and balanced group. Your calm happiness will face challenges.

Image

The waters are raised above the earth. The wise man has his weapons of war put in good repair, to be prepared against unforeseen contingencies.

A large group is open to threat, so precautions must be taken. Be on the alert.

Line readings

Line 1: *One has a sincere desire for union but is unable to carry it out, so that disorder is brought into the sphere of union. If one cries out for help to another, all at once one's tears will give place to smiles. One need not mind the temporary difficulty; as one goes forward, there will be no error.*

Put your faith and trust in a person of strong virtue and steady character, who will help you to solve your problems.

Line 2: *One is led forward by another. There will be good fortune, and freedom from error. There is entire sincerity, and in that case even the small offerings of the spring sacrifice are acceptable.*

Be guided by your intuition and if you feel in tune with a person or group then seek to bond with them.

Line 3: *One sighs after union and sighs, yet nowhere finds any advantage. If one goes forward, one will not err, though there may be some small cause for regret.*

As an outsider you are drawn to a group and wish to join it, but you are hesitant. You should approach the group and seek admission to it: you will be welcomed.

Line 4: *If one be greatly fortunate, one will receive no blame.*

Selfless work for the benefit of others will bring harmony and good fortune closer.

Line 5: *One is in the place of dignity and unites all under one. There will be no error. If any do not have confidence in one, see to it that one's virtue be great, long continued, and firmly correct, and all occasion for repentance will disappear.*

All members of a group must be open and honest with each other so that harmony can be established.

Line 6: *One sighs and weeps; but there will be no error.*

Openness, honesty, and the expression of feelings, is the way to strengthen the bonds within a group and thus strengthen the group.

Hexagram 46 Sheng—Ascending

Component Trigrams

Primary: K'un—Earth (upper), Sun—Wind (lower). Nuclear: Chen—Thunder (above), Tui—Marsh (below).

Keywords

Earth, wood, growth, fertility, patience, attentiveness, accumulating virtue, progress.

Commentary

This hexagram indicates that your fortunes are slowly improving. By making steady, small improvements in your character you will eventually overcome all obstacles to reach your goal and be honoured and lauded. Keep attending to these minor matters and your successful progress is assured.

Judgement

There will be great progress and success. Seeking to meet with the great man, one need have no anxiety. Advance to the south will be fortunate.

Everything is in your favour. There are no obstacles between you and your goal. Begin working toward it now and expect the help of others.

Interpretation

The trigrams signify earth and wood (Sun is wood, as well as wind). Specifically, a tree growing ever upwards, straight and true, from the earth to the heavens. From a small beginning as a sapling, the tree slowly persisted and grew beyond its initial obstacles into free, unhindered growth. Your slow, steady growth will emulate the tree's eventual, spectacular success.

Image

Wood grows within the earth. The wise man pays careful attention to his virtue, and accumulates the small developments of it till it is high and great.

From small acorns, great oaks grow. You must persist in your slow, steady growth like the tree, and you will become remarkably favoured.

Line readings

Line 1: *One advances upwards with the welcome of those above one. There will be great good fortune.*

Remain determined in the face of the length of the journey you have to make in order to reach your goal. You will get there, one small step at a time.

Line 2: *One's sincerity will make even the small offerings of the spring sacrifice acceptable. There will be no error.*

Although you still have a long way to go towards your goal, your honesty and sincerity winsfavour and sympathy from others.

Line 3: *One ascends upwards as into an empty city.*

There are no obstacles in your way. Make sure you are on the right path and remember that things could change and bring difficulty.

Line 4: *One is employed by the king to present his offerings on the mountain. There will be good fortune; there will be no mistake.*

This line suggests a new opportunity or the according of reward or honour.

Line 5: *One is firmly correct, and therefore enjoying good fortune; there will be no mistake.*

Although you are near your goal don't get excited or overconfident. Continue in the same, calm steady way until you reach your goal. Don't do anything different or anything impetuous.

Line 6: *One advances upwards blindly. Advantage will be found in a ceaseless maintenance of firm correctness.*

Ambition for its own sake will push on blindly and will ultimately fail. You need to have a clear goal so that you can work towards it, and then be aware that you have reached it. You must remain sincere and honest, and work hard towards your aims.

Hexagram 47
K'un—Exhaustion

Component Trigrams
Primary: Tui—Marsh (upper), K'an—Water (lower). Nuclear: Sun—Wind (above), Li—Fire (below).

Keywords
Marshes, water, scarcity, trial, self-discipline, opposition, endurance.

Commentary
The situation is hard and difficult. The usual, necessary resources for coping have been exhausted. There is no order or control. And you face a time of conflict, disorder and fatigue. You will have to be self-sufficient and improvize a way through the testing difficulties that inescapably confront you. You will have to rely on deep, inner strength and a willed determination to remain optimistic and cheerful no matter what. Others may be not be very understanding. You may have to make some material sacrifice. But if you have a worthy goal and persist in your path towards it, maintaining self-control and a sense of humour, you will survive the pressures on you, and your situation will gradually improve.

Judgement
There may yet be progress and success. For the firm and correct, the really great man,

there will be good fortune. He will fall into no error. If one makes speeches, one is not heard.

Times of hardship can also be times of learning and growth. Remain optimistic and use your setbacks as salutary lessons. Follow the precept that actions speak louder than words.

Interpretation

The water is beneath the marshes. What is essential has been drained away. The two primary trigrams, representing delight and danger, taken together suggest a time of joy in the face of scarcity and adversity. The person of character and virtue will win through a perilous time by remaining in good spirits and acting correctly.

Image

The marsh drains away into a water-course. The wise man will sacrifice his life in order to carry out his purpose. When bad fortune assails you and strips you of your resources, accept it as your fate, and concentrate on being self-sufficient.

Line readings

Line 1: *One sits in rags and despondency under the stump of a tree. One enters a dark valley, and for three years has no prospect of deliverance.*

You have given up and slumped into a debilitating depression, which makes your situation seem darker that it is. You must use your inner resources to help you find a way out of this depression.

Line 2: *One is despondent amidst wine and meat. The ruler comes to one's help. It will be well for one to maintain one's sincerity as in sacrificing. Active operations will lead to evil, but one will be free from blame.*

You have a sufficiency but are offered even more. You are forced to think about it.

Line 3: *One is oppressed before a frowning rock. One lays hold of thorns. One enters the palace and does not see one's wife. There will be misfortune.*

You strive to go forward but seem unable to make any progress, being blocked by obstacles at every turn. Perhaps the problems stem from your attitudes or actions. Try to look at them clearly and objectively and discuss the matter with those close to you.

Line 4: *One proceeds very slowly to help another who is oppressed by the carriage adorned with metal in front of him. There will be occasion for regret, but the end all will be good.*

Your status may make you feel aloof from those who are in a less powerful situation, this may be compounded by feelings of guilt. Accept that you are only separated by the trappings of success and seek contact with them and possible help.

Line 5: *One is wounded. One is oppressed by the ministers. One is leisurely in one's movements however, and is satisfied. It will be well for one to be as sincere as in sacrificing to spiritual beings.*

You will have to wait patiently and wisely for things to slowly improve.

Line 6: *One is oppressed as if bound with creepers; or one is in a high and dangerous position and saying to oneself, 'If I move, I shall repent it.' If one repents of former errors, there will be good fortune in going forward.*

You feel held back and unable to move, but in fact it is only in your mind. Act now.

Hexagram 48
Ching—The Well

Component Trigrams

Primary: K'an—Water (upper), Sun—Wind (lower). Nuclear: Li—Fire (above), Tui—Marshes (below).

Keywords

Water, wood, community, propriety, order, nourishment.

Commentary

As a well nourishes the community that depends on it, so must your character have its own deep and lasting resources that will always sustain you. From your position of self-sufficient strength and energy you will be able to invest your energies in your community for the benefit of all. You must strive to maintain correctly the harmony of the community, and by so doing you will have success. If harmony is not maintained, there will be misfortune.

Judgement

A town may change but its wells remain unchanged. The water of a well never disappears and never receives any great increase. Those who come and go draw water from the well and enjoy the benefit. If one is about to draw water from the well, but the rope is too short or the bucket breaks, then there is misfortune.

Things change but the workings of human nature stay the same. One must be able to draw on one's inner resources, otherwise there will be an unfortunate lack.

Interpretation

Sun signifies wood as well as water. The hexagram as a whole represents a well with a bucket that brings up the life-sustaining substance from the unfailing spring. The idea communicated is that of the correct maintenance of communal resources. From the well of human nature we learn from our personal and communal pasts. It is important not to get too far away from what sustains us. Being guided in the present by your inner nature is vital, as is reflection on events in the past.

Image
Water raised by wood. The wise man comforts the people, and stimulates them to mutual helpfulness.

Working in harmony with others for the benefit of all is of the highest importance.

Line readings
Line 1: *The well is so muddy that men will not drink from it; neither birds nor other creatures will resort to an old well.*

It is important to remain in touch with the present moment and also to retain your independence of mind and action. Overstretching yourself for others can lead to depletion of your resources and a loss of individuality. You will also be taken for granted.

Line 2: *From a hole in the well the water escapes and flows away to the shrimps and such small creatures among the grass; the water of the well leaks away from a broken bucket.*

You deliberately and perversely have nothing to do with others because you believe you won't be able to stay in control of relations. This is a waste of your resources and assets as an individual, of your potential value to yourself and others—who respond to your disdain by ignoring you.

Line 3: *The well has been cleared out, but is not used. Our hearts are sorry for this, for the water might be drawn out and used. If the king were only of the same mind as us, both he and we might receive the benefit of it.*

Someone's valuable practical abilities are not being used. He is despondent, feeling unwanted and undervalued. He could do much good for the community.

Line 4: *The well has a well-laid lining. There will be no error.*

This is a time to make yourself your number one priority. You have to rest and recuperate, restore your energies. This is not selfish indulgence but the correct thing to do, and others will have rely on their own resources for the present.

Line 5: *A clear limpid well, the waters of its cold spring are freely drunk.*

Another is offering something valuable to you and you may not be aware of this as yet. You should seek this person out and pay attention to them.

Line 6: *The water from the well is brought to the top, which is not allowed to be covered. This suggests the idea of sincerity. There will be great good fortune.*

There is a never-failing source of valuable learning in human nature and life. There are also deep spiritual resources in human nature which can be drawn on for the benefit of all. Be sympathetic to those who wish to learn.

Hexagram 49
Ko—Change

Component Trigrams
Primary: Tui—Marsh (upper), Li—Fire (lower). Nuclear: Ch'ien—Heaven (above), Sun—Wind (below).

Keywords
Marshes, fire, progression, appropriateness, preparation, renovation, reform.

Commentary
Dramatic and necessary change is taking place in your life, or is about to. Accept and become involved in making the required changes, but make sure they happen at the right and appropriate time. If you are working with others in a new enterprise then ensure that you bring clear-sightedness and clear-headedness to it, and supply a fund of optimism. You cannot rely on automatic support though, even for an undertaking with obvious attractions. You will have to be persuasive. Don't let the process of change unbalance your individual way of seeing and doing things. Make sure that the change is for a definite and necessary purpose, and is required at this time. Act selflessly and with humility, honesty and sincerity when dealing with new situations.

Judgement
Only when something has been accomplished will it be believed in. There will be great progress and success. Advantage will come from being firm and correct. In that case occasion for repentance will disappear.

We must learn to accept change properly and this means learning and profiting from change. We also have to time our actions correctly and to take the right direction. It is wrong to act for materialist or self-seeking reasons. Other people must be taken into account.

Interpretation
In the trigrams, fire within the marshes means that major change is

imminent. Fire evaporates water, and water extinguishes fire. Li also indicates a clear-sighted intelligence and Tui signifies delight. The change intimated is not a wilful, spontaneous or chance overthrow or rebellion, but a natural and inescapable change which is nevertheless well-planned and measured, and is directed at a clearly defined purpose.

Image
Fire within the waters of the marsh. The wise man regulates his astronomical calculations, and makes clear the seasons and times.

As the seasons change so must we, responding appropriately to what is asked of us.

Line readings
Line 1: *One is bound with the skin of a yellow ox.*

You should not enact any changes until it is the right time for them, though sometimes circumstances force you into premature change. In either case exercise patience and self-control.

Line 2: *One makes one's changes after some time has passed. Action taken will be fortunate. There will be no error.*

Being well-prepared for change will enable you to deal with it much more successfully.

Line 3: *One's action will bring misfortune. Though one is firm and correct, one's position is perilous. If the change one contemplates has been three times fully discussed, one will be believed in.*

Don't be too impetuous or too dilatory in meeting change. Proper timing is all. Consider the situation before you commit yourself to action and take on board the thoughts and advice of others.

Line 4: *Occasion for repentance disappears from one. Let one be believed in; and though one change existing ordinances, there will be good fortune.*

There are radical changes taking place. If you participate in these changes from an irreproachable moral standpoint and conduct yourself with integrity, then you will inevitably receive help from others.

Line 5: *The great man produces his changes as the tiger does when he changes his stripes. Before he divines and proceeds to action, faith has been reposed in him.*

If you make it completely clear to others what is informing the change, why it is taking place and the aim it has, then they will be glad to support it. Otherwise they will not.

Line 6: *The wise man produces his changes as the leopard does when he changes his spots, while small men change their faces and show their obedience. To go forward now would lead to evil, but there will be good fortune in abiding firm and correct.*

In the aftermath of great change, smaller changes will still reverberate for a time. You should only become involved with those that you can cope with.

Hexagram 50
Ting—The Cauldron

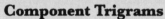

Component Trigrams

Primary: Li—Fire (upper), Sun—Wind (lower). Nuclear: Tui—Marsh (above), Ch'ien—Heaven (below).

Keywords

Fire, wood, order, stability, alliances, nourishment.

Commentary

You should use whatever means you can to look after, encourage and generally support those people of your circle who possess wisdom and ability, and have a significant contribution to make to the community. Be receptive to the original and creative ideas which are produced by these gifted people. Maintain correct and harmonious relations with these people of influence and status and it will be good for you. If you are offered the chance to join an influential group, do so with suitable grace and decorum. You should come significantly closer to a desired and worthy goal.

Judgement

Great progress and success.

The nourishing of the material and spiritual aspects of life are both equally important. Their health and well-being must always be attended to if wisdom and fruitfulness are to flourish.

Interpretation

In the trigrams we have wood below fire. This becomes the fire below a large cauldron. The hexagram's physical shape suggests the cauldron, with the bottom line as the legs, the three solid lines the vessel's body, the next two lines the handles and the top line the lid or cover. The cauldron is at the heart of the house and the source of all the nourishment for the household, material and spiritual. When the cauldron is replete, then all is harmony and well-being.

Image

Wood within fire. The wise man keeps his every position correct, and maintains secure the appointment of heaven.

Living in harmony with oneself and with others is the sure way to the light of wisdom, which the wise man will thus use to illuminate the world.

Line readings

Line 1: *The cauldron is overthrown and its feet turned up. But there will be advantage in its getting rid of what was bad in it. It shows us the concubine whose position is improved by means of her son. There will be no error.*

Recognition and success, power and influence are possible for even the humblest and lowliest. Look within yourself, cleanse and clarify where it is necessary.

Line 2: *The cauldron has food to be cooked in it. If one can say, 'My enemy dislikes me, but he cannot approach me,' there will be good fortune.*

You are successful and prospering and may incur the jealousy of others. Don't let this bother you or make you feel guilty. If you are true to yourself and your worthy path then you have nothing to fear, and nothing for others or yourself to accuse you of.

Line 3: *The cauldron has the places of its handles changed. One's progress is thus halted. The fat flesh of the pheasant which is in the cauldron will not be eaten. But the genial rain will come, and the grounds for repentance will disappear. There will be good fortune in the end.*

You are prevented from sharing your bounty and good fortune with others, and consequently feel frustrated and full of chagrin. But persist in your good intention and eventually the situation will change and you will be able to accomplish your task.

Line 4: *The cauldron has its feet broken; and its contents, designed for the ruler's use, are overturned and spilt. One will be made to blush for shame. There will be misfortune.*

You are feeling tense and vulnerable at the moment because of stress and pressure. Be careful you don't crack because of it.

Line 5: *The cauldron has golden handles and rings of metal in them. There will be advantage through being firm and correct.*

Those around you can see your genuine, inner worth and merit and would like to help you, but there is something in your attitudes or conduct which prevents them from doing so. And this also makes you unable to share your good fortune with them.

Line 6: *The cauldron has carrying-rings of jade.*

The benefits of your good fortune can be shared with others.

Hexagram 51
Chen—Thunder

Component Trigrams
Primary: Chen—Thunder (upper), Chen—Thunder (lower). Nuclear:
K'an—Water (above), Ken—The Mountain (below).

Keywords
Thunder, surprise, poise, movement, expansion, beginnings.

Commentary
You must make yourself aware of the dangers around you and take the
necessary precautions. Maintaining your course on the right path and
keeping your life and conduct in good order and discipline, is the best
way to overcome the obstacles in front of you and reach your goal. You
must stay determined and committed. Do not hesitate to act as the
situation and your conscience prompts you. Be bold and brave and
whatever comes against you, you can meet and master. If you are calm
and disciplined, fully in control of yourself, then you will be able to
dominate the troubled situation and even gain advantage from it.

Judgement
*Ease and development. When the time of movement comes one will be found looking
out with apprehension, and yet smiling and talking cheerfully. When the movement
like a crash of thunder terrifies all within a hundred miles, one will be like the sincere
worshipper who is not startled into letting go of his ladle and cup of sacrificial spirits.*

The only thing to fear in a fearful situation, is your fear itself. Your growth
and development depend on you learning this and taking it to heart.

Interpretation
Thunder above thunder, brings a resounding clamour. The hexagram
signifies a severe sudden outburst of noise or a sudden and shocking
jolt of movement. It deals with the appropriate response to situations of
abrupt and shocking change.

Image
Thunder redoubled. The wise man is fearful and apprehensive, cultivates his virtue and examines his faults.

Look at your inner values, your motives and conduct. Recognise your
own shortcomings and correct the faults and weaknesses that you find.

Line readings
Line 1: *When the movement approaches, one looks out and around with apprehension,
and afterwards smiles and talks cheerfully. There will be good fortune.*

One you realize that it is not you alone who is affected by the present circumstances your morale will improve.

Line 2: *When the movement approaches, one is in a position of peril. One judges it better to let go the articles in one's possession, and to ascend to a very lofty height. There is no occasion for one to pursue the things one has let go; in seven days one will find them.*

Don't worry about any material losses you suffer because of your present situation. Better to ask yourself if they were important anyway.

Line 3: *One is distraught amid the startling movements going on. If these movements excite one to right action, there will be no mistake.*

Don't let disturbing events affect your balance. For the time being, go along with what fate decides for you, and in time you will be able to take some positive action.

Line 4: *Amid the startling movements, one sinks supinely deeper into the mud.*

When the situation becomes clearer, and you are able to think more clearly about it, then you will be able to do something. In the meantime, bide your time and be prepared to accommodate yourself a little to the circumstances you find yourself in. Don't be untrue to yourself though. Be prepared to take advantage of any early opportunities that may unexpectedly present themselves.

Line 5: *One comes and goes amid the startling movements of the time, and always in peril; but perhaps one will not incur loss, and find business which one can accomplish.*

Though others may think it folly and disapprove, there are certain actions you must undertake just now. If they are done in the right spirit and in the proper manner, you will come to no harm.

Line 6: *Amidst the startling movements of the time, in breathless dismay one looks around with trembling apprehension. If one takes action, there will be misfortune. If, while the startling movements have not reached one's own person and neighbourhood, one were to take precautions, there would be no error, though one's relatives might still speak against one.*

It would be better for your mental, emotional and spiritual balance if you withdrew into yourself just now. Among those others affected by the present turmoil there will be much strife and contention. Ignore any wounding comments about you made by those close to you.

Hexagram 52
Ken—The mountain

Component Trigrams

Primary: Ken—The Mountain (upper), Ken—The Mountain (lower).
Nuclear: Chen—Thunder (above), K'an—Water (below).

Keywords

Mountain, stillness, correct action, observation, appropriate restraint of action.

Commentary

You must base all you do on the firmest and soundest principles, which will endure and guide you in all situations. Act only at the right time and do not act selfishly. After assessing the overall situation, act only in a way that accords with your particular circumstances and character. You will discover the most appropriate way, whether direct or indirect.

Judgement

When one's back is at rest, one loses all consciousness of self; when one walks in the courtyard and does not see any of the persons in it, there will be no error.

In calmness and stillness, we can often find what we have been looking for. Now is the time to sit in stillness.

Interpretation

Both trigrams represent the mountain, signifying great stillness. The mountain sitting immobile on the earth suggests great poise and inner resolution. The mountain also thrusts upwards from the earth to the heavens. And in its position it is an obstacle to those who want to go beyond it.

Image

A mountain within a mountain. The wise man does not go in his thoughts beyond the duties of the position in which he is.

You must direct your thoughts to yourself and your situation, and also examine your inner self.

Line readings

Line 1: *One keeps one's toes at rest. There will be no error; but it will be advantageous for one to be persistently firm and correct.*

Don't lose your strength of purpose, but be directed by your intuition if you feel unsure about a situation. Retain your patience and exercise caution.

Line 2: *One keeps the calves of one's legs at rest. One cannot help another whom one follows, and one is dissatisfied in one's mind.*

This is one of those occasions when you are unable to help someone, though you would like to. Be strong and remain true to yourself.

Line 3: *One keeps one's loins at rest and makes one's back rigid. The situation is perilous, and the heart glows with suppressed excitement.*

Being inflexible and stubborn causes problems. It may, among other things, result in self-willed as distinct from appropriate action, or being overbearing with others. Be wary of these faults, and take care to avoid being inflexible.

Line 4: *One keeps one's trunk at rest. There will be no error.*

Knowing when to act and when not to act is an attribute of wisdom. You must strive still to attain such clarity, becoming more selfless on the way. Then you will find peace.

Line 5: *One keeps one's jawbones at rest, so that one's words are all orderly. Occasion for repentance will disappear.*

Exercise caution and control over what you say, and let others contribute their comments and opinions.

Line 6: *One devotedly maintains one's restfulness. There will be good fortune.*

Tranquillity and peace are attained, a settled composure of mind and spirit. This is true harmony.

Hexagram 53
Chien—Gradually progressing

Component Trigrams
Primary: Sun—Wind (upper), Ken—The Mountain (lower). Nuclear: Li—Fire (above), K'an—Water (below).

Keywords
Wood, the mountain, patience, order, growth, steady advancement, deliberation.

Commentary
You will have to persist in a gradual progress towards the attainment of real self-improvement and the ability to exercise a good influence on others. By progressing in small, successive steps you will be assured of omitting nothing important. You will also be a laudable example to others around you. And when you finally attain your goal you will then be able to savour the sense of satisfaction and achievement. Make sure as you progress that your conduct and motives remain correct and orderly. This, in conjunction with your conscientious sense of purpose, will result in improvement for yourself and for those in your close circle. Maintaining this constant effort at self-improvement on a long-term plan which does not look for short-term rewards, is no different from making steady progress to a worthy outcome that has benefits for all.

Judgement

The marriage of a young lady: good fortune. There will be advantage in being firm and correct.

Undertakings must proceed at their own particular pace, you can't just force them to proceed at your arbitrarily willed pace. This is particularly true of those undertakings involving other people. To effect your own self-improvement and heighten your awareness will also take the length of time that is required.

Interpretation

The trigrams represent a tree on top of a mountain. The tree's development is slow and gradual, and as it grows it is able to increasingly provide shade and other kinds of enrichment for its environment.

Image

A tree above a mountain. The wise man attains to and maintains his extraordinary virtue, and makes the manners of the people good.

In order to have an influence for the good on others you have to have reached a position of authority and respect, where your attitude and conduct is regarded as providing an example to be followed. These things only happen over a long period of time.

Line readings

Line 1: *The wild geese gradually approach the shore. A young officer in similar circumstances will be in a position of danger, and be spoken against; but there will be no error.*

You are setting out on a journey and will be crossing uncharted territory, with no familiar landmarks or people to guide you. You will have to progress cautiously. It would be advisable to pay attention to others who have something to say to you.

Line 2: *The wild geese gradually approach the large rocks, where they eat and drink joyfully and at ease. There will be good fortune.*

You feel more secure but the situation remains somewhat volatile and nervy. It would be a good idea to accept what other people may want to share with you.

Line 3: *The wild geese gradually advance to the dry plains. A husband goes on an expedition from which he does not return. A wife is pregnant, but will not nourish her child. There will be misfortune.*

You have been too forceful and impatient and have overstretched yourself. You are now in a precarious situation but you have no alternative but to continue forward with caution and vigilance.

Line 4: *The wild geese gradually advance to the trees. They may light on the flat branches. There will be no error.*

You find yourself in a situation that you were unprepared for, and that you are struggling to comprehend and cope with. You will have to sit tight and lay low for a while.

Line 5: *The wild geese gradually advance to the high mound. A wife for three years does not become pregnant; but in the end the natural issue cannot be prevented. There will be good fortune.*

Those in your close circle have been disturbed and unsettled by your achievements. Some are perhaps jealous and resentful and may wish to see you fail. Give them time. As you continue in your path they will become accustomed to the changes that you bring.

Line 6: *The wild geese gradually advance to the large heights beyond. Their feathers can be used as ornaments. There will be good fortune.*

Having attained your goal it is now time to turn in a new direction and aim for a new goal. You are now respected and admired by others. They are prepared to follow you and your example.

This is the beginning of favourable times for you. You can look forward to many new opportunities.

Hexagram 54
Kuei—The younger maiden marries

Component Trigrams
Primary: Chen—Thunder (upper), Tui—Marsh (lower). Nuclear: K'an—Water (above), Li—Fire (below).

Keywords
Thunder, marshes, autumn, decay, renewal, transitoriness.

Commentary
You are in a deteriorating situation when you may expect to have to face decay, shady-dealing and perhaps public scandal and disgrace. There may be turmoil and loss. Your relations with others may become frustratingly antagonistic and acrimonious. Even existing harmonious relationships may be disrupted and disordered, with painful consequences for all. Console yourself with the knowledge that these times are part of a cycle of change and will inevitably come to an end, and harmony will be restored. In the meantime you have no other recourse but to stoically endure your afflictions and sufferings as your inescapable fate.

Judgement
Action will bring misfortune and is in no way advantageous.

When a young maiden marries into a family she has to learn to adapt to and respect their ways of doing things; she cannot try and impose her own, or expect everyone to fit around her. She must be quietly observant and exercise tact, demonstrating an awareness and under-standing of her position and role in the family. She has to keep in mind that she is just one individual within a greater group.

Interpretation

The trigrams represent thunder over the marshes, indicating a time of autumnal decline. They also signify eldest son and youngest daughter. The hexagram as a whole concerns a young daughter marrying of her own free choice, and before her elder sister. Both these acts were for-bidden and regarded as serious challenges to the stability of the family and hence society. Also forbidden was the marriage of a young woman to an older man, as its motives were considered to be merely sensual and unstable. It is a highly inauspicious hexagram about the ending of harmonious social and political structures and practices. The hexa-gram conveys a sense of enormously significant and far-reaching end-ings and subsequent beginnings.

Image

Thunder above the waters of a marsh. The wise man having regard to the far-distant end, knows the mischief that may be done at the begin-ning.

When times are troubled and hard, when you suffer personal disap-pointments, and when you are keenly affected and afflicted by the break-down of harmonious relations with others, the wisest attitude to adopt is one of fatalism and stoic patience, consoled and comforted by the realization that in time things will calm down and become bearable again.

Line readings

Line 1: *The younger sister is married off in a position secondary to the first wife. A person lame on one leg who yet manages to tramp along. Going forward will be fortunate.*

You are in a situation where you may be tempted to act for your own improvement, but you must restrain yourself. The wisest thing just now is to adopt a low profile: do and say nothing that will draw attention to yourself.

Line 2: *The younger sister is blind of one eye, and yet able to see. There will advantage in her maintaining the firm correctness of a solitary widow.*

You are in a relationship with someone who has disillusioned you by their attitude or behaviour towards you. Others around you are aware of this.

Line 3: *The younger sister is in a mean position. She returns and accepts an ancillary position.*

You are never satisfied with what you have. Perhaps you are pursuing an unreal ideal.

Line 4: *The younger sister protracts the time. She may be late in being married, but the time will come.*

Don't be despondent about your long-desired but unrealized hopes or ambitions. Retain your optimism and your integrity and wait patiently for your desired opportunity. It will eventually come and everything will be fine.

Line 5: *The younger sister of the king was married, but her gown was not equal to the still younger sister who accompanied her in an inferior capacity. The moon almost full. There will be good fortune.*

Those who don't jump at the first opportunity that comes their way but are prepared to wait, are often the best rewarded. Perhaps you are being too ambitious or unrealistic in what you want, and it would therefore be better to chose a more attainable goal. Your chances of success may then improve and you will find what you are looking for.

Line 6: *The young lady bears a basket, but without anything in it. The gentleman slaughters the sheep, but without blood flowing from it. There will be no advantage in any way.*

You have to accept that you can't always satisfy the needs and desires of others or yourself. And anyway, it could be the case that something which seems valuable and desirable is in reality not that great at all.

Hexagram 55
Feng—Abundance

Component Trigrams
Primary: Chen—Thunder (upper), Li—Fire (lower). Nuclear: Tui—Marsh (above), Sun—Wind (below).

Keywords
Thunder, lightning, power, plenty, judicious action, opportunity.

Commentary
There is a powerful force for positive change in your life and you should take full advantage of it, as the auspicious period in front of you will end some time. Use good judgement in the actions you take. Settle any

unresolved disagreements. This is the time to launch new undertakings designed to further your fortunes. If you run your affairs with a shrewd intelligence and a readiness to take bold action when required, then you may be able to prolong your period of prosperity beyond the time when it would otherwise have come to a natural end. In your relations with others you should demonstrate the enthusiasm and optimism appropriate to one who is enjoying success and good fortune. Don't make the serious error of seeing each new rewarding opportunity as just another added and troublesome burden. Enjoy the rare feeling of being able to tackle almost anything and make a success of it.

Judgement

There will be progress and development. When a king has reached the point of abundance, there is no occasion to be anxious through fear of a change. Let him be as the sun at noon.

Although your time of great good fortune will not last forever, yet still you can relish it and enjoy it, enriching yourself and others by so doing. Perhaps it would be wise to move in the direction of a spiritual goal, having achieved your material goals.

Interpretation

In the hexagram, thunder is above lightning. Together they convey the idea of a dramatic thunderstorm which dispels all murkiness and negativity, and results in an all-illuminating brilliance and clarity. From this we have the suggestions of fullness and abundance, and the sweeping away of all obstacles. But even such an irresistible force is subject to change in time.

Image

Thunder and lightning combine. The wise man decides cases of litigation, and apportions punishments with exactness.

It is necessary to have peace of mind and a clear and untroubled spirit to be in harmony and at one with yourself. Then you can see clearly and act judiciously.

Line readings

Line 1: *One meets with one's mate. Though both be of the same character, there will be no error. Advance will call forth approval.*

It would be a good thing to work for a time with another who has an attribute or resource that you lack. But you must remember that the partnership will be temporary and so be prepared to end it when the time comes.

Line 2: *One is surrounded by screens so large and thick that at midday one can see*

*from them the stars. If one go and try to enlighten the ruler, one will make oneself be
viewed with suspicion and dislike. Let one cherish one's feeling of sincere devotion
that one may thereby move the ruler's mind, and there will be good fortune.*

Someone has deliberately and maliciously set out to 'eclipse' you and
they are beginning to achieve their aim. Accept it and do nothing about
it, as good will come of it.

Line 3: *One has an additional screen of a large and thick banner, through which at
midday one can see the small star. In the darkness one breaks one's right arm; but
there will be no error.*

There is nothing you can do except patiently wait.

Line 4: *One is in a tent so large and thick that at midday one can see from it the
stars. But one meets with another, undivided like oneself. There will be good fortune.*

The situation is improving for you. You have encountered the person
referred to in line one.

Line 5: *One brings around one the men of brilliant ability. There will be occasion
for congratulation and praise. There will be good fortune.*

In your moment of imminent success you do not forget those who
are around you. You consolidate your bonds with them and listen respectfully to them.

Line 6: *One has made one's house large, but it only serves as a screen to one's
household. When one looks at one's door, it is still, and there is nobody about it. For
three years no-one is to be seen. There will be misfortune.*

You cannot enjoy your just rewards as you have deliberately removed
yourself from others and cannot share your good fortune with them.
You are isolated and alone. This emotional and spiritual barrenness in
the midst of plenty is your creation and your responsibility.

Hexagram 56
Lu—The traveller abroad

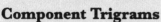

Component Trigrams

Primary: Li—Fire (upper), Ken—The Mountain (lower). Nuclear: Tui—
Marsh (above), Sun—Wind (below).

Keywords

Fire, the mountain, the stranger, restraint, exclusion, humility.

Commentary

You should not look for any lasting outcomes or rewards from your
present situation. It is only a temporary place for you and you will not
be able to change your status as an outsider. If you maintain your mod-

esty and integrity, though, you will come to no harm and will remain on target for your goal. Rely on your inner strength to see you through the present difficulties, and accept the fact that you will make little headway towards your chosen goal during this time. Don't try to force any issues or try to impose yourself on the situation. Instead of trying to combat your unsatisfactory status as an outsider, focus instead on your own virtues and qualities and learn to appreciate what can be gained from your condition of solitariness.

Judgement

There may be some little attainment and progress. If the stranger or traveller be firm and correct as he ought to be, there will be good fortune.

A selfless regard for those he meets as he passes is a worthy and admirable quality in a traveller. His small kindnesses will have a greater reward.

Interpretation

In the trigrams, fire burns on the mountain. The mountain is immobile but the fire moves around in every direction, with no fixed aim. The image suggest is that of the traveller, who is a stranger in a strange land. The trigrams move in opposite directions—the fire burns upwards, and the mountain forces downwards—and this indicates that the contact between them will be of a temporary nature. However, things can still be learned as one moves around, even if one is not explicitly promoting progress towards an aim.

Image

Fire atop the mountain. The wise man exerts his wisdom and caution in the use of punishments and not allowing litigations to continue.

If you find you have to judge others, try to do it as quickly and as objectively as possible, showing fair-mindedness.

Line readings

Line 1: *The stranger is mean and meanly occupied. It is thus that he brings on himself further calamity.*

To waste time on things which are of no importance is to squander opportunities for making progress towards a worthwhile goal

Line 2: *The stranger occupies his lodging-house, carrying with him his means of livelihood, and is provided with good and trusty servants.*

Wherever he is a wise man has a clarity of self-knowledge, never feels lost to himself. He is always true to himself. No matter where he finds himself, he can rely on his own inner resources and remain calm and truly himself.

Line 3: *The stranger burns his lodging-house and loses his servants. However firm and correct he try to be, he will be in peril.*

If you try to get involved in something which doesn't really concern you, you will get your fingers burned. Exercise self-restraint and discipline. Perhaps your friends don't seem to be in tune with you at the moment. Be patient and they will join you once again.

Line 4: *The traveller is in a resting-place, and has also the means of livelihood and the axe, but is still saying, 'I am not at ease in my mind.'*

If you seem to have resolved the difficulties and problems that have been bothering you, be cautious. This is only a temporary respite and you cannot rely on it. You must look for real and permanent answers to your difficulties.

Line 5: *One shoots a pheasant. One will lose one's arrow, but in the end will obtain praise and a high position.*

Even though you are among new and unknown people you will be able to establish a rapport or a working accord with them. This helps you feel more secure.

Line 6: *A bird burns its nest. The stranger first laughs, then cries out. He has lost his ox-like docility too readily and too easily. There will be misfortune.*

You have relaxed your self-discipline and restraint in this situation and acted unwisely, with painful and upsetting consequences for yourself and others. You have behaved like a fool and shown a lack of respect for other people. What's done is done, you cannot undo it. All you can do is find ways of coping and dealing with the situation you have created.

Hexagram 57
Sun—Wind

Component Trigrams

Primary: Sun—Wind (upper), Sun—Wind (lower). Nuclear: Li—Fire (above), Tui—Marsh (below).

Keywords

wind, gentle, repetition, penetration, communication, authority, subtlety, harmony, obedience.

Commentary

In order to succeed in a worthy aim you will have to be persistent, and seek to exercise your influence on others. Others will be necessary to help you overcome any problems. You will have to make fully clear to others what you require of them, repeating your instructions if necessary, so that they can understand and fulfil your wishes. It may not be easy to communicate what you want, but if others don't understand you and your project is stymied then the fault is yours, not theirs. It may be a good idea to call on the help of someone more experienced who you respect and value. Tactics such as emphasizing your status or prestige or trying to insist on your authority in order to bring others to do what you want, will merely be futile gestures. You will have to concentrate, and be resourceful in finding ways to get your message across and your intention fulfilled. You also have to ensure that the message you are sending out is the one that is being received. If you succeed in effective communication and are given relevant and useful help, then you will make some moderate progress.

Judgement
There will be some little attainment and progress. There will be advantage in movement in any direction whatsoever. It will be advantageous to see the great man.

Chose your goal and persevere towards it with unfailing calmness, gentleness and humility, and you will succeed. Seeking guidance from a wiser person would be good for you.

Interpretation
Wind is represented in the upper and lower trigrams. Two attributes of wind are gentleness and penetration. The topic of the hexagram is the persistent, pervasive and penetrating power of influence that a superior has over his subordinates; their obedience to his will—like a blade of grass that bends before a strong wind. The hexagram emphasizes the need for subtlety and repetition as required, in our efforts to get others to do our bidding. There must be thoughtfulness and intelligence in communications with subordinates; and assignments and tasks delegated by a superior should be faithfully implemented.

Image
Winds following each other. The wise man reiterates his orders and secures the practice of his affairs.

In order to exercise your influence effectively it may be better to consult with your own inner wisdom or seek the wise help of another, before you attempt to do anything with other people.

Line readings
Line 1: *Now one advances, now one recedes. It would be advantageous of one to have the firm correctness of the brave soldier.*

Don't vacillate. Decide promptly what you want and then set out immediately to achieve it.

Line 2: *One is beneath a couch, and employs diviners and exorcists in a way bordering on confusion. There will be good fortune and no error.*

You must find out what malicious or malevolent level of activity or plotting is going on behind closed doors and who are the perpetrators or plotters. Obtain help from others who are experienced and capable of dealing with such a situation.

Line 3: *One penetrates only by violent and repeated efforts. There will be occasion for regret.*

Now is not the time to wait and give something further thought. You must act now or you will live to regret it.

Line 4: *All occasion for repentance has passed away. One takes game for its threefold use in one's hunting.*

Maintaining your integrity and self-respect, and the correctness of your motives and conduct, will give you the peace of mind and the strength to help others.

Line 5: *With firm correctness there will be good fortune. All occasion for repentance will disappear, and all one's movements will be advantageous. There may have been no good beginning, but there will be a good end. Three days before making any changes, let one give notice of them; and three days after, let one reconsider them. There will thus be good fortune.*

If things aren't going well then it is time to stop and think about the situation and decide on the best action to take in order to remedy it. After acting you should then assess the results. If you haven't fully achieved what you set out to do, no matter. You have done your best for the time being and it is time to move on.

Line 6: *One is beneath a couch, having lost the axe with which one executed one's decisions. However firm and correct one may try to be, there will be misfortune.*

Be very careful. You have overreached yourself and become too involved in a very dark and disturbing situation. Withdraw from it without delay as it is a threat and a danger to you, and you do not have the experience to deal with it or the necessary resources to protect yourself.

Hexagram 58
Tui—The delighted

Component Trigrams

Primary: Tui—Marsh (upper), Tui—Marsh (lower). Nuclear: Sun—Wind (above), Li—Fire (below).

Keywords

Marsh, serenity, contentment, satisfaction, freedom from anxiety and doubt.

Commentary

This is an auspicious hexagram. Your are in harmony with yourself, materially and spiritually, and have an honest integrity that makes you true to yourself and others. You have no need, have no use, for negative or fearful thoughts and feelings. In your relations with others be generous, modest and sincere and strive to comprehend and sympathize with their troubles and worries. If you are able to do all this with true joy, you will experience serene happiness and will be well-equipped to overcome any obstacles you come across.

Judgement

There will be progress and attainment. It will be advantageous to be firm and correct.

Through strength of purpose, persistent effort, and faithfulness to the integrity of one's true nature, you have attained harmony and happiness and are an example and a willing source of guidance to others.

Interpretation

The hexagram has the trigram Tui as both primary trigrams. It represents peaceful water as in a marsh or a lake, and suggests delight and joy. The hexagram signifies a state of serene happiness that consists of a sense of personal wholeness and well-being, and the best of relations with others. The hexagram does not wholly exclude the presence or possibility of adversity, but its concern is to emphasize the all-powerful and ultimately all-conquering human faculty of chosing to live joyfully, no matter what the circumstances.

Image

A double lake. The wise man encourages the conversation of friends and the stimulus of their common practice.

Mutual and reciprocal influence and help, brings reward and happiness.

Line readings

Line 1: *The pleasure of inward harmony. There will be good fortune.*

You are happy with your circumstances and achievements.

Line 2: *The pleasure arising from inward sincerity. There will be good fortune. Occasion for good fortune will disappear.*

Treat others with sincere respect and don't flaunt or gloat over your successes.

Line 3: *One brings round oneself whatever can give pleasure. There will be misfortune.*

You are not nourishing or cultivating your inner self, seeming to be shallowly content with superficial, material sources and means of pleasure. You will lose touch with yourself and lose your way completely unless you mend your ways.

Line 4: *One deliberates about what to seek one's pleasure in, and one is not at rest. One borders on what would be injurious, but there will be cause for joy.*

You are unhappy because you are putting everything in your life under an analytical microscope. Open your eyes and life to the higher things above. Set yourself to achieve the highest goals.

Line 5: *One trusts in another who would injure one. The situation is perilous.*

Your situation is becoming vulnerable and there is a strong likelihood that you will be exploited. Be vigilant and cautious.

Line 6: *One's pleasure leads and attracts others.*

To revel in pleasure for its own sake is dangerous. It leads eventually to an enervating sense of boredom and restless dissatisfaction. You have lost touch with yourself and your sense of direction. You must restore your self-discipline and sense of purpose. Only then can you experience true delight.

Hexagram 59
Huan—Dispersal

Component Trigrams.
Primary: Sun—Wind (upper), K'an—Water (lower). Nuclear: Ken—Mountain (upper), Chen—Thunder.

Keywords
Wind, water, division, dissipation, piety, righteousness, order, correct action.

Commentary
There are disruptive influences at work but if you adopt the right attitude and conduct you will be able to resist these influences and maintain proper order. You must apply yourself to attaining a worthy goal and cultivating a virtuous character and you will have the ability to overcome any threats to stability and harmony. Seek help and guidance from the wisdom of your elders. It may be necessary for you to commit yourself to a large and perilous enterprise. As long as you act with sincerity and honesty, and remain true to your principles, there will be no danger to you.

Judgement

There will be progress and success. The king goes to his ancestral temple; it will be advantageous to cross the great stream. It will be advantageous to be firm and correct.

Seeking spiritual union with others who share your spiritual concerns and attributes is the way to overcome problems. Cooperation and harmonious relations is the way forward.

Interpretation

In the hexagram there is wind above water, and the water ripples and disperses. The hexagram cautions against the spreading and cumulative effects of an individual or a group's divergence from the right and true course. These aimless and divisive forces can be combated by an honest and sincere commitment to worthy aims. Persevering in this course will restore proper order. The upper trigram also signifies wood, which suggests the boat that will be used to 'cross the great stream': carry out a crucial task.

Image

Wind moves above the water. The ancient kings presented offerings to God and established the ancestral temple.

Individuals can become isolated from each other and their own spiritual natures. They must come together as a people with one spiritual purpose; this will truly unite them.

Line readings

Line 1: *One is engaged in rescuing from the impending misfortune, and having the assistance of, a strong horse. There will be good fortune.*

You must do something about the conflict and confusion around you. If you don't act promptly the situation will get even more complicated and difficult too solve.

Line 2: *Amid the confusion, one hurries to one's contrivance for security. All occasion for repentance will disappear.*

You are taking a good look at yourself and don't like what you see. You must make the effort and cultivate the self-discipline to correct what is at fault in your character and principles.

Line 3: *One discards any regard for one's own person. There will be no occasion for repentance.*

Jettisoning unnecessary personal needs and wants is a good and worthy thing to do.

Line 4: *One scatters the different parties in the state; which leads to good fortune.*

From the dispersion he collects again good men standing out, a crowd like a mound, which is what ordinary men would not have thought of.

Withdrawing from those around you will allow you to concentrate on a task and bring it to a successful conclusion. It also permits you a clearer view of your companions and allows you to make sounder judgements about them.

Line 5: *Amidst the dispersion, one issues great announcements as the perspiration flows from one's body. One scatters abroad also the accumulations in the royal granaries. There will be no error.*

You are the linchpin of others' cooperative efforts, a focal point of ideas and inspiration for correcting the faults of the past. This is a good position.

Line 6: *One disposes of one's bloody wounds, and goes and separates oneself from one's anxious fears. There will be no error.*

You must pull back from the activities and concerns that you have been wholeheartedly and enthusiastically involved in, as you are getting carried away and losing sight of yourself and your aims. You need a sobering rest and a chance to rediscover yourself and your priorities.

Hexagram 60
Chieh—Restraint

Component Trigrams
Primary: K'an—Water (upper), Tui—Marsh (lower). Nuclear: Ken—The Mountain (above), Chen—Thunder (below).

Keywords
Water, marshes, regulation, proper restraint, moderation, time, regular division.

Commentary
This is a situation where observing restraint and self-imposed limitations will be necessary in order to avoid the dangers caused by lack of control and poor judgement. Moderation, flexibility and appropriateness must be the watchwords. You must apply constraints to your dealings with others which are appropriate to the circumstances and help to maintain good order and relations. You will have to monitor the distribution of resources, fine-tuning when necessary to cope with changes in the situation. Rigid adherence to strict rules and regulations will be ineffectual and will encourage a destructive lack of thought and judgement. If a certain amount of sensible flexibility is promoted, con-

cerning adherence to established standards, then you will meet with success in your undertakings. But if you rely on the unthinking application of familiar procedures then you will be severely disillusioned. Be moderate and show good judgement in your relations with others and you will progress.

Judgement
There will be progress and attainment. If the limitations are severe and difficult, they should not be made permanent.

Constraints and limitations are necessary for balance and good order. But there must be moderation and flexibility. Wise discernment and judgement are required.

Interpretation
In the trigram structure there is water above marshes. If the marsh is allocated too much water it will flood and overflow; if it receives too little water it will dry up. The concept of the hexagram is proper regulation, sensitive restraint and ordered distribution. The lines of the hexagram reproduce the pattern of the joints on a bamboo stalk. This also contributes to the idea of standardized rules and necessary limitation. The hexagram teaches about the correct application of regulatory power in dealing with people and allocating resources.

Image
Water fills the lake. The wise man constructs his methods of numbering and measurement, and discusses points of virtue and conduct.

You have to discover for yourself your limitations. Exceeding your limitations is a waste of time and energy and ends in failure.

Line readings
Line 1: *One does not quit the courtyard outside one's door. There will be no error.*

This is not the time to act. You should look within yourself for answers you seek, and when the time comes to act, you will know it.

Line 2: *One does not quit the courtyard inside one's gate. There will be misfortune.*

Grasp opportunities when they present themselves. You may not get a second chance.

Line 3: *One does not observe the proper regulations, in which case one shall lament. But there will be no-one to blame but oneself.*

You have shown no moderation and have wallowed in excess. You are now feeling responsible and remorseful. You realize the harm caused by exceeding your limitations and abandoning restraint.

Line 4: *One is quietly and naturally attentive to all regulations. There will be progress and success.*

You must learn to be able to calmly take the moderate path of sensible and comfortable restraint, creating a reservoir of energy for yourself.

Line 5: *One sweetly and acceptably enacts one's regulations. There will be good fortune. The onward progress with them will afford ground for admiration.*

Make sure that the limitations you set yourself or others observe the needs of the individual as well as the needs of the situation.

Line 6: *One enacts severe and difficult regulations. Even with firmness and correctness there will be misfortune. But though there be cause for repentance, it will by and by disappear.*

You have been too severe on yourself or others. Relax a little.

Hexagram 61
Chung Fu—The truth within

Component Trigrams
Primary: Sun—Wind (upper), Tui—Marsh (lower). Nuclear: Ken—The Mountain (above), Chen—Thunder (below).

Keywords
Wind, marshes, truth, transformation, flawlessness, deliberation, wisdom, humility.

Commentary
This is a highly auspicious time for your spiritual development. Cultivate the strength and power of your inner self and you will be able to accomplish any difficult undertaking. If there is such an undertaking at hand you should tackle it now, applying yourself to it with confidence in the worthiness of your aims and the integrity of your character. Your ultimate aim will not be to impose yourself on others but to become as humble and selfless as possible, and move forward with great sincerity and honesty on the right path.

Judgement
The truth within moves even pigs and fish, and leads to good fortune. There will be advantage in crossing the great stream. There will be advantage in being firm and correct.

There is great power and influence in the inner virtues of truth and sincerity. You can reach and communicate with the different inner natures of individuals, and can unite them in harmony to cooperate in the accomplishment of a great undertaking, which will have a favourable outcome.

Interpretation

The hexagram's structure has wind above the marsh. The wind penetrates in all directions and energizes the collected waters of the marsh. Even secret and cloistered things are reached by the wind's power. The wind signifies the limitless and unassailable power of complete sincerity and truth. The two broken yin lines in the centre of the hexagram associate perfect truth with emptiness, absence—perhaps of ego, materialism, illusion etc. The Sun trigram also represents wood and here suggest a boat of special emptiness which will allow the undertaking of a special and important task i.e. 'crossing the great stream.'

Image

Wind above the waters of a marsh. The wise man deliberates about cases of litigation and delays the infliction of death.

You need to recognize and respect the innermost nature of others if you want to truly understand them and gain their respect in return.

Line readings

Line 1: *One rests in oneself. There will be good fortune. If one looks to another, one would not find rest.*

You are being dishonest and insincere with others in order to exploit them for selfish reasons.

Line 2: *One is like the crane crying out in her hidden place and her young ones responding to her. It is as if it were said, 'I have a cup of good spirits,' and the response were, 'I will partake of it with you.'*

You will experience the need to respond to the promptings of inner truth, either from your own inner nature or that of another.

Line 3: *One has met with one's mate. Now one beats one's drum, now one leaves off. Now one weeps, and now one sings.*

You have lost your integrity and self-respect by identifying too closely with another person.

Line 4: *One is like the moon nearly full, and like a horse in a chariot whose fellow disappears. There will be no error.*

You must seek solace and strength within as someone close withdraws from you.

Line 5: *One is perfectly sincere and links others to one in closest union. There will be no error.*

Your sincerity and honesty is the core around which your group coheres. You must decide if you want the group to continue. It is not your responsibility if the group fails after you withdraw.

Line 6: *One is like the crowing cock trying to mount to heaven. Even with firm correctness there will be misfortune.*

Don't seek to make what you say more impressive than its truth sufficiently makes it. Take care over how you express your self and avoid exaggerating.

Hexagram 62
Hsiao Kua—Exceeding in smallness

Component Trigrams
Primary: Chen—Thunder (upper), Ken—The Mountain (lower). Nuclear: Tui—Marshes (above), Sun—Wind (below).

Keywords
Thunder, the mountain, appropriateness, humility, discretion.

Commentary
This is a time for you to modestly rein in your ambitions and efforts, and put them on hold. Only when appropriate circumstances present themselves should you look to humbly progress a little way along the path to your goals. You are not abandoning the correct and true path, though. You will remain committed to the perfection of honesty and sincerity, but you will proceed by more humble directions towards that worthy goal. Persist with determination in this new path of small achievements in the correct spirit of humility and virtue and you will gain noteworthy success. These small changes that you modestly embark on will accrue disproportionately great rewards.

Judgement
There will be progress and attainment. But it will be advantageous to be firm and correct. Efforts in small affairs are advised. Efforts in large affairs are not advised. The notes of the bird on the wing descend, and it is better to descend than to rise up. There will in this way be great good fortune.

If you strive for more modest aims and show persistence and virtue in your efforts, then you will receive significant rewards.

Interpretation
There is thunder above the mountain. The sound echoes with great power and volume, but this fades as the thunder recedes. The hexagram is concerned with modest ambition, astute self-restraint and the sensible knack of knowing when not to go for big changes. The shape of the hexagram suggests a bird. Its wings are the pairs of yin lines at the top and bottom. The action of the bird demonstrates the wisdom of

humility. It is sensible to descend to a handy branch rather than continue to soar into the attractive but inhospitable wild blue yonder.

Image

Thunder beyond the hill. The wise man in his conduct exceeds in humility, in mourning exceeds in sorrow, and in his expenditure exceeds in economy.

Be humble and modest in your conduct and your ambitions. Attend to self-knowledge and integrity. Be sensitive and responsive to the changing times.

Line readings

Line 1: *A bird flies and ascends till the issue is misfortune.*

You have jumped the gun and acted before the time was right and you were properly prepared. You cannot carry out what you intended to do and you are now in a vulnerable and dangerous position. You will have to be very careful.

Line 2: *One passes by one's grandfather and meets with one's grandmother; not attempting anything against one's ruler, but meeting him as his minister. There will be no error.*

Don't be overambitious. Be satisfied with what you have already achieved.

Line 3: *One takes no extraordinary precautions against danger; and some in consequence find opportunity to assail and injure one. There will be misfortune.*

If you don't show caution then you foolishly put yourself at risk. Given the opportunity, others will take advantage of your naivety.

Line 4: *One falls into no error but meets the exigencies of the situation, without exceeding one's natural course. If one goes forward, there will be peril, and one must be cautious. There is no occasion to be using firmness perpetually.*

This is not a good time for you to take the lead in anything. You will provoke conflict with another. Withdraw from action and modestly and discreetly retire into the background. Remain true to yourself.

Line 5: *Dense clouds, but no rain, coming from the borders in the west. The prince shoots his arrow, and takes the bird in a cave.*

This is not the time for great advancement in your fortunes. Don't expect it or try for it, because you will suffer disappointment if you do.

Line 6: *One does not meet the exigency of the situation, and exceeds one's proper course. A bird flying far aloft. There will be misfortune. Calamity and self-produced injury.*

You are following an unwise and unrealistic path of ambition that will only lead you to failure. You should swallow your pride and come back down to earth. But the choice is yours.

Hexagram 63
Chi Chi—Having crossed the stream

Component Trigrams

Primary: K'an—Water (upper), Li—Fire (lower). Nuclear: Li—Fire (above), K'an—Water (below).

Keywords

Fire, water, balance, imbalance, caution, prudence, consolidation.

Commentary

You have worked hard in difficult circumstances to achieve your aim of balance and harmony, and at this point you may feel that you can withdraw, as the situation is all but resolved and success achieved. But to do this would be an error. It would disturb the balance and order you have already achieved. And though the major work has been done, something still remains to be done.

There are small tasks required to ensure that the gains already made are not lost. In a modest and calm manner you must go on, remaining committed to the true and proper way of doing things, and finish the job you started. You must do this while remembering, with due and humble acceptance of fate, that nothing ever lasts and everything is subject to change. With astute and refining adjustments your efforts should be consummated with final and rewarding success. Afterwards, however, you must expect an inevitable decline from the heights of success.

Judgement

Progress and success in small matters. There will be advantage in being firm and correct. There has been good fortune in the beginning; there may be disorder in the end.

Keep in mind that a situation that has been brought to order and harmony can quickly become unbalanced and disorganized again. You must persevere and pay attention to small details. Remain cautious and prepared.

Interpretation

The hexagram suggests water hanging above fire. Release the water and it douses the fire. Heighten the flames and the water evaporates. But neither happens as the elements of the situation are in balance, neither invading the other's position. This suggestion of order and balance is added to by the regularly alternating yin and yang lines. Also in relation to the idea of symmetrical balance: the upper primary trigram

247

represents danger, but the lower represents intelligent foresight. (Note also the symmetrical inversion of the nuclear trigrams). The name of the hexagram refers to a situation of completeness and success at the end of a long and testing undertaking. However, there are still some things to be done to finally secure the success.

Image

Water above fire. The wise man thinks of evil that may come, and beforehand guards against it.

At a time of balance and order the wise man begins preparing for the bad times that will follow.

Line readings

Line 1: *A driver drags back his wheel; a fox has wet his tail. There will be no error.*

Don't get just get swept along with the changes and developments that are taking place. You must go at your own pace and follow only the dictates of your conscience and your judgement.

Line 2: *A wife has lost her carriage-screen. There is no occasion to go in pursuit of it. In seven days she will find it.*

A recognition or a union that you seek is not being granted. You must accept this. Cultivate your inner self and bide your time. The situation will change.

Line 3: *One attacked the Demon region, but was three years in subduing it. Small men should not be employed in such enterprises.*

When you are in the process of developing your knowledge, your curiosity and desire to learn may inadvertently lead you into intimidating or upsetting others. Take care over this.

Line 4: *One has rags provided against any leak in one's boat, and is on guard all day long.*

Even the most favourable of times will end, and change into times of misfortune and hardship. Remain prepared at all times for unexpected problems and setbacks.

Line 5: *The neighbour in the east slaughters an ox for his sacrifice; but this is not equal to the small spring sacrifice of the neighbour in the west, whose sincerity receives the blessing.*

Don't try to fool people or show them disrespect. Be honest and sincere. Remain true to yourself.

Line 6: *One has even one's head immersed. The situation is perilous.*

Having completed an undertaking and effected a change, whether for the good or the worse, you must continue to move on. You cannot stay where you are. Neither can you return to the way things were. Things done, are as they always will be. Leave them behind and keep going forward.

Hexagram 64
Wei Chi—Having not yet
crossed the stream

Component Trigrams

Primary: Li—Fire (upper), K'an—Water (lower). Nuclear: K'an—Water (above), Li—Fire (below).

Keywords

Fire, water, disharmony, incoherence, lack of order, caution, prudence.

Commentary

The time of harmony and balance has passed and disorder has taken its place. This is the new situation you find yourself in. Big challenges lie ahead as you strive to restore coherence. But disorder and disharmony are natural aspects of human life and the ability to respond appropriately to such situations is a great advantage. Examine closely the basis of the present situation and make sensible and realistic assessments about what it is possible to achieve. You must tackle the problems with careful thought and planning. Don't try to be clever in any way, or to take short-cuts. You should spend time and effort in developing harmonious relations with others. Your action to turn the situation around should be characterized by honest and humble persistence and a determination never to deviate from your principled motives and conduct. In this way you will be promoting the emergence of new order and harmony.

Judgement

Progress and success. Yet for a young fox that has nearly crossed the stream, but has immersed his tail in the water, there will be no advantage in any way.

Immature bravado, naivety and inexperience will find only trouble and problems when it tries to act or make real progress. Caution and preparedness are required, particularly at the moment of success.

Interpretation

In the hexagram, fire is above water. Fire burns upwards. Water flows downwards. And never the twain shall meet. The two forces are not in harmony and neither can affect the other. The hexagram suggests forces which are polar opposites but are not arranged so that they are complementary to each other. The arduous effort to create order out of such disorder will also require great caution and firm discipline. The hexagram's name refers to the tremendous undertaking not yet completed.

Image

Fire above water. The wise man carefully discriminates among the qualities of things, and the different positions they naturally occupy.

Striving to ensure that things are in their proper places and in their proper relations to one another is how order is created. When things are in balance and harmony then all is well.

Line readings

Line 1: *One is like a fox whose tail gets immersed. There will be occasion for regret.*
It is not yet time to act. Be more patient and less impulsive.

Line 2: *One drags back one's carriage-wheel. With firmness and correctness there will be good fortune.*
Keep waiting patiently, but prepare for action by planning well.

Line 3: *With the state of things not yet remedied, one advances on; which will lead to evil. But there will be advantage in trying to cross the great stream.*
Don't leap into action. It may be better to enlist the help of others in taking a new direction rather than attempting to forge ahead on your own.

Line 4: *By firm correctness one obtains good fortune, so that all occasion for repentance disappears. Let one stir oneself up, as if one were invading the Demon region, where for three years rewards will come to one and one's troops from the great kingdom.*
You must act now, and expect to encounter trying difficulties as you go forward. You must not deviate from your course as you engage with problems. Your struggle is wresting order from disorder.

Line 5: *By firm correctness one obtains good fortune, and has no occasion for repentance. One has the brightness of a wise man, and the possession of sincerity. There will be good fortune.*
You have accomplished what you set out to do and things are falling into their final places. You are in the midst of a new beginning and you feel satisfied and full of clarity. Others around you are aware of this.

Line 6: *One is full of confidence and therefore feasting quietly. There will be no error. If one cherish this confidence till one is like the fox who gets his head immersed, one will fail of what is right.*
You can celebrate final success with others. But don't forsake your principles or lose your integrity by indulging in excess.

Palmistry

Introduction

Palmistry ranks among the most ancient forms of learning and knowledge. Some palmists justify its study by a text from the Book of Job (Job 37:7—'He sealeth up the hand of every man; that all men may know his work'), but it is known to have been understood in Egypt and, farther back still, among the Hindus.

The art of palmistry takes its place as a serious study in which the deductions are as reliable, if the student can be earnest and intelligent, as those of any other system founded on ordered knowledge.

Here the art of palmistry is reduced to its clearest and simplest form.

Whether we like to think so or not, in our first impression of someone at least, we all tend to judge a person's face to be an index of their character, and from its form and expression predicate the qualities of its owner. Painters and sculptors pay enormous attention to the faithful rendering of the faces of their subjects; the best examples being those that truly show a personality behind the artistry. There are also those who claim that certain physical characteristics of the face point to certain emotional and intellectual characteristics in the personality.

The hand

An expression of character

To a great extent the personal qualities of the hand have also been recognized, the expressions 'a useful hand,' 'an artistic hand,' and so forth, being commonly heard. But too often hands are neglected, and even eminent painters and sculptors frequently give unreal, characterless hands to their subjects.

Fingertips

There are an infinite variety of papillary ridges on the finger tips, and their arrangement is used as a means of identification. An impression of the fingertips, i.e. the process of fingerprinting, is very often used by the forensic division of the police for this purpose because each person's fingerprints have the property of being unique.

Variety in hands

What is true of the part is, in this case, true of the whole, as the marking of the hands generally presents just as great a variety as the marking of the finger tips, no two hands being alike in this way. This is easily seen in living hands, and is well shown in the nature-printed plates in this volume.

But the markings of the hands are not the only difference: colour, size, shape, and relative bulk of parts, also vary. All these qualities and the lines have a certain connection, and one observer dealing only with the outline, and another dealing only with the lines, will discover many things in common. Of course, the observer who deals with all these differences will observe most.

Hand lore

From the earliest ages of which we have record, there have been some who have paid great attention to the hands, and by much study have learned not only to judge the character, but to read past events, and even profess to foretell the future. In recent years there has been a great revival of the study. Different writers have compared readings, and these readings have been verified in large numbers of hands, so that year by year the results are becoming more exact.

Interdependence of parts

To understand why hands vary so much it is important to know something about their structure, and to remember that all parts of the body are interdependent, as, owing to nervous connection, one part cannot be affected without influencing to a greater or lesser degree one or more other parts.

Bony framework

The framework of the hand is the bony skeleton, the appearance of which is now familiar owing to modern radiography. The framework regulates in great part the size of the hand. The eight small bones of the wrist are arranged in two rows; from these start the five metacarpal bones, which form the palm of the hand (as far as the first knuckles), one supporting the thumb, and one supporting each of the fingers. Each finger contains three phalanges, the last being widened out to form a support for the nail. These are named by anatomists, 'first', 'second', and 'third', from the palm down (however, palmists have reversed this order, calling the nail-bearing phalanx the first). The thumb is attached to a short metacarpal, which is much more freely movable than the others, and has only two phalanges.

The joints

These bones are joined together by capsules surrounding the joints, by ligaments strengthening the capsules, and by the tendons which pass over the joints. Sometimes the joints have very little movement, but in all the phalanges, and in the metacarpal bone of the thumb, there is free movement.

The muscles

The muscles or flesh, and the tendons form a considerable part of the bulk of the hand. Some of these tendons come from the muscles of the forearm. The muscles of the palm are those which run to the fingers, forming the 'mounts' at the base of each finger and rather inclining to the little finger side, and the large mass forming the ball of the thumb. These muscles assist the thumb to perform its varied movements, the smaller mass of muscles running along the opposite edge of the hand to the little finger.

The skin

To understand the lines on the hand, the structure and function of the skin of the hand must be first understood.

The skin consists of two layers. The deeper is the dermis or true skin. It contains a large number of nerves and blood vessels, and is joined to the structures below by connective tissue containing fat in the meshes, while above, it is protected by the upper scaly layer of the skin—the epidermis.

Papillary ridges

The organs of touch are contained in papillae. These papillae are very numerous in the palm of the hand, and on the palm surface of the fingers, there being on the fingertips about 2400 to the square inch. They are arranged in rows, and so form ridges. These ridges are notched by short transverse furrows, into which the ducts of the sweat glands open. The epidermis covers these papillae, being thicker over the hollows than over the summits of the ridges. The papillae do not show as plainly on the surface of the epidermis as they do on the true skin when the epidermis has been removed, as by blistering. They can, however, be easily seen through a magnifying glass, and it is the papillary ridges which give rise to the peculiar fine markings shown on the finger tips and elsewhere in the accompanying prints.

Nerves of the papillae

In most of the papillae are tactile corpuscles. These are the true organs of touch, and delicacy of touch depends to a large extent on their number. Each tactile corpuscle contains a filament of nerve, and is freely supplied with bloodvessels. Each nerve communicates directly with the brain, and the size of small objects is estimated through touch by the number of tactile corpuscles which send impressions along their special nerve-path to the brain.

The lines

The lines on the hand must not be confounded with the papillary markings. They are spaces where the papillae are wanting, and where the surface of the epidermis is comparatively smooth, flat, and depressed.

Fold lines

The larger lines correspond to folds, and vary in position with the varying bulk of the muscles. By contracting the hands in different ways, the coincidence of these lines with the folds can be seen.

Lines produced in connection with the nervous system

There are, however, numerous lines that cannot be turned into folds by any contraction of muscles. Their existence must be due to some other cause. It is at this point that we must look at their connection with the nervous system.

During the course of an illness in which the nervous system is much affected, crowds of new lines will develop, of which, when health is restored, some may disappear. Similarly, in mental illness many crossing and interlocking fine lines may appear.

You may well be sceptical. But think of how a physical or mental illness can alter a person's appearance. A physical illness might change the appearance of a person's skin and leave a lasting effect. Lines might develop through the influence of nerves, if it is remembered that the crowds of nerves going to the papillae are each in separate communication with the brain. Undue excitation of some of these nerves may cause extra growth of tissue in the papillae, or in their neighbourhood, or, if the action is too strong, may lead to wasting of the papillae.

These nervous changes also affect the development of the neighbouring tissues, and may cause deposit or absorption of fat, etc. Such changes as these may separate the papillary ridges and papillae, causing lines to appear, or may bring papillae together, causing the disappearance of lines.

Why certain lines should always be associated with certain conditions is a question that has long aroused speculation. This can be answered by looking at the physiological connection between brain and body. There is a direct link between parts of the brain with portions of the hand. The *cerebral cortex*, the outer layer of the brain, which is crucial for complex mental processes such as thinking, memory and voluntary action, receives messages from our senses and gives out motor commands to the various muscles in our bodies. A region in the frontal lobe known as the *motor projection area* controls movement. Experiments have been carried out on animal and human subjects under local anaesthetic where parts of this area were electrically stimulated giving a concurrent reaction in a specific part of the body. The portion allocated to the hands and fingers is proportionally very large because they are capable of such complex movements and coordination. The palmist's view has always been that there is a connection between the lines on the hand with certain traits or conditions of personality. Perhaps it is possible that the correlation between brain and motor function is reflected in the alleged link between palm and personality?

Prediction

There is one other point of great interest that can be only briefly dealt with. Palmists of the highest standing claim that it has been shown over and over again that coming events are shown on the hand. This is beyond the domain of the anatomist, physiologist and psychologist. To a certain extent future tendencies could be diagnosed from symptoms showing themselves in the hand. For example, a physician, seeing a patient with bluish coloured fingertips, fears heart disease.

Many predictions of palmists cannot, however, be explained in this way, and the most reasonable suggestion made is that we have a sense so little used that it is generally unrecognized—the sense that deals with the future. This sense is seen in the lower animals, and helps to account for hibernation, migration, etc. Country people traditionally foretold the quality of the weather and of the seasons from observing the actions of animals. In human beings this sense is occasionally manifested in the form of forebodings and dreams. It is suggested that in man the use of reason has supplanted this power; but that it is not gone, only dormant, and that it may be through its automatic and unconscious action that future events are able to influence the nerve centres, and through them mark the hand.

Chiromancy

While the ancient subject of palmistry amply repays more profound study by those who wish to devote themselves to it, it is possible to read any hand thoroughly, to tell the character, the weak points, and the actual events from the beginning to the end of life, from a knowledge of the principles and practice as described.

Whether it be palmistry, however, or any of the other methods of forecasting events, telling fortunes or reading character, the chief point to strike us is the age of all these methods. With practically no modification they have been handed down to us through the ages. They do not change with the march of time and their very antiquity should bring them veneration and respect.

Many of the superstitions in particular are not confined to our own land but prevail in other countries. In the Middle Ages palmistry, or *chiromancy* as it was then called, was numbered among the forbidden black arts.

The anatomy of the hand

Bones and muscles

The human hand is made up of the metacarpal bones and the phalangeal bones. Between the hand and the bones of the forearm—the radius and ulna—are the eight carpal bones of the wrist, in two rows. Between the carpal bones and the fingers and thumb come the metacarpals. These are similar to the phalangeals, or finger bones, in shape but are longer. They are contained in the muscular envelope of the palm. Jointed to the metacarpals at the knuckles are the bones of the phalanges in three rows, the bones tapering towards the fingertips.

An opposable thumb

The thumb has only two phalangeal bones and these, like its metacarpal, are shorter than those of the fingers. The metacarpal of the thumb is capable of free movement, and it is this characteristic that makes the thumb an 'opposable' digit. Because of this we are able to grasp objects and use our hands in such complex operations as sewing, writing, draw-

The bones of the hand

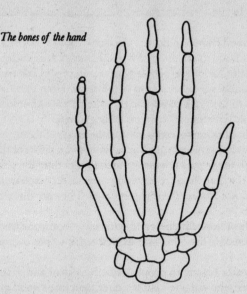

ing and working with tools. There are twenty-seven bones in the hand and wrist—eight carpals, five metacarpals and fourteen phalangeal bones.

Flexibility causes lines

One result of the great flexibility of the hand is that its palmar surface is thickly padded in between the lines of flexion, or bending, while at these lines the skin is bound down to the tendons that move the digits, and to the deeper layers. This combination of loose and firm surfaces gives the necessary steadiness and adaptability to the grasp. It is obvious that if the padding of the palm were loose and free to slip about, a firm grasp would be impossible.

The"bracelet' lines at the wrist have a similar origin. The monticuli—prominences that we see at the base of the thumb and fingers—are composed of muscle tissue. So too are those on the phalanges. Nature has endowed the hand with the characteristics of flexibility and firmness, and has cushioned the palm against shocks that would otherwise injure its framework.

The size and shape of the hands
• **Large hands** show order, method, obedience and detail.

- **Small hands** show energy, government, ability to rule and executive power.
- **Medium-sized hands** indicate a character with a capacity for turning his or her hand to anything. When the fingers are exactly as long as the palm, they belong to people who are successful in business but not in any highly specialized kind of business. Note that this hand belongs also to the 'Jack-of-all-trades'—the person who does many things capably but none of them exceedingly well.

  Hands with palms long in comparison to the length of the fingers, show an ability to make big plans, a quick grasp of things, a dislike of detail.

  Hands with the fingers relatively much longer than the palm cannot plan but they can 'finish' everything they do. A person with hands like these will not neglect the slightest detail. They are the 'slow-but-sure' people.
- **Wide hands** indicate kindness and sympathy—someone who is able to see and consider the other side as well as his or her own point of view.
- **Narrow hands** belong to people who are critical and exacting by nature—those who see one's faults rather than one's good qualities. It is said that the best husbands and wives are not found with this kind of hand, but if the life partner's hand is too short and too wide, fate may draw them together.
- **Hands wide open with the fingers well apart** show originality, initiative and courage.
- **Hands with fingers close together** show convention, fear of consequences and cowardice.
- **White hands** show a selfish nature.
- **Red hands** show passionate feeling, anger and energy.
- **Hands of warmish pink** show a warm heart.

Soft hands indicate laziness, which may coexist with distinct and probably unused talent. But, hands that are only moderately soft, or soft on the mounts, may belong to people who work best in short bursts only.
- **Very hard hands** demonstrate energy and the love of work for its own sake. These are people who should ask themselves what it is that they want out of life and then set out to get it, cultivating mental disciplines so that they do not waste their nervous energy too extravagantly.
- **Square hands** show reason, consistency, common sense and accuracy.
- **Pointed hands** show spirituality and idealism.

Note that a hard and very square hand belongs to a person who always has reason on his or her side. He or she is never wrong.

- **Peaky hands**. The extremely 'peaky' hand—especially if it lacks 'grip' and feels unreal when it is grasped—belongs to the dreamer, the impractical person. With very pointed fingertips, these hands will have no sense of reality—they will take up and support the wildest notions. Tapering fingertips show a lack of executive power.
- **Spatulate hands**. There is a third hand, called the spatulate hand, which is the opposite of the pointed hand. It is rare and inclines to be distinctly ugly, with fingers that bulge at the top. This is the useful hand. Its owner is concerned only with material things, but this hand, when not excessively spatulate, belongs to the person of action—the worldly person. Its owner is practical, technically adept and would feel at home working with engines or machinery.

For a person to be an inventor or a really original thinker who can translate his or her thoughts into action, the hand must partake of all these three types, and every one of the fingertips must vary.

The mixed hand is the most difficult to read.

Palmists have, over many years, defined seven well-marked types of hands:
The elemental
The spatulate or active
The conical or temperamental
The square or utilitarian
The knotty or philosophic
The pointed or idealistic
The mixed

The elemental

This hand is the mark of primitive races; it is characteristic of peoples, such as the Laplanders, who inhabit Polar regions, and was also a feature of the Tartar and Slav races. The palm is large, and the fingers short and thick. It is intrinsically the hand of the peasant or the serf of times long past, it is seen in all lands among those who for generations have come from the stock that furnishes the 'hewers of wood and drawers of water'. These people have, in the course of centuries evolved as a type who have adapted to making a living by hard and rough labour; their acquisitive and self-preservative faculties have developed to predominance. What significance is to be attached to the possession of an elemental hand in our subject? It depends, of course, on the degree of relation to the archetype, for the pure elemental is uncommon outside those regions that have been mentioned. Superstitious, narrow-minded and unintellectual, this type has nevertheless produced, on occasion, great leaders—in religious persecutions and in the rare and dreadful peasant risings in European history.

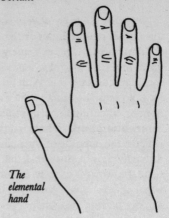

The elemental hand

The spatulate or active

This hand is large and broad, with blunt, thick fingers that are broad at the tips. The digits are long. It is the mark of someone of action rather than a great thinker, of the tireless, restless agitator who seeks to improve the lot of others by his or her endeavours and adventure; of the bold and daring navigator of Polar seas, or of the courageous pioneer.

People with the spatulate hand have certainly played their part in history, linking the Atlantic and the Pacific oceans by railway, in cutting canals such as the Suez and the Panama, in opening up air routes across continents and oceans. They are generally intolerant of convention, and are highly original in thought and action. Women of the spatulate type are endowed with a large measure of intuition.

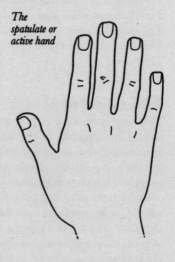

The spatulate or active hand

In games and athletics they may excel, and usually they are musical. Some of the greatest painters of all time have belonged to the spatulate type. In general, this hand denotes the executive rather than the administrator. Rulers of this group have made history by their failures rather than by their achievements.

The conical or temperamental

This type of hand marks the emotional or temperamental subject—impetuous, impulsive and exuberant. The aesthetic perception is strongly developed, and beauty in all forms and guises appeals strongly to this person. He or she is sensitive to the emotional stimulus of music and pictures. A somewhat unstable nature is indicated—the temperament being coloured by varying moods which never endure long. Although generally cheerful and optimistic, this person is, however, easily depressed by any misfortune or by lack of success in trivial enterprises, and the mood of satisfaction may change suddenly to one of black despair.

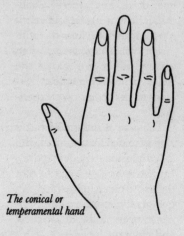

The conical or temperamental hand

The content of his or her mind is coloured by the conversation of any and every person he or she meets. Lacking skill in constructive thought, this type reflects the moods and opinions of those stronger surrounding personalities.

The wife or husband of this type is a somewhat difficult person. He or she does not easily tolerate discipline, dislikes mundane routine, and craves for pleasure and excitement—for something new or different. Whilst hot-tempered, this person is soon repentant after an outburst of passion, and so avoids making enemies.

The square or utilitarian

This type of hand denotes the methodical, matter-of-fact individual, who is a steady, law-abiding member of society. Though this person may not rise to great heights in intellectual matters, he or she is a plodder who very often reaps rewards as a result of industry and perseverance. In contrast to the owner of a spatulate hand, the utilitarian hand generally represents a conservative outlook and a sturdy support of the existing order of things—in religion, in politics and in business. He or she often responds to change with immediate and intense opposition.

A very valuable member of the community, he or she appears as the successful lawyer, politician or teacher who makes progress as much through self-restraint as through good deeds. The owner of a utilitarian hand is a good soldier but a poor leader, because the utilitarian type is nonplussed when an opponent disregards the 'rules' or does something contrary to his or her own experience.

The man of this group makes a good match for a woman who is not passionately demanding. In matrimony, he is apt to take things too much for granted, frequently forgetting that his partner expects material, physical and emotional evidence of his love.

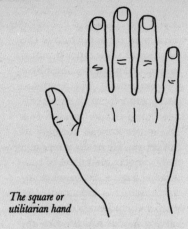

The square or utilitarian hand

The knotty or philosophic

This hand is noticeable for its bluntly conical fingertips, its large joints and its broad third phalanges. It denotes a materialistic type of mind—logical, methodical and systematic. This is the hand of the seeker of life's truths.

Such a person is inclined to be reserved and to appear 'standoffish' . This is quite undeserved; the reserve arises merely from a profound knowledge of and an interest in matters that only a few people will care to talk about. In the absence of people with similar interests, the philosophic appears aloof; but place him *en rapport* with a kindred spirit and his or her reserve vanishes. In the young person this temperament inevitably leads to a somewhat introspective tendency, and the subject is, generally, not a 'good mixer'.

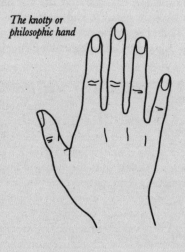

The knotty or philosophic hand

Philosophic types have few delusions about themselves, though they will always back their own opinions when they eventually arrive at them. They endeavour to keep an open mind during investigation or analysis of evidence. Although the philosophic may not be ideal as a choice of partner, he or she is generally a good parent, though just and stern. He or she may be sceptical about religion, but, nevertheless, might maintain a firm commitment to some creed.

The pointed or idealistic

This hand marks the possessor as one who worships at the shrine of beauty—not material beauty so much as beauty of the mind, though the artistic perception is usually well developed and the subject appreciates true beauty in everything. As a rule, the idealistic type is rather impractical in mundane matters, and has little idea of thrift or provision for future wants—like the grasshopper in the fable, who sings during the sunny hours, but may starve in the winter of life.

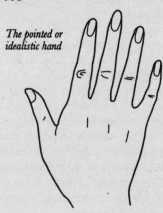

The pointed or idealistic hand

Gifted with a vivid and creative imagination, people of this type love verse and literature, and frequently write, paint or compose. A marriage of two such persons is usually an ideally happy one, though the parties may have to suffer poverty. On the other hand, should the similarity of temperament be merely superficial, then intense unhappiness may result. Being naturally fickle and inconstant, idealistic types are in need of a very strong bond of love to hold them to their life partners.

He or she is religious and worships wholeheartedly . Beautiful music, pictures, lights etc, fit in best with his or her idea of devotion. The less aesthetic side of religion holds less attraction for the idealistic type.

The mixed

This hand is one that cannot be readily classified in any of the other six groups, for it contains characteristics of some of all of them. Thus, the palm may be large and the fingers long, thick at the lower phalange and then tapering. It thus has points of the idealistic type and others that associate it more with the utilitarian. In another subject we may observe characteristics of both the active and philosophic types of hand. The rule of interpretation is to give value to the most important features. If these are contradictory an average is indicated.

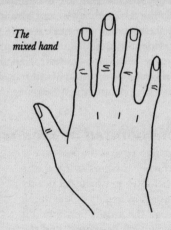

The mixed hand

Generally, a mixed hand indicates an adaptable temperament and some versatility. The latter quality may be so much in evidence that the subject turns out to be a 'Jack-of-all-trades'. Many brilliant engineers, inventors and research workers have belonged to this type, spending their life in pursuit of new technologies and developments. However, when they have solved their problems they are not materially better off—though the world has profited from their discoveries.

The attributes indicated in a mixed hand are those of the types to which it is nearest in form. There are many varieties, and each must be analysed on its merits.

The female hand

Though the female hand, as well as the male, is classified in the seven types identified, the distinguishing features are not so strongly marked. A woman's hands are softer, smoother and more modelled, but the characteristics which have been highlighted can be identified.

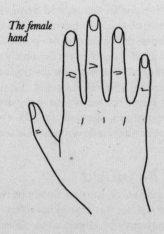

The female hand

The elemental hand is rare in the female, and the spatulate and knotty types are less conspicuous than in the male. When any one of these three is found with strongly marked features, the attributes are present in large measure. As to the temperamental and idealistic, the interpreter may here fall into the error of over-evaluation, for in many women the hand has something of these features without, however, belonging really to either type. The square or utilitarian type is more easily recognized; and the mixed type, too, can usually be distinguished.

The fingers and the mounts

The fingers
- The first or index finger is the finger of Jupiter.
- The second or middle finger is the finger of Saturn.
- The third or wedding-ring finger is the finger of Apollo.
- The fourth or little finger is the finger of Mercury.

The natural bend of the fingers is important, and the palmist should be quick to notice its natural attitude before examining the interior of the hand.

Some fingers are distinguished by their independent, prominent position over the rest. When the tips are inclined to curl to the palm, a plodding, determined nature is indicated—one that does not easily relinquish a set aim or purpose because of obstacles.

A wide space between Jupiter and Saturn shows unconventionality, and originality of thought and outlook.

When the Jupiter finger is upright and straight, and of normal length, a just, candid nature is revealed. Should its position be in advance of the other fingers, a respect for authority is indicated. If it falls slightly behind, this indicates dependency on others and a reluctance to take the initiative and the burden of responsibility. If the finger is short this denotes ingratitude and no enthusiasm. If it is pointed it is an indication of tact, comprehension, and sympathy. A square finger is a sign of integrity, but also of someone who may be thoughtlessly frank in expressing opinions.

The generous and broad phalanges of Saturn show gravity, depth of character, and a sense of proportion. A short Saturn signifies imprudence and an inclination to act on impulse and behave rashly—spatulate implies energy, and square indicates cool, clear-headed, thought before action and absence of hasty judgements.

If the finger of Apollo is well developed this shows artistic tendencies. If its position is slightly forward, the talent lies in painting, drawing, or sculpture. A pointed finger is a sign that the artistic ability is greater than the practical. A spatulate shape shows a sense of the beautiful in form and colour, and possession of dramatic powers.

Mercury, set lower than the other fingers, reveals the fact that many adverse circumstances have been battled with. A pointed finger of Mercury indicates tact, discrimination and intuition. If it is square, it shows a love of scientific pursuits and good reasoning powers.

The mounts

The mounts under each bear the same names as the fingers above them. Thus we have the mounts of Jupiter, Saturn, Apollo and Mercury, as shown in the diagram.

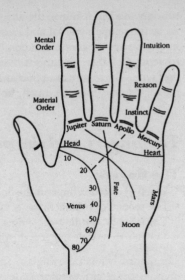

The human hand as delineated for the purposes of palmistry

The mount at the base of the thumb is the mount of Venus, and that opposite to it on the fleshy outer base of the hand, is the mount of Luna or of the Moon. There are, in addition, two mounts of Mars situated respectively above the mount of Venus and below the mount of Jupiter; this is Mars Positive. On the outer side of the hand, above the mount of Luna and below that of the mount of Mercury, is situated Mars Negative.

As the fingers and their supporting mounts represent the same qualities, it is easier to simultaneously learn what the fingers and mounts stand for. However, note that an exceptionally long or large finger stands for the nobler overdevelopment of the qualities, whereas an overdevelopment of the mounts stands for their more fatalistic or baser over-expression. The hand is like the head in this respect—in the top part we read of the intellectual qualities, and at the base of the animal instincts.

Fingers that are weak or small and mounts that are quite flat, show absence of the qualities represented. Mounts that seem to be almost hollow—though this *may* be due to the very high development of the 'neighbouring' mount—indicate the qualities opposite to those for which the fingers stand.

Remember that in palmistry, as in most everything else, *excess* is not a good thing. In real life the excess of any virtue may prove a vice! The wise ever seek to direct their actions in line with:

'. . .the happy mean,
A Vice at each side and the Virtue between.'

Thus, the excess of prudence is the vice of miserliness on one side, and its absence is prodigality on the other.

Jupiter

Jupiter stands for veneration, worship, religion. A very dominant first finger indicates the hands of great religious leaders and all those whose sense of honour is extremely high. With the mount big and out of proportion, then religious mania or enthusiasm run wild. If the mount is hard, fanaticism is indicated—if it is soft and high then the subject is said to be of sympathetic nature but with strange beliefs.

Saturn

Saturn stands for knowledge, thought, occultism, superstition. This second mount, if unusually high, will denote fatalism, melancholy and esoteric knowledge. The subject will say—

'I cannot do or undo. What must be, will be.'

When the second finger is big and square, this indicates a thoughtful but not a practical person—a pointed finger is a sign of unbalanced thought.

When Saturn's mount is flat, there is a total lack of imagination, and people without imagination are apt to be cruel. But this mount may appear flat, because of the height of Apollo which denotes joyousness, as distinct from the sadness of Saturn.

Apollo

Apollo signifies art, beauty, wealth and joy in living.

This mount is highly developed in all artists who have an inborn love of colour and of beauty. But if the hand is soft, there may be an overstrong enjoyment of pleasure through the senses. If the mount of Apollo is flat it illustrates a nature that detests joy and almost seems to dislike beauty and dread happiness.

A long thin finger of Apollo indicates a love of colour, and if the thumb is strong there will be capacity to express this in some form of art.

Mercury

Mercury denotes persuasive speech, business and worldly shrewdness.

If the mount is very high and the finger pointed, it indicates a person who is perhaps 'too clever' or even tricky, especially if Jupiter is poor. A crooked little finger indicates a thief, one who steals not because the person needs to steal, but because he or she likes to do so. The mount of Mercury, if very flat, shows an individual with no foresight and the inability to seize a chance when it presents itself. Mercury's finger, if square at the top, shows one who can both buy and sell to advantage.

So much for the mounts that distinctly belong to the fingers.

The thumb

The possession of a thumb, a digit that can be placed in opposition to the fingers, differentiates man from all the animals except certain apes and monkeys. It is a most valuable addition, for humans could never have developed without it. The ability to make and use crude and rough tools enabled our primitive ancestors to set out on the evolutionary path that has led to our civilization of today. From rough tools man could fashion finer and more efficient ones—first of flint, then of bronze and iron—and utilize them to build and construct. No wonder the thumb is such a valuable index to character and temperament.

The characteristics of the thumb, in general, are those of the type of hand to which it belongs; but there are certain special features of the thumb that are worthy of attention. First of all, let us mention the rare case where the thumb is absent or is very small—this is perhaps a sign denoting degeneration to a primitive type. Ordinarily the thumb, when placed close to the index finger, reaches to the joint or just below it. If it does not reach this joint it is a short thumb. If it goes beyond the joint the thumb is said to be long.

The thumb has only two phalanges—the first, or topmost, one is associated with willpower and executive ability, and the second with logical perception and reasoning powers. The size of the first phalange is important in reading the hand, for if the phalange is large it denotes that other tendencies indicated by the fingers and other parts of the hand are likely to be effective. If the contrary is the case, tendencies remain dormant unless there is enough willpower to ensure that these gifts can be actively employed.

The thumb, then, is a real index to character. By the proportionate size of the two phalanges it denotes whether will or reason will have the upper hand in guiding the actions of the subject. If both phalanges are much the same in size, the individual will employ both these mental faculties equally in determining his or her way of life. At the base of the thumb is the mount of Venus, indicating the love propensity. If well developed, it shows that the subject is wayed by his or her heart a good deal in coming to decisions. Palmists sometimes describe the part of the thumb beneath the mount as the third phalange.

If the thumb lies close to the fingers we can say that the owner is careful with money and not too generous. A looser thumb, standing away from the hand, denotes a freer, more open nature. Then, too, we can note whether the thumb is supple at the top joint, or stiff and unyielding. In the former case we may say the subject is broad-minded, generous, tolerant and good-humoured. Moreover, he or she can readily adapt to different circumstances. In the man with the stiff-jointed thumb we should expect qualities that are almost the opposite of those just mentioned—caution, reserve, an obstinate adherence to somewhat narrow views of life and morals, and a determination to obtain what he regards as his rights. With this sign should be considered the relative sizes of the first and second phalange.

It is useful to have some standard by which to measure the relative size of the two phalanges of the thumb. Various proportions have been suggested as the normal one. It may be taken that the first, or end phalange should be nearly half the length of the thumb, the second being slightly longer. In the left hand it is likely that the phalanges will show quite a different proportional size, when examining a left-handed subject the left hand should be taken as the representative one.

Sometimes the thumb is broadened and 'clubbed' at the tip, which is full and plump. This denotes a passionate, hot-tempered individual, swayed excessively by his emotions and easily roused to intense anger.

More about the fingers

The fingers, as you will see, are divided by two knuckles or 'knots' into three divisions.

The top space, which includes the tips with the nails at the back, is the first phalange, devoted to will, as is the top of the thumb. If this is long, fine, or pointed, there is also imagination—length indicates the will to express artistic imagination. If thick, an obstinate will. If thick and long, a strong, dominating will. But the thumb ought not to be set low on the hand if the talent is original or creative.

The middle, or second phalange belongs to reason. If this is long, then the person thinks things out and, if the hand is fairly square and capable-looking, they are able to plan ahead. Good organizers have a strong second phalange. A short space stands for those who have no use for reason. But with a clever hand, their intuition will serve them well. They will 'get there' if they trust their own perceptions, and act on their first impressions.

The third phalange, if thick and long, belongs to people of a passionate nature. But this phalange of the fingers shows the nobler aspect of the animal nature, just as that at the very base of the hand under Venus, coming as it does in the lowest part of the hand, expresses the physical side.

As for the knots that divide the phalanges, the upper knot dividing the first from the second phalange is the knot of philosophy. Large and well developed, it shows a love of accurate thinking, of exact knowledge. If small, it indicates those who are not at all philosophical; those whose acts are not ruled by their heads. Impetuous people generally have poor knots of philosophy.

The lower knot, which divides the second from the third phalange, is the knot of order. It belongs to great talkers. These are also good talkers, for we generally do well in what we enjoy doing most. People who talk well must have a well-developed sense of order, though they are seldom credited with this. Yet, without it, how could they find the right word and set it in the right place at the right moment?

In a long and narrow hand, a knot that is prominent will show a contradictory,, quarrelsome person. But in a clever, short hand that is wide, indicating kindness, it means a love of debate, a talent for 'stating a case' and ability to prove things. With a crooked little finger, you might get a clever liar, if this knot is strong. But where there is sympathy (a wide hand), and a thumb set low (talent), and good head and heart lines, these talkers generally turn their charming talent to their own advantage.

The fingernails

The nails are developed from skin tissues, and so partake of the intimate nature of the flesh. It is remarkable that in people of mixed blood the nails may denote this fact. Even when the blood has been thinned down for a number of generations, the nails may still show signs of ancestry. Then, too, the nails show signs of disease, for example, becoming brittle if blood circulation is poor. It is common knowledge that in some cases of poisoning the harmful substance may show its presence when the nails are subjected to chemical examination.

Long nails denote a calm, phlegmatic temperament—short ones suggest a more impetuous nature. When the fingernails are well formed, with good crescents and a rounded, shapely base, we may expect an equable nature and sound judgement. A broad and curved top, associated with the last-named characteristics, denotes an open, generous and frank mind. Narrow, elongated nails are found on people of somewhat delicate constitution, and are often pale and bloodless or even bluish in colour. When unaccompanied by any signs of ill health, the long and moderately narrow nail suggests a refined and idealistic or psychic type of individual. Nails with a spatulate end, especially when broad in proportion to their length, denote pugnacity. When the nails show a reddish colouring, this attribute is strengthened.

In general, the nails should be pinkish to reddish in hue, and not pale or bluish. Ridged or grooved nails suggest a naturally nervous temperament, though this sign may denote nothing more than an alert and sensitive mind. Any irregularities in the shape, form, or colouring of the nails are signs of health defects. Blueness that persists is a sign of some defect of the circulatory system. The nails are of secondary importance to the fingers as an index to character, though they may afford useful indications to health and temperament.

The lines of the hand

- The **line of life** (A) runs around the base of the mount of Venus.
- The **line of head** (B) runs across the centre of the hand, starting under Jupiter.
- The **line of heart** (C) runs across the upper part of the palm directly under the mounts.
- The **line of fate** (D) (or **line of destiny**) is one of the two most important lines on the hand, the other being the line of life. It runs from low down on the hand straight through the centre, up towards the finger of Saturn.
- The **line of fortune** (E) (or the **line of Apollo** or the **Sun**) also runs up the hand towards the finger of Apollo, or the ring finger.
- The **line of intuition** (F) is rare in its perfect form. It is a semicircle, a longish semicircle or oval line running round, or partly round the mount of Luna.

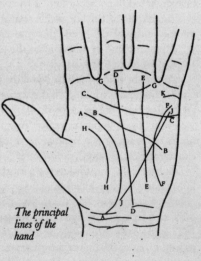

The principal lines of the hand

271

- The **girdle of Venus** (G) is rare. When found, it is above the heart line, a small semicircular mark around, or partly around the two middle mounts of Jupiter and Saturn.
- The **line of Mars** (H) is a smaller semicircle sometimes found within the line of life.
- The **line of health** (J) (or the line of Mercury) on which business affairs is also read, is a third line running up the hand, but somewhat transversely, towards the finger of Mercury
- Finally come the **bracelets**, three lines (or two, or only one in some cases), that run halfway around the wrists, under the front of the hand.

It will be observed that the line of life, line of head and line of health between them form a triangle, which is called the Great Triangle. Note also that the line of Sun, line of destiny, line of head and line of heart form the Quadrangle at their intersection.

Age and time calculations

Time is calculated on these lines of the hands, as you will see by looking at the diagram. We have one hundred years to be read on the line of life at its fullest and longest—that is, when it actually goes round and almost behind the thumb base. The age at which certain events, represented by crosses, squares, triangles, and other marks will happen, can be calculated fairly accurately if the palmist remembers the following:

- the middle of the line of life stands for the fiftieth year
- the centre of the head line represents the age of thirty-five
- where the line of fate touches the head line at its centre is this same important age of thirty-five
- the age of thirty-five is read on the line of heart under the centre of the finger of Apollo. Palmistry gives the larger half of heart events, to the years before thirty-five.

In real life, as in palmistry, we 'count time by heart beats' and not by hours or years. It is a mistake to think that all hours—or years—are exactly the same length.

Doubtless the most interesting marks to be found among the minor lines of the hand, which indicate voyages, change of environment, talents and ambitions, are those that concern the attachments, love affairs, and future marriage of the subject.

These are the influence lines, which may be discerned running from mount Luna to the line of fate, from mount Venus to the line of life, and on the mount of Mercury. Their depth, length, and clarity depend upon the enduring nature of the sentiment involved. When crossed, barred, or cut, they demonstrate the fact that difficulties and opposition from parents, friends, or relatives are to be encountered, or it may be that the influence was merely a fleeting infatuation.

These signs should be compared with the age calculated upon the fate line—it will then be discovered whether the influence lines are of the past, present, or future. Only constant practice and experience can aid the reader to a correct estimate of the period of these happenings.

How to read the lines

Date lines

The chronology used in palmistry is based upon a division of certain of the lines into year-periods. The line of heart, line of head, line of destiny, line of Sun and line of life are those chiefly used for determining ages or dates. The span of someone's life can be taken at seventy-five years for the purpose of these readings, and the lines are graduated accordingly. The line of life reads downwards, and the lines of destiny and the Sun are read upwards. The lines of heart and head are read from their origin at the thumb side of the palm.

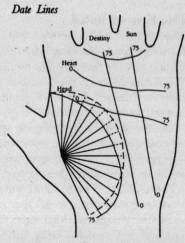

Date Lines

These lines can be divided into four-, six- or seven-year intervals, or as in this text, a five-year interval.

The line of life

The line of life, long, even and clear, represents a long and healthy life. If broken in one hand, this life line tells of a serious illness. If completely broken in both hands, then life may end at that age. However, the life line may grow again and the broken lines join together, especially if more than five years lie between the date at which the hand is read and the time when the life lines in both hands end. Thus, no serious palmist would pretend to be able to tell the age at which death occurs.

Note that this life line, if chained, tells of delicacy and illness, caused by anxiety, unhappiness, or worry. If the line is red, there is a tendency to fevers. If it is purple, it shows a tendency to inherited illnesses. One often sees a faint purplish shade on part of the line of life of one hand. If in the left hand only, this shows actual illness has been avoided.

Both hands must be read, and when the life line shows a series of fine crosses set closely together, this indicates the occurrence of neuralgic pains and aches at the time indicated. If these are repeated on the line of head, then this indicates pain of a more serious nature, occurring in the head. This life line, pale or thin, tells of poor health generally during those years. But the smaller line of Mars inside the life line promises survival, and corrects or modifies indications of poor health or of short life.

Branches upwards from the line of life tell of honours or successes that are purely fortuitous. Thus, if an individual achieves high office his palm will show a branch upwards from the line of fate. This individual's partner, for whom this honour is fortuitous, might show a branch on the life line.

The line of head

When this line is long there is talent and a naturally good memory. But if it is too closely linked up with the beginning of the line of life (thus making only one line under the mount of Jupiter) there is a marked lack of self-confidence. If they continue as one for over 1 centimetre ($^1/_2$ inch), then this self-distrust will greatly hamper and delay success, however talented the subject is.

The line of head starting slightly apart from the life line gives a steady self-confidence. But if the space between is very wide (7mm is very wide here) this shows rash impulsiveness. Review and re-evaluation will always be advisable for these people.

The head line, if short, shows impulse, prejudice, a lack of reasoning power and a tendency to act first and think afterwards. The line of head when straight and long shows thrift and economy (with no imagination, if very straight). Long, and tending slightly downwards at the end shows sympathy and an ability to see the viewpoint of other people. If drooping low down to the base of the hand, the subject has too much imagination. If apparent in both hands, along with a weak thumb, then it may indicate mental weakness.

If the line of head is divided into a large fork at the end, one branch of which goes straight across the hand and the other turns down on to the mount of Luna or even towards the wrist, this shows that life has two sides—the practical side, which will be efficiently conducted, and a vivid and very real life of the imagination. The hands of novelists typically show this handsome forking on the head lines.

If the head line is blurred this indicates an illness in which there has been delirium. If it is broken in one hand, the subject may commit a serious error of judgement. A line broken in both hands, is a warning that the subject may suffer an accident where his or her head is injured in some way.

The line of heart

When this is clear and long, it gives a happy life, rich in affection. But if it misses the mount of Jupiter, rising from up between that mount and the next one (the mount of Saturn) there is coldness as regards love, with a tormenting capacity for jealousy. If this is apparent on one hand only, this tendency is kept under control admirably. Hands in which the heart line misses Jupiter do not find happiness in love. When it starts under Saturn there is coldness and a lack of feeling.

A short heart line denotes selfishness in love, where flirting takes the place of affection and may be mistaken for it. A series of very small crosses on the heart line indicates suffering through the unworthiness of those loved.

A broken heart line shows a broken engagement or similar emotional trauma. Breaks under the mount of Jupiter indicate the cause was honour; under Saturn, this indicates that the cause was a fatality, perhaps death; under Apollo, pride with some mystery. The subject does not know *why* the break came, and is too proud to find out. Under Mercury, the broken heart line means that the person who was loved was thoroughly unworthy.

The girdle of Venus

The girdle of Venus used to be read as a sign of an evil life. Now, however, it is more correctly taken to mean the likelihood of some great unhappiness in relation to an emotional attachment. Its ugly aspect will have passed over by the time the subject reaches his or her thirty-fifth year.

If a man has this half-ring, he will be well advised not to marry until that age has passed, nor indeed to form any important partnerships. If a married woman is seen to have this girdle, the wise palmist will tell her to 'sit tight' until this difficult period passes. She will surely get on better with her unsatisfactory life partner *after* she has turned thirty-five. This ill-omened mark also tells of sudden death touching the life. The girdle of Venus always tells of a catastrophe that has occurred in the earlier part of the life.

The line of fate

This may start from four places:

- From the bracelets—this indicates an uncommon destiny, that may mean great happiness or misery, according to the way in which the life is lived. However, the circumstances are, as a rule, out of the subject's choice with this 'start' of the fate line.
- From the line of life—this indicates that the subject will have a good life with good chances and will make his or her own way in life.
- From the mount of the Moon—fate is made by marriage or entirely through the decisions or doings of other people.
- From the middle of the hand—a hard life, troubled and hampered by poverty or cruel circumstances.

But the line of fate that ends high up in the hand, even though it starts over high up, *does* spell success at the end. Breaks in this line are not negative, they represent changes. If the line goes on straight and clear, these may be good changes. Branches towards the Moon tell of travels; towards Jupiter, of honours and dignities earned.

Branches that rise from the outer side and touch the fate line denote affairs of the heart. Those that are clear and touch the fate lines of both hands indicate marriage at the age where they touch. A good cross on Jupiter ought to confirm this indication.

Sometimes the fate line, after starting well and low down in the hand, disappears for some years and then reappears. This means that the life is uneventful during those years. The money line also disappears sometimes. Widowhood, represented by a line from the fate line touching the heart line and ending in a cross, often brings out both the fate line and the money line again, later on in life. This only if the widow obtains control of money because of her bereavement.

Absence of the fate line does not mean anxiety. It shows that the person is only 'vegetating' when there is no fate line. Small lines across the fate line are troubles.

The line of fortune

This tells of money matters. When it drops for some time it has the same meaning as the fading of the fate line. This line, chained or blurred, tells of actual struggling, of 'hard times' due to the absence of money or to expenditure being greater than income.

A long clear line going right up to the mount of Apollo tells of riches, a successful life as regards financial fortune. If it bites into the finger, then there is a kind of 'glorious' fortune; great inheritance or a fortune received through some kind of 'luck'.

The line of business and of health

This shows the career, if indeed there is one. This line, standing out prominently and going straight up to the mount of Mercury, speaks of a successful career. Branches jutting out signify tests, adventures and experiences in new lines of work. If these last while the original line fades out, then this indicates that there will be a clear change of occupation. If forked at the top, this line shows there is great practical ability in the individual. If it is thick, this indicates a delicate old age; if it is red and thin, this shows feverish tendencies. Beware of excitement if this line looks 'angry'.

The line of intuition

The line of intuition gives great sympathy, instinctive cleverness, intuitive judgement. Perfectly formed, this line belongs to the 'seer', the clairvoyant. Being on the mount of the Moon, it implies sadness, even unhappiness:

'For foresight is a melancholy gift
Which bares the bald and speeds the all-too swift.'

The bracelets

These tell of successful life, money, and gains in general. It is said that each of these lines, if it is clear and deep (but not too wide), indicates some thirty years of joyful living. But if one of the lines or some part of any of them is chained, there is a fight against poverty and difficult circumstances during that period of thirty years, or the part of them, that is chained.

The bracelets are read as beginning from the end under the thumb. The one nearest the hand stands for the first thirty years of life; the centre line for the period between thirty and sixty years. These are years of effort and struggle in any life that is lived in an honourable way. The lowest line represents the period between sixty and ninety years. You can understand why few hands have these three lines clear and unbroken!

Branches on any age of the lines tell of legacies. The year, in which the legacy or the various legacies are received can be accurately computed by means of the age instructions already given.

The triangle

Note that the lines of head, life and fate should form a well-defined triangle under the two middle fingers. If this triangle is weak at the junction of any two of the three lines, look for failure or disappointment affecting the destiny of the subject in connection with the qualities represented by those two lines.

Thus, if the triangle is cramped owing to the head line being joined to the life line, then a lack of self-confidence hinders success. If the head line spoils the triangle, owing to its going far down on the mount of Luna instead of straight across the middle of the hand, a too active imagination is the enemy. With warm affections, a too imaginative head line spells jealousy!

If the life line stops short and so spoils the triangle, then life may be cut short or this may signify the hindrance of success. The fate line may be weak or poor or absent in the early part of life and sometimes spoils the shape of the triangle. In this case this sindicates that early hardships, struggles, lack of friends, etc, are likely to cause failure.

The plain of Mars

The plain of Mars is the space between the two mounts of that name. It lies between the lines of the heart and of the head, and should be clear and wide. That is, the heart line should not drop into it nor the head line rise up on to it. If it is hollow, then this plain is said to show early exile from home. If this plain is clear and well defined in the left hand, it indicates skill in chess and in strategy—in the right hand, with other indications of courage, it shows bravery with skill.

Reading both hands

Note that the left hand stands for the natural and the *fated* things, the right hand for what we do with them. The right hand is the hand of *free will*. If one hand is distinctly 'bad', showing a poor fate line, crossed and broken, or a badly broken line of fortune, it is better for this to be the left hand, because the right hand *may* show improvement. In this case, there will have been a brave fight and the fighter has made things better than they were originally.

If the left hand is 'good' and the right one 'bad', then this says that good health has been completely wasted, money prospects lost sight of, and positive chances thrown away. It is imperative never to 'tell' anything really important until you have found that it is certainly so in both hands. Now let us study the small signs and symbols on the lines and the mounts.

Crosses

Crosses are bad when they are badly formed. A well-formed cross on Jupiter's mount stands for a good marriage. On Saturn's mount, ill-luck. When Saturn's line (the line of fate) goes up into the actual finger, ending there with a cross, there is a great and uncommon destiny, with tragedy at the ending.

A cross on the line of fate is always an obstacle, a 'check' to the fate.

A cross lying near it, but not on it, is an obstacle to a life near. Note that the line of fate that stops short in the middle of the hand indicates failure, however well it starts up.

A cross on Apollo's mount, means ill-luck connected with art or literature. On the mount of Mercury, it shows a loss of money or ill-gotten gains. On the line of intuition it shows delusions, on the line of life, it indicates an illness. A cross beside the line of life, points to illness or trouble to some life near. A cross in the plain of Mars (in the middle of the palm under Saturn) signifies love of the occult, attraction to magic, etc.

Stars

Stars are fatalities. One on the mount of Jupiter indicates honours. On mount of Saturn, you find the signs of danger of death by violence. On the mount of Apollo, it indicates unhappy riches. On the mount of Mercury, theft or dishonour may be indicated. A star in the plain of Mars, that is, between the two mounts of Mars, signifies military glory. On the mount of Luna, a star may be indicative of danger of drowning. A star low on the head line, points to insanity in the family—high up on the head line, it is a signal of danger of loss of sight. A star on the line of fortune signifies catastrophe.

Squares

Squares are good. They add force and strength to the qualities indicated by the mounts where they appear. But a square on the inside of the line of life, represents imprisonment or seclusion of some kind. Note the age at which the square touches the life line.

Triangles

Triangles indicate some special talent or aptitude—on Jupiter, for diplomacy; on Saturn, for magic; on Apollo, for art or literature; on Mercury, for success (money success) in politics. A triangle on the mount of Venus tells of a prudent marriage. Triangles also represent deliverance from danger and misfortune.

Dots

Dots are sometimes of good *or* evil omen. White dots on the heart line tell of success in love. Red dots on the heart line, point to emotional love affairs. Dark dots on the head line indicate eye trouble. White dots on the head line, show success in invention, according to which mount they appear under.

Islands

Islands that are made by the line dividing and then joining up again about 1 centimetre ($^1/_2$ inch) further on are always bad. On the life line, they tell of hereditary illness. On the heart line, an unworthy attachment is indicated. On the health line they tell of the same illness as on the life line, but, though serious, this is not fatal.

Grills

Grills or crossed lines always show obstacles. They take from the good effects of the qualities indicated by the mounts, just as squares add to these qualities. A grill on Jupiter tells of tyranny and superstition. On Saturn it denotes misfortune. On Apollo a grill indicates folly, vanity and extravagance. On Mercury it is a sign of hypocrisy, lying and theft. A grill on Mars tells of sudden death, and on Luna it signifies anxiety, discontent, sadness.

Marriage

Marriage is indicated by a large cross on the mount of Jupiter. Again, the marriage line comes up from the outer side of the hand under the mount of the little finger and crosses Mercury. The branches that rise on either side of this clear line are indicative of children. If it drops on to the line of the heart, widowhood is likely. If it crosses the heart line to the plain of Mars, this tells of a possible separation, also to be read in the lines of influence that rise on Luna's mount and go up to the fate line. When these touch in both hands, there is a strong likelihood of marriage taking place at that age.

Tea-leaf Fortunes

The secret of success in this art consists of concentration, which enables the seer, who has a mind empty of all outside matters, to seize at a glance the symbols thrown up in the teacups and to read them intelligently so that the subject, or person whose cup is being read, can understand.

The cup must be passed directly to the seer by the person who has drunk the tea. If the cup passes from hand to hand before it reaches the seer, the fortune will be confused and undefined, and most likely untrue.

It is also desirable that the subject should sit near the seer when the cup has been given up. But the cup ought to be turned over on to the saucer to allow for 'tears' to be drained off the leaves before it is handed to the seer. It is extraordinary how tears, or drops of tea, will stay in the cup, however long it has remained turned over on the saucer, if there is matter for grief in the fortune of the subject.

Some subjects turn the cup round three times and touch the edge of the saucer with the cup, 'wishing the wish of the heart' as they do so. But unless there is a clear or outstanding star near the top on the inner side of the teacup, no more is heard of this 'wish of the heart'. (Wishes properly belong to card-reading.)

The seer or reader picks up the turned-over cup from the saucer, which the subject hands over.

You (if 'you' are the seer) hold the cup in your right hand. Note that the handle of the teacup is the house or home of the subject or 'place'. For someone whose interest is entirely in business, the handle may stand for 'the office'; for an actress it may mean 'the theatre', for a doctor, 'the surgery'. But for the average man or woman you will do well to read it as 'the home'.

The near or inner side of the cup, as you hold it in your right hand, is 'the fortune', the things that are happening or are sure to happen.

On the outer or farther side we read thoughts, things that may come, that are likely or possible but that are now very much 'in the air', unfulfilled, uncertain. If you read the same person's cup tomorrow or in a week's time, there may be quite a different story to be read from the outer side of the cup.

Some seers read a month's time in the depths of the cup, dividing it into two and reading the immediate fortnight that is coming from the top half, and the third and fourth weeks from now in the lower half of the cup's side. Happenings of a month ahead are near the bottom of the side. The very top is today. The rim is now. Close to the rim is by first post tomorrow morning. A leaf or sprig sticking out on the rim, startling news, now. Any sign sticking out implies surprise, even shock.

Note that the leaves or sprigs of tea dust—any combination of symbols, in fact—that lie on the bottom of the cup stand for trouble, annoyance, anxiety, mishap, bad luck, misfortune. Even if it is a star, it is a wish or a 'glory' that will cause the subject more sorrow than joy. And drops, moisture, liquid, things that stand for 'tears' always cling to the bottom of the cup. Notice especially that whatever you read in the bottom of the cup is timed as *now*. This is all to the good. Your subject's cup may be quite clear at the bottom tomorrow!

Sometimes, especially if the seer is reading a person's cup for the first time, and more especially if they are meeting for the first time, the skilled reader will rule out all 'time' and will read from the cup a fortune that goes far ahead and may cover the whole life of the subject.

The most experienced reader of teacups cannot tell what it is that impels him or her to do this, but does know that he or she is actually and truly reading what is sure to come true, and feels, with the feeling that is stronger than all knowledge, that what is 'seen' must be said. This rare and inexplicable state of mind looks beyond all symbolism. Symbols are no longer there; for the seer is now really clairvoyant, seeing nothing, but 'telling' of what is surely in the veiled future.

The Meaning of the Symbols

All the signs explained here are to be read as important or negligible according to size and clearness. Signs that disappear almost as they are read are true things that are ceasing to matter.

animals horses and dogs are friends. A lion represents a powerful friend. A tiger is an unreliable rich man, not necessarily an enemy. Leopards and wolves are enemies. A cat or a cow is a deceitful woman. Monkeys are mischievous people, especially if they are grinning.

baby a sign that one may be expected. If a cradle is near it, all will be well.

birds if they are in flight, birds say that news is coming. A bird standing is not such a good sign. A bird standing on one leg indicates plans frustrated or things changed for the worse since news was received.

circles *see* RINGS.

crosses symbolize things earned. A large, well-made cross tells of painful ambition realized. A small or ill-made cross implies obstacles, with danger of losses. A cross beside a grave, a funeral. Near to a wreath of flowers, a death. Not 'near' if there are no tears in the bottom of the cup.

dots are news, but of things of the mind, scholarship, science. Dots set as a triangle denote a wish, a successful but not exactly a material one. Dots are 'fine' things, sometimes ideas. Dots set inside small circles are money through business or affairs.

faces these are described to the subject, saying whether they stand for men or women, old or young, sad or joyful people. The subject must identify them. Sometimes the subject's own face is formed clearly by dots. Notice its position and the signs near it. But the fact that it is there, means that the day or the time is important.

gardens represent flirtations.

hearts two hearts tell of an engagement. If there is a ring around them or near them, this denotes a happy marriage. A crown over the joined hearts is a very auspicious sign.

letters denote the arrival of something by post. A dot in the middle of a square or 'long square' letter, tells of money by post.

letters of the alphabet alphabet letters are often thrown up in the teacup with astonishing clarity. These do not always stand for the initials of a name; they may indicate a town. But two or three capital letters together are, as a rule, the initials of someone with whom the subject ought to get into communication. Figures must be read in conjunction with the symbols that are near to it.

lines lines stand for distance. Two lines are journeys by train or car. A ship is a voyage. Cars, engines and such things stand for themselves, but notice how they are placed and where.

masses or **heaps** masses or heaps of tea leaves are prosperity. The larger or higher they are, the more money or good luck is indicated. But masses in the bottom of the cup indicate that there is much anxiety even concerning what should be unmitigated good.

rings if they are small, rings mean business offers; if large, a proposal of marriage. Rings are always something that involves a question or an offer. A circle with a letter near it says the offer will be made in writing.

A ring formed of dots denotes an offer that is not so definite. A half or a part circle, not fully closed, is an indefinite offer or a half-question thrown out as a 'feeler' or with some hesitation. The same rule applying to smallness or largeness applies to the complete ring. It denotes business if small and marriage if large.

sprigs stand for people. Tightly curled sprigs are men, and more loosely furled ones are women. When upstanding, these are straightforward people, although if there is any kind of a weapon pointed at them, or from them, the message is 'Beware'. Sprigs set across are people who have been vexed. Look at the nearby symbols to find out why. Sprigs set sideways are people who are not quite trustworthy. People are also represented by faces, initials and signs, which the subject must identify.

squares tell of safety from a feared danger or deliverance. With a half-moon, squares denote danger of drowning escaped. But squares say that the subject is, for the time being, 'taking one step forward and two steps backwards' and, at best, is merely 'marking time', even if the square is set in the clear of the cup's side.

stars indicate successes, desires fulfilled, 'glory' achieved and startling success. If they appear in the bottom, something in the nature of fatality accompanies the good happenings.

triangles symbolize prevention of ill or trouble avoided. Look at the symbols nearby to interpret these more fully.

Enough has been said to show how the teacups ought to be read. 'The way to do it, is to do it.' A last word to the would-be seer: Never hesitate to say what you see clearly in the cup you are reading.

If you are sincere (selfless) in the matter and the subject is intelligent and anxious to know things, what you say is sure to be true or to come true.

Dice and Good Luck

Dice have been used for many games of chance and fortune throughout history. From ancient Egypt and classical Greece to the Far East, numbered cubes made of wood, glass, ivory or metal with their sides inscribed from 1-6 were popular for games and as a means of consultation. It was found through their medium that future happenings and events could be predicted.

Test this ancient form of fortune-telling:

Draw a chalk ring on the table or tablecloth. Three new dice and a new cup or shaker box are needed. All three dice must be shaken in the box, with the box held in the left hand.

If you throw all the dice outside this ring, ask no more, and, above all, steer clear of quarrels! One or two of the dice falling outside the ring indicates the same warning in a milder form. But the thrower, in this case, may throw again.

The following are the common interpretations of the sum total of the numbers on the faces that fall uppermost:

one (that is one dice with one point and two with blanks) says 'Nothing doing!'

two slight trouble, and rather a lack of good news. Nothing to worry about.

three good. Seize the chance that comes *today*. Your wish will be fulfilled, or a pleasing or happy event will take place.

four a disappointment; but it will turn out to be for the best.

five news of a death, but no surprise about the news.

six a marriage, news of which will surprise if not distress the thrower. Also a sign of the loss of a portion of wealth.

seven an omen of good luck. All will go well in the matter about which you are now anxious.

eight disagreeable news through the post. 'Sit tight'. Better news will follow.

nine this is a good throw. It is a sign of good happenings but with some touch of scandal. Success in love or reconciliation of a quarrel or disagreement could also occur.

ten uncertainty, but nothing worse. 'Wait till the clouds roll by.'

eleven danger of loss of money through treachery. This also indicates the illness of someone close.

twelve someone seeks to involve you in an intrigue. Refuse to grant favours that are asked of you. There is danger of you being made a cat's paw. Do not act without seeking advice from a friend.

thirteen warns you that an enemy seeks your downfall. Throw again, and if the number is higher, he or she will not succeed.

fourteen long voyaging but not yet. Your travels will prove profitable but not easily. Always have hope. This is also an indication of a new friendship to come.

fifteen some domestic trouble. Examine whether there are people making mischief in your home. Sort it out!

sixteen you are going to be lucky in a matter of which you are not hopeful. Tell no one of your gains for a week after you know of them. Sixteen also warns you not to think too much about money. Other important things are being neglected by you. You will not want for money ever, but it will not supply the need of friendship.

seventeen indicates something very good indeed, unearned, unsought, even undeserved. You may well be thankful when this comes. Perhaps a suggestion or proposal from a stranger.

eighteen this is the very best throw of all. It tells of a high destiny, great luck and happiness. But beware of inconstancy when your luck is at its highest. 'The full cup needs a steady hand.'